Visual
GAMES

FRANCO AGOSTINI

Visual
GAMES

Macdonald Orbis

Drawings
Maria Chiara Molinaroli
Vittorio Salarolo
Lino Simeoni
Pietro Vanessi

A *Macdonald Orbis* BOOK

© 1986 by Arnoldo Mondadori Editore S.p.A., Milan
© 1988 in the English translation Arnoldo Mondadori Editore S.p.A., Milan

Translated by Geoffrey Culverwell and John Gilbert

First published in Great Britain in 1988
by Macdonald & Co. (Publishers) Ltd
London & Sydney

A Pergamon Press plc company

British Library Cataloguing in Publication Data
Agostini, Franco, *1946–*
    Visual Games
    1. Pictorial Puzzles-Collection
    I. Title
    793.73

    ISBN 0-356-15726-1

Filmset by Rowland Phototypesetting Ltd,
Bury St Edmunds, Suffolk

Printed and bound in Italy by
Officine Grafiche Arnoldo Mondadori Editore, Verona

Macdonald & Co. (Publishers) Ltd
Greater London House
Hampstead Road
London NW1 7QX

Jacket by Don Macpherson based on an original design by CDE Gruppo Mondadori

Contents

Introduction

This book is designed to enlist the direct participation of you, the reader, in a series of tests and experiments, sometimes simple, sometimes intricate, but always enlightening, which, by improving your visual perception, will lead to a greater awareness of the reality of the world we live in.

At several points in the book you will be invited to solve puzzles – in the form of short tests and exercises – which involve picking out one particular shape from large numbers of other similar ones, composing or unravelling figures and identifying specific elements of symmetry. There are also experiments that call for your active participation: in order to understand some explanations you may have to turn a figure upside-down or rotate it; you will be asked to bend down and look at an illustration while holding the book between your legs; on other occasions you will have to hold a page perpendicular to your eyes and then look at it with one eye closed. Some of the games are, in fact, proper, established laboratory experiments, which can, however, easily be performed by anyone. Others are merely demonstrations of curious phenomena that help us recognize certain aspects of visual perception of which most people are unaware.

This book then is much more than a mere compendium of games. Behind all the diagrams and illustrations, which do indeed provide the basis for amusing games and anecdotes, are critical and theoretical explanations linked to the more serious problems of perception as an element of psychology. The illustrative contents are not only fascinating subjects for observation: they are real and thought-provoking visual experiences. Often, in order to understand a particular figure, readers will be encouraged to stop, think and ask themselves certain questions before going on to try and find an answer.

If you ask people why they see things in the way they do, they will generally look rather puzzled and then reply: "Because that's how I see them." This is the attitude most of us have toward the world about us: we take for granted that it is just as we see it. It never crosses our minds that it could be in any way different and that what we see is merely the result of the way in which our organs of perception function.

This book is primarily intended to demonstrate that the perception of objects is not just the result of passive reflection, but a process of active collation, the product of the compilation and processing of data by the brain and the organs of sensory perception. This does not mean that the objects which we see have no existence in time or space, but rather that we do not see their physical reality, only the reality as perceived by our eyes. Although common sense would normally prevent us from accepting this subjective principle, we feel sure you, as the reader will feel differently once you have carried out the experiments outlined in this book. In particular, we are convinced that you will look through different eyes at the countless images that surround you every day of your life. And this, in our opinion, is a very worthwhile goal. Gaining awareness of the mechanisms that lie at the basis of visual perception, recognizing the relationship between the eye and the brain, and freeing oneself from the conventional, superficial way of looking at the world, means not only expanding the potential of one's experience, but also of being alive to the existence of a more "real" world.

Everyone will agree that we live in a world dominated by images. Even though it would perhaps be premature, as yet, to proclaim the supremacy of images over words, it cannot be denied that visual communication is continually extending its powers, frequently integrating with verbal communication, sometimes replacing it altogether. This being the case, then it becomes extremely important to know and be able to decipher this language which modern society uses to communicate with the individual.

This book, although light-hearted in tone, is also designed to give the reader an understanding of the subconscious mechanisms that determine how we perceive the world and our surroundings. An image conveys an infinite number of messages that a word can either not communicate at all or can only do so less efficiently. The average person is generally in no position to cope with the constant flood of information that comes to him in visual form. This can be seen in advertising, which conditions people, creates unnatural needs and encourages us to use a particular product; in tele-

vision, which is able to sway public opinion; in newspapers, magazines and films. Being able to read the "text" implicit in these images and to decipher the mass of visual messages that surround us in our daily life means being able to live with greater freedom and greater awareness. This is, however, only the negative side of the problem. By mastering visual language we can also increase our own capacity for self-expression and improve our ability to communicate with others. Another point to consider is that if we are members of a society that tends to communicate increasingly through visual language, then an understanding of the techniques and devices used, can help us to know ourselves better. In this respect, Visual Games is also of value as an educational book.

Although it is true that the discussion of images develops along essentially gestalt lines, individual scientific concepts are introduced as entertaining curiosities, with constant reference to the experiences of everyday life. The psychology of perception is, in fact, nothing more than a critical explanation of the way in which our visual experience is conditioned. Achieving this involves examining the world which we all share — everyday life — from a different angle. Seeing the same things, but with a critical and rational mind, often means becoming aware of new aspects and new qualities. The aim of this book is to make you, the reader, conscious of the existence of a whole group of hitherto ignored phenomena and also to highlight their complexity. If, therefore, the book acts as a means of broadening your sense of awareness, it may also be regarded as a way of encouraging the development of a basic scientific mentality.

This book does not illustrate complex or rarefied experiments; in physics, for example, some experiments are the domain of specialists. The perceptive phenomena with which we deal here, the games, the exercises, the curious facts and anecdotes, refer to our everyday experiences. The brief theoretical analyses and concepts to which we resort, and the references to the psychology of perception, are all related to things which form part of our daily lives; things that each of us can recreate by ourselves. In this sense, the book is also an informative scientific work.

A world of images

*All it often needs is the slightest detail
to give a photograph a meaning that is
diametrically opposed to the one intended.
[. . .] The objectivity of images
is only an illusion.* (Gisèle Freund)

On the island of Wainatu

The following story is based on fact, even though we have had to change the names, the location and several other details.

Wainatu was a large and lush island, inhabited by tribes that until a generation ago had practised cannibalism. Very few visitors, apart from missionaries or intrepid explorers, had dared land on the island to make contact with its inhabitants. There were tales of bloodcurdling customs and practices that kept outsiders at bay. The discovery of large mineral deposits, however, particularly oil, forced the inhabitants into the mainstream of Western civilization in a single generation.

The first arrivals came as invaders; they were followed by technicians, geologists and engineers and their huge machines. Roads were built, huts were replaced by houses, and very soon the villages had become small civic centers, replete with multi-storey buildings and skyscrapers, shops and supermarkets; the vast riches concealed beneath the ground had completely transformed the island and its inhabitants. But the cultural leap had been too sudden and rumour had it that some of the old customs still lingered on, especially those connected with cannibalism. The government had long since abolished any rituals or religious practices that could in any way lead to the revival of customs that were now deemed to be repugnant. But one could never be sure.

The supermarkets were filled with every type of merchandise, mainly Western products, which by now had become necessities, but also with luxury goods: bottles of champagne, perfumes and expensive clothes. There were also the usual displays of cans of meat, fish, vegetables etc, with pictures on the labels to enable people to identify the contents. The authorities in charge of food distribution suddenly became aware that there had been a run on a certain canned product bearing the picture of a plump and smiling little boy. Given the wide range of products available, why was this particular brand so popular?

Imagine the dismay of the authorities when they discovered that people were buying these cans because they were convinced they were eating the tender young flesh of a child, whereas in reality the cans contained beef. Cannibalism, abolished by law, had come into its own again: its abolition had not meant its cultural death. Beneath the veneer of civilization the inhabitants of Wainatu were still cannibals.

This story says a lot about the effects on culture of certain changes carried out in the name of progress. Our concern here, however, is to investigate another, possibly more thought-provoking aspect of this story: why had the island's inhabitants interpreted the picture on the label as referring to the can's contents rather than as a decorative motif?

At this point we would ask our readers to read no further, but to pause a while and try to answer this question. There is much to be gained from comparing your own conclusions with those we shall suggest. This book is not solely or even predominantly a book for reading; it is a text on which you must bring your own mind to bear and make your own comparative judgements.

The plump child

If we see a can of meat with a fine, healthy-looking cow on the label, we conclude that it contains good quality beef. In the same way, if we see a can bearing pictures of tuna, sardines or anchovies, for example, we expect it to contain the meat of these particular fish. If, on the other hand, we see a happy healthy child on a can, we would never think that it contained human flesh; we would conclude that children eating the contents would grow up to be happy and healthy. Imagine, however, that this can, as happened in our story, landed in the middle of a tribe or people among whom cannibalism had been widely practised and who regarded it as culturally acceptable; who could deny the possibility that the same picture would be interpreted as an announcement that the can contained the succulent flesh of a fine plump child?

The meaning of an image, the message it conveys, is closely linked to personal experience and knowledge. Normally, the images on cans are a "shorthand" message informing us of what they contain. But if we see a representation of a smiling child, we would never assume that it could be an indication of the contents, since eating children is not a part of our cultural heritage. There is thus a basic cultural rationale that helps us to interpret visual messages in the correct way.

The role of the viewer

Let us pass from cans of meat to the contemplation of a pear in a basket of fruit. If you think that in order to perceive a pear all you have to do is "see" it (i.e. receive the stimuli of light emanating from a particular fruit), then you are sadly mistaken. Without seeking to be too philosophical, even an act as simple as looking at a pear is not performed as automatically as one might imagine. Seeing a pear is, without any exaggeration, a cultural act. The reason for this statement will become clearer to the reader after reading all, or almost all, of this book, because it is something we shall be referring to on several occasions, but which we must now start to discuss. You will already have realized that by the word "culture" we are not referring to something that can be acquired from books at school; we are using it in its more general, modern sense, to mean the sum total of all the customs, practices and traditions of a people. So, in order to recognize an ordinary pear, we must first know what a "pear" is. In other words, we must have learned how to distinguish the shape, colour range and surface texture of pears from all other shapes, colours and surface textures.

But that is not all; it is also necessary to have learned how to distinguish these characteristics in individual pears. Just as no two people or no two dogs are alike, so all pears are different. You must of course use your eyes to see these differences. Just try asking a shepherd if the sheep in his flock are all alike, as they seem to you. Not only will he tell you that they are all different, he will also be able to say in what respects they

How we interpret a visual message is inextricably linked to experience and acquired knowledge. Messages that are clear to one culture may prove difficult or even impossible to comprehend for people from a different cultural background. An example of this is the so-called "candelabra" of Paracas, in the southern part of Peru, which covers the entire face of a mountain and is clearly visible from far out at sea. The meaning and purpose of this gigantic work, created by people of an ancient civilization, remain a mystery to us.

differ. In fact, the way in which we see and characterize the world and the objects in it is conditioned by past experience and depends largely on culture and on acquired knowledge. Somewhere in our minds these images from the past are all stored, together with their particular characteristics. Even an ordinary pear will only represent a visual message if it forms part of an already familiar store of experience and knowledge.

A surfeit of images

We live in a world of images. Throughout the day we are constantly assailed by signals and information transmitted via images. When we open the morning newspaper, for example, much of the news is accompanied by photographs of men, women and events. It is a fact of life that in recent years the entertainment pages, those dealing with the cinema, television and theater, have increased considerably. If you remain unconvinced, just consult any newspaper published fifteen or twenty years ago and notice how little space was devoted to entertainments. These same entertainment pages show how even a news medium as traditional as the newspaper has had to come to terms with visual communication; papers are filled with pictures of actors, actresses or scenes from the films or plays being reviewed in the adjoining articles. There is not a single daily newspaper that does not provide a guide to the day's television programmes or criticism of ones screened the night before. This shows how even newspapers, which are essentially based on the written word, have had to make allowances for the vast development in visual communication that has occurred in recent years.

If we go out to work, we pass through streets that are lined with large expanses of posters and advertising hoardings trying to attract our attention and make us feel the need to look attractive or healthy, or indicating new ways to satisfy our hunger and thirst. Quite often our work will bring us into contact with images: photographs, sketches, plans, maps, diagrams etc. When we return home in the evening, we relax in front of the television and immerse ourselves in the myriad images it projects at us. And so the day ends with a true surfeit of images.

The special power of the image

What power do images possess that words lack? Not every phrase or every thought can be translated into images. This fact is cited by some to support the superiority of verbal communication, but images have an emotional capacity that words do not. The Greek and Roman orators of the ancient world were well aware of this, as were the preachers of the Middle Ages, who, in order to give their message more weight, delivered it in emotional tones, accompanied by gestures and actions designed to fire the imagination of their listeners and make them react. Teachers know how useful pictures can be in making certain concepts and notions immediately comprehensible; it is no coincidence that the principal medium of mass communication, television, with its power to bring past and present events alive, is now so widespread in schools as an irreplaceable audio-visual aid. It should also be remembered that visual communication is not limited solely to figures and images. At a road junction, for example, the red colour of a traffic light suggests danger. Some modern paintings, which are merely compositions of differently coloured lines with only the remotest relation to concrete objects, make us feel a variety of emotions. Diffused colour in a nightclub imparts a feeling of warmth and creates a pleasant atmosphere. The emotive power of images is thus wide and varied.

An improvised example of abstract representation. Even a composition that does not represent objects or other concrete forms will still convey a message with its own communicative function.

A modern means of communication

In the increasingly communicative world we live in today, the old means of disseminating information, based mainly on words, have proved to be inadequate. Images, on the other hand, with their ability to transmit a large amount of information concisely and rapidly, have become a particularly appropriate instrument for fulfilling the communication requirements of today.

As a result, all the expressive possibilities of the language of images have been investigated and developed. New techniques, new solutions and new figurative devices have revealed the creative potential of the human imagination in a variety of fields. Simple, basic, easy to read and easy to understand, images have become ever more widespread.

If we examine the images in the first column we can see that they each convey an easily decipherable piece of information. Working from top to bottom, they indicate, *sun, moon, woman, rain, splendour* (the sun and the moon together), *peace* (a woman inside a house), *rest* (a man beneath a tree) and *snow* (rain that can be caught in the hand). The illustration portrays the development from pictographs (first column) to ideograms (last column) in Japanese writing.

Their aim is to bring to mind a particular meaning in the fastest possible way. If we see a sign representing a beer tankard, for example, we know that beneath it there should be an establishment where we can refresh ourselves with a good glass of beer. If we then see next to it a board with the symbols of a knife and fork, we know that it is also possible to eat there. A little man made out of tyres tells us that we are near a service station. And there are countless other examples of this type.

Often, in order to remind ourselves to do something, we will tie a knot in our handkerchief, which thus becomes an image of something to resolve, a knotty problem that needs to be unravelled. Knots, amulets, symbolic shapes, magical signs carved on pieces of wood or animal bones, totems and other figures have all been used since prehistory, as they are still today, as vehicles for the transmission of particular messages.

In the beginning was the image

When an image has to meet the need for precise and clear information, the actual objects that it portrays have to be simplified and reduced to their essential characteristics. They then become *pictographs*, the name commonly applied to the written signs used at the dawn of civilization by peoples such as the ancient Sumerians, which consisted basically of a schematic drawing of the object in question. A head with two horns, for instance, recalls the skull of an ox and therefore leads us to believe that it contains some information relating to a member of the bovine species.

In the earliest forms of writing there was the image, the sign, but this underwent a process of abstraction and simplification that transformed it into lines that no longer had anything to do with the object originally portrayed. Pictographs then became *ideograms*, which are symbols, representations of objects so stylized as to be no longer recognizable. This is the system of writing still used by the Chinese today. A pictograph representing a standard type of vase or an ideogram with the same meaning will both give us generic information concerning a vase, but they do not specify exactly what sort of vase we are dealing with. As economic transactions intensified, people felt the need for a more flexible and sophisticated system of conveying information. The transition from ideograms to phonetic writing (initially syllabic, because each syllable represented a sound, and then literal, meaning that there was one sign for each letter) was designed to answer this need. The system of literal writing proved to be capable of registering and relaying an almost infinite number of messages, of crystallizing and developing even the most subtle concepts and of describing the most complex of relationships.

It is thus in images that one must seek the origins of the written word. Later on we will deal in greater depth with the complicated relationship that exists between words and images and between visual and verbal communication.

Modern pictographs

Here are a number of modern pictographs: see if you can work out what they mean and where you would be likely to find them. The answers are on the next page.

1a

1b

2a

2b

1c

1d

3a

3b

2c

2d

4a

4b

3c

3d

5a

5b

4c

4d

The language of languages

There are certain circumstances in which words are inadequate as a means of communication and where resorting to images can prove a positive advantage. Such occasions may take the form of meetings attended by people from different countries, speaking languages with different origins and different grammatical structures. More frequently, however, it is international sporting events, such as the Olympic Games, international athletics meetings or World Cup football matches, which pose considerable problems as to the best means of conveying information. In other words, we are

"Modern pictographs" – explaining the signs (previous page)

Series *a* shows various different means of public transport. *Fig. 1a* shows a means of travelling on rails and thus means *train*, a sign found mainly in large towns. The same applies to *Fig. 2a*, which is the generic symbol for an airport. *Fig. 3a* indicates a heliport, an airport equipped for the landing and take-off of helicopters. *Fig. 4a* indicates a *seaport*, where people can catch a ferry. *Fig. 5a* brings to mind the most common methods of urban transport, *taxis* and *buses*. Let us now try to describe, after analyzing the individual drawings, where and in what context we would be likely to find the pictographs that appear in series *b*.

Fig. 1b seems to be telling us about a place where cases can be safely locked away. It may therefore indicate the presence of a *safe deposit box*. A key combined with a car, as in *Fig. 2b*, is also an unmistakable symbol: it informs us of the existence of a lock-up garage. *Fig. 3b*, with its question mark, seems to be asking passersby the question: "Are you sleepy?" "Do you need a bed?" It therefore signals the presence of a place where people can find a *bed*, somewhere to *sleep*. If it is accompanied by *Figs. 4b* and *5b*, then it means that visitors can have breakfast (with a cup of coffee, milk, tea etc.) or even a more substantial meal involving a knife and fork. In passing

from *Fig. 1b* to *5b* we have described some of the most important services that a good motel can offer its clients.

Series *c* takes us inside an airport. *Fig. 1c* shows the moment when a person behind some sort of counter (we cannot see the lower part of the body) is handing a piece of paper – probably a ticket – to another person standing on the other side (here we see the whole body): it therefore indicates a *ticket office*. *Fig. 2c* indicates a place for baggage and suitcases. *Figs. 3c* and *4c* both contain the image of a policeman (with his unmistakable peaked cap and bandoleer strung across his chest and attached to a belt at his hip) looking into an open suitcase and then inspecting a sort of booklet. They are thus signs indicating the place where baggage is searched and passports are checked.

Series *d* may form part of the pictographs often found at large stations, at any point where travellers arrive and depart or at frontier posts. *Fig. 1d* indicates a *telephone*, while *2d* shows a *post office* where letters can be posted. *3d* has a much more complex message to convey: by means of the symbols for different currencies (the dollar, the French franc, the British pound and the Japanese yen) it indicates the presence of a *Bureau de Change*. Finally, a symbol with which everyone is familiar, *Fig. 4d*, which indicates a *First Aid station*.

dealing with circumstances in which the number and variety of spoken languages make communication between individuals a problematical affair. Using national languages in such situations just means increasing the linguistic Babel, with all the consequences which that entails. It therefore becomes necessary to create a clear and universal "sign language," which can cross linguistic frontiers and be readily understood by everybody. It is significant that research in this field has led toward images, figures and signs as a means of communication capable of transmitting messages and information in the most immediate, simple and concise way.

But perhaps we are straying too far into the realms of abstraction. Let us therefore take an example which will give a better idea of what we are trying to say.

The word "dog" is written in different ways in different languages: in French it is "chien," in Spanish "perro," in German "Hund," in Italian "cane" and so on. But all these ways of saying "dog" have nothing to do with the flesh-and-bone reality of a dog; they are conventional terms made up of sounds and letters. There are as many ways of saying "dog" as there are languages in the world. If, however, we use a picture of a dog, we can clearly communicate the idea in a way that transcends language and is universally and immediately comprehensible. This is what we mean by the idea that "the image is mightier than the word."

The figures shown on the opposite page convey messages that do not need words to be universally understood.

It should, however, be remembered that the understanding of such symbols is linked not only to their context, but also to prior experience. If, for instance, an illustration of a clothes hanger were used as a shop sign, we would know that the shop dealt in such commodities, whereas the same sign in a hotel lobby indicates the cloakroom. As we have already seen, people from a different cultural background would probably interpret the message in yet another way.

Which sport?

Sporting events, especially those at international level, are a time when people from different countries, sometimes from opposite ends of the earth, meet and share a common experience. They therefore represent an important factor in fostering international friendship and understanding. The ancient Greeks were aware of this fact when they suspended all hostilities between different city states during the Olympic Games, but they, of course, did not have the same problems as those faced by present-day organizers and contestants. The modern Olympic authorities have invented a universal and easily decipherable language based on images to cope with these problems. The symbols shown on this and the following page indicate various sporting disciplines: some of them identify specialist events within a single sport, while others merely give a general indication. Try yourself to identify the different sporting activities they represent.

Ball games

It is easy to recognize football in the first two symbols, but can you name the other ball games as well? Try also to identify and describe which detail gives the most obvious clue. The answers are on page 17.

Snow sports

Winter sports enthusiasts can test their knowledge by correctly identifying the different events pictured below. The symbols shown here relate to sports performed on ice or snow, all of which have many elements in common. Each sport is distinguished from the others by details that relate more to the equipment (skis, ski-sticks etc.) than to the way in which they are practised. For this reason the reader's eye should concentrate on the posture adopted by the figures to identify the name of the sport concerned. Here, too, the most important thing is to describe the details that give the strongest overall impression. The answers can be found on the opposite page.

"Ball games" – explaining the signs (page 15)

Fig. 1 represents a person running with the ball at his feet: as we have already said, these elements clearly bring to mind the game of *football*. Observe how the images describe the essential characteristic of this sport, the aim of which is to get the ball into the opponent's goal using one's feet (or head). The two images thus rely on the factor that distinguishes this ball game from others: the use of the foot.

In *Fig. 2* the information is conveyed by the type of ball used in football, in this case soccer. It is aimed at people who know how to distinguish the different types of ball: those used in football and those used in basketball, volleyball etc. Therefore, fewer people will be able to interpret *Fig. 2* correctly.

The sport referred to in *Fig. 3* is *rugby*: we know this from the shape of the ball, which is oval, and the stance of the players. The image, in fact, shows one player tackling another as he tries to get away holding the ball. It contains more than enough information for us to be able to identify the game of rugby, which is one of the few ball games where players are allowed to tackle opponents round the legs to bring them down.

In order to realize that the sport portrayed in *Fig. 4* is basketball, we have to stop and analyze the details provided by the two players who are stretching up toward a small net or "basket." It is not, in itself, a clear and immediately comprehensible image. *Fig. 5*, on the other hand, shows clearly that the sport in question is basketball. It should be noted that it is not so much the shape of the ball and its distinguishing characteristics that provide the clues to the sport as its position above the basket.

Figs. 6, 7 and *8* portray other ball games. Let us try to identify and describe them from the few details that distinguish them from each other. *Fig. 6* shows a player in the act of hitting a ball with his hand in order to project it over an obstacle placed above his head. One immediately thinks of *volleyball*, with the horizontal line representing the net that characterizes this game. *Fig. 7* also shows a game in which the ball is handled, but one in which it is held above the head during play. But the two horizontal lines and the position of the body, which is relaxed and not tense as in volleyball, bring to mind a man playing with a ball in water and trying to keep his head above the surface: the sport must therefore be *water polo*. *Fig. 8* is hard to recognize, because it depicts a little-known and little-played game. The game is *softball*, a variation of baseball that differs from the latter in that it is played on a smaller field, with larger and, as the name suggests, softer balls and shorter bats. It is less exhausting and less demanding than baseball.

The player shown in *Fig. 9* is holding a small bat, while the line cutting across the figure at waist level gives the idea of a flat surface. These are all elements characteristic of *table tennis*. The way in which the player holds the bat also helps us identify the game being played.

A similar detail, combined with the shape of the racket, clearly identifies the game in *Fig. 10* as *tennis*, even though the symbol does not actually make any reference to the presence of a net.

In *Fig. 11*, as in the two previous ones, it is the shape of the equipment held by the player (in this case, a bat), and also his stance, which tells us that the game in question is *baseball*.

Fig. 12 shows a player throwing a ball which he holds in his hand; in this example, it is the player's stance in particular which tells us that the game in question is *bowling*.

"Snow sports" – explaining the signs (page 16)

Fig. 1 represents the form of skiing accessible to the largest number of people: *cross-country* skiing. The most telling details, apart from the rather disjointed posture of the figure, are the raised position of the rear ski, and the way in which the front hand presses down on the ski-stick.

Similarly, in *Fig. 2*, it is primarily the position of the body which brings to mind *slalom* skiing, even though this particular symbol is not as informative as it might be and does leave some room for doubt. This is certainly not the case with *Fig. 9*, in which the idea of a slalom race is clearly conveyed by the frontal position of the figure, and, more specifically, by the curving lines that echo the winding slalom course. Slalom racing is, in fact, an event in which the contestants have to negotiate a series of gates by means of constant twisting and turning; in *giant slalom* there are normally no fewer than twenty of these gates, placed on a gradient of 300 meters (975 feet).

Figs. 3 and *4* represent *downhill* racing. The idea is conveyed particularly by the aerodynamic stance of the figure and by the way in which the ski-sticks are both tucked under the arms. The pictograph that gets the idea across in the clearest and most effective way would seem to be *Fig. 3*.

Apart from the stance of the body, *Fig. 5* contains a further piece of information to indicate that it represents *ski-jumping*: the absence of ski-sticks, items of equipment which are not required for this specialized discipline.

In *Fig. 6*, the way in which the contestant is steering the sled tells us that the sport is *tobogganing*.

In *Fig. 7*, the outline of a sort of "sidecar," reminiscent of the special type of sled known as a "bobsleigh," together with the two figures placed one behind the other, tell us that the sport in question is the *two-man bobsleigh*.

Fig. 8 recalls one of the classically graceful poses adopted by practitioners of *figure skating*.

Figs. 9, 10, 11 and *12* depict the *slalom*, as we have already mentioned, *downhill*, *ski-jumping* and *cross-country* respectively. These pictographs have been grouped together because they all share the same lines which, as we have already noted, not only convey a feeling of rapid movement, meaning that they are not purely decorative elements, but also portray details that inform us as to the type of specialized skiing discipline involved. They were used in 1968 at Grenoble, France, for the Winter Olympics.

A glimpse at history

Were images more widely used as a means of communication in antiquity than in the modern world?

This is not an easy question to answer. Certainly the remains of the civilization of Ancient Egypt are littered with images: paintings, sculptures and bas-reliefs tell of events in the lives of the Pharaohs, as well as portraying the gods and scenes of everyday life: labouring in the fields, tending cattle, hunting and fishing. These representations make use of such characteristic symbols as the sun and the vulture (with wings outstretched to signify protection), fantastic shapes and decorative motifs based on palms or lotus flowers. The Minoans of Crete adorned their pottery and the walls of the palace of Knossos with floral, marine and naturalistic motifs inspired by their maritime heritage and the splendours of court life.

And what of the ancient Greeks with their statues and sculptures, models of perfection and beauty that still fascinate us today? When one thinks in addition of their extraordinarily widespread use of pottery (the word "ceramic" itself comes from the Greek *keramikós*), it does not seem too improbable to suggest that through their terra-cotta vases they were indirectly responsible for the invention of an early form of mass communication based on images and on the ability to transmit information and knowledge at a glance. The ancient Greeks embellished millions of terra-cotta vases with a variety of images, portraying either scenes of everyday life or legendary episodes from their religious and mythological heritage. Today we are able to reconstruct their mode of dress, their way of life and their attitudes by means of the innumerable figures that appear on their pottery. Other, less sophisticated peoples, however, have also left reminders of their existence through drawings, as can be seen from rock carvings dating from prehistoric and historical times.

The ancient Romans delighted in decorating their homes with images characterized by a heightened sense of realism.

Opposite page: below left, rock paintings depicting bison and horses (Santimamiña Cave, Spain), which show how the language of images has been part of human history since its earliest beginnings. The upper illustration in the box to the right (opposite) shows examples of Egyptian hieroglyphs, a type of writing whose signs often retain clear outlines of the objects to which they refer; below, a number of Egyptian (Nos. 1–6) and Cretan (Nos. 7–14) hieroglyphs.
Their meanings are as follows: 1, sun, time; 2, mountain; 3, sea, water; 4, to eat; 5, to walk; 6, to fight; 7, ox; 8, double-headed axe; 9, plough; 10, ship; 11, vase; 12, palace; 13, tree; 14, country.

This page: above, Greek vase painting showing a warrior urging on the two horses drawing his chariot. Greek vase painting is regarded by many as an early example of image-based communication, designed to act as a means of making the cultural and religious heritage of mythology accessible to a mass audience.
The illustration below reproduces the bill presented in 1830 by an illiterate English mason to a man for whom he had done some work. The drawings mean: two men and a child for three-quarters of a day; two buckets of mortar, total ten shillings and tenpence. The hanged man at the end of the sequence signifies that the bill has been paid.

A visit to that unique monument of the Roman world, Pompeii, will give an idea of what we mean; there one can admire large numbers of Roman frescoes and mosaics in a variety of forms, portraying a variety of subjects.

During the Middle Ages, when the common people were unable either to read or write, the Church used images to tell stories from the Bible, from the life of Christ and the lives of the saints: these took the form of mosaics and wall-paintings, sometimes both, containing a long series of pictures, rather like a strip cartoon (if that is not being irreverent), which could convey religious and moral principles in a form that was accessible to all.

Although it is true that the Church has always favoured the spoken word as a means of conveying the basic truths of

How communication is achieved

An image represents a message that we are able to identify through the information provided. Every message presupposes the existence of one person, or several, to issue the message (the *transmitter*), and one, or several, to receive the message (the *receiver*). If, in addition, it contains information, this will relate to one or more specific facts (the *reference*), which in *their* turn are related to their setting (the *context*).

We have of necessity been somewhat vague and sketchy in our explanation thus far, but let us now remedy the situation by providing a concrete example. This alone can sometimes be enough to simplify and clarify concepts which, when considered in the abstract, seem complex and almost incomprehensible. Let us therefore examine the signs below and try to describe what they indicate.

Christianity, it felt unable to renounce the persuasive powers of the image, despite the ever-present danger of idolatry. The statement by St Gregory that "figures are to the illiterate what letters are to the learned" justified recourse to the language of imagery as a necessity of the times. In fact, the Church has always recognized the value of this means of communication, which has constantly retained its effectiveness, as can be seen from the way in which the figurative arts have evolved. In fact, one could say that painting, sculpture and also architecture have become irreplaceable as a means by which the Church divulges its teachings.

It is true that fewer frescoes are painted today and fewer mosaics are created, but that does not mean that images are any less present. Just take a look at any old photograph of your local town – one from the beginning of the century will do – and you can see immediately how its appearance has changed. The streets and buildings are now covered in signs, pictures, symbols and posters. There are advertisements everywhere, in buses, on the walls and along the roads, all trying to attract our attention. But the most striking difference is the overwhelming presence of traffic signs; these, as we shall see later, represent a unique coded language, made up of a group of conventional signs composed of special images.

The illustration above shows four conventional signs, some more common than others, which you may well see during your travels: can you remember what they mean? They indicate, from left to right and from top to bottom, a camp site, a point where overtaking is forbidden, a stretch of unprotected water and the presence of a nearby school.

The first portrays a glass with part of it broken off and, in itself, tells us nothing. The second one, however, shows an open umbrella; it could therefore possibly be interpreted as a warning that it is raining, but such a warning seems to serve no useful purpose; perhaps, then, it is the sign for a shop where umbrellas are sold. The third one appears to tell us nothing at all: what could two hands stretching out to grasp some sort of cube possibly mean? If, however, we say that they are all labels placed on freight or postal packages, then their meaning immediately becomes apparent and their message clear. The first indicates that the package contains glass, not necessarily glasses as such, which can be easily broken. The second warns that the package must be protected from the rain, while the third shows that it should be held in both hands in a certain position. All that is needed is to show their context for the signs to lose their ambiguity and assume a specific and unmistakable meaning.

In this case the reference was clear, but the images themselves had no meaning outside their context. Let us now try another exercise, but one that calls for a little more effort on your part because it will be up to you to describe the context.

The meaning of "context"

Can you say in what context the signs shown on the opposite page will appear? Give the matter some thought and, before hazarding a guess, try to describe the message they convey.

Let us first observe what all these signs have in common: the red bar running across them, which makes it clear that they are expressing a prohibition. In addition, all four show a staircase with one significant detail: the steps are separated by a deep gap.

The first sign warns people not to go up the stairs barefoot, probably because it could cause injury. The second advises people not to insert the tips of umbrellas into the gaps because they may break off. Similarly, the third warns people of the danger of having the toes of their shoes caught in the gaps, while the fourth forbids people to sit on the stairs. Taking into consideration all the individual factors, it should not be difficult to work out that all these warnings are aimed at people travelling on an escalator of the type found in large stores and subways.

What is a code?

Once we have understood how communication is achieved, all that remains is to explain what is meant by a *code*, to provide a precise and clear definition of the term.

All the signals that we use (gestures, sounds, images) mean nothing by themselves. In order for them to have any particular significance, there must be some sort of agreement between those who transmit a message or piece of information and those who receive it. A green light, for example, has no intrinsic meaning, but less than a hundred years ago, when the first cars began to foreshadow traffic problems yet to come, it was agreed this signal should mean "permission to proceed." The same conventional system was applied to the red light and later to every other sign using red as the colour of warning and prohibition; red flags on a beach during heavy seas, for example, warn bathers that it is dangerous to swim. The device that makes us interpret red as a warning or prohibition is a code.

We are therefore now in a position to understand what a code is: it is a conventional device whereby meanings are attributed to different signals. Every system of communication, by virtue of its definition, possesses a code, a system of rules that indicates the conventional signals, their meaning and their usage. The very word "conventional" is itself an indication that these rules are the result of common accord between mankind. And as mankind changes, so can the rules. The important thing is to respect them and to abide by them, otherwise there can be no communication and thus no comprehension. The Morse code, the system of road signs, the nuances of spoken language are all examples of codes. Codes therefore represent the key to understanding messages, but in order to accomplish their aim, these messages need some channel of communication. When we speak to another person, for example, our voice is transmitted through the air by means of sound waves which are received by the listener's organ of hearing, the ear. The conduit, the link between the two people, represents the channel, in this particular case *sound waves*. There are, however, other channels through which messages can pass, for example, *light waves*, which are the vehicle for conveying the language of images and other visual communications.

Man communicates and gains knowledge through his senses. Each of these senses has its own particular language, and for every language there is a different code and channel of communication.

A few everyday examples

The highway code, with all its signs and signals, is a very eloquent example of a system of universally comprehensible symbols.

The correct reading of a code is dependent on its context as well as its text to reveal its meaning. If, for example, we see a sign showing a horn crossed by a red line, we know that we are in an area where use of the car horn is forbidden, not that trumpets are for sale.

Have you ever seen people in train corridors holding an unlit cigarette in their hands as they search anxiously for a seat? They are, in fact, looking for a sign showing a lighted cigarette. And when they finally locate one they look about them in search of a free seat. If they are successful, they sit down and enjoy a quiet smoke. This describes the classic behaviour of a dedicated smoker. People who detest smoking may also be on the lookout for the same symbol, albeit for the opposite reason. The important thing is that neither party sees that symbol in a train compartment as meaning "cigarettes sold here." The ability to read a signal correctly depends not only on what it says or what it represents, but also on the context in which it is said.

The best known signs nowadays, because they are the ones most frequently encountered, are traffic signs. They rely for their communicative powers not only on their content, but also on their shape, which may be circular, triangular, rectangular or square. Circular signs generally express an order, triangular signs warn drivers of a possible danger while square signs provide information on particular circumstances such as parking restrictions and directions.

These conventions, because of their widespread familiarity, have also ended up being used in other contexts, often completely unrelated to their original function.

A curious code

Beggars have never had an easy life, not only because of their circumstances, but also because of the way in which they are treated by the community at large. Their "difference" is seen as something dangerous; they are seen as "outsiders" to be wary of. People give alms partly to be rid of these unknown people, who are believed to be prone to stealing and all sorts of criminal behaviour.

There have been times when beggars were pursued by the law. In England, prior to the Industrial Revolution, there were laws threatening prison to anyone caught begging. But even when tolerated, beggars inspired feelings of mistrust and rejection. It was thus natural that a sort of solidarity would develop among those faced by the same hardships. And so tramps and beggars, who travelled from town to town, created a strange code language made up of a group of symbols that would be of help to those in the know and as obscure as possible to conventional mortals. These signs were drawn on walls and on gateposts and were based on symbolism that may now seem somewhat arbitrary.

We illustrate some of these signs on this page; it is up to the reader to try and decipher their underlying message by analyzing their shapes and meanings. You can then compare your answers with those given on the page opposite.

"Noise" in images

It has to be admitted that some of the most irritating and intolerable noises of modern life emanate from traffic congestion. It may be because it is such an "unnatural" noise that our ears react against it. Truly natural and therefore more receptive to the ear are sounds that conjure up pleasant images in our mind and give us a feeling of peace, such as the sound of

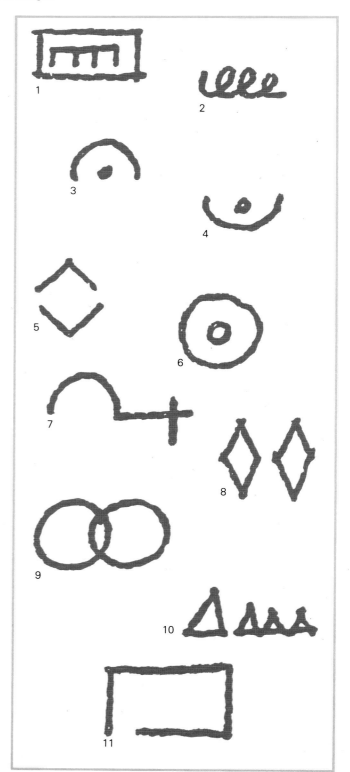

rain, which lulls us to sleep, the murmur of the sea, which instils in us a sense of tranquillity, or the rustle of leaves in the wind. Some sounds, however, such as the crash of thunder, can bring to the minds of some people, horrific memories of the sound of falling bombs in wartime.

Have you ever tried to make noise with images? Although it may seem unusual it is possible to speak of "noise" when dealing with visual communication.

Speaking in a general context, "noise" is a sound that prevents us from properly hearing voices or other meaningful sounds, as for example, the crackling noise we sometimes hear on the radio or the telephone which makes it difficult to understand what is being said, in other words, any combination of factors that hinders the process of communication.

We have no problems understanding the meaning of "noise" when referred to the language of sounds: poor pronunciation, the use of unknown, inappropriate or obscure words, extraneous sounds that interfere with a speech we are listening to etc. In written communication, "noise" may derive from printing errors, lettering that is faint or too small, illegible handwriting and so on.

What is "noise" then in visual language? Look at the photograph in the top left-hand corner of the following page: it is not difficult to make out a shirt (the collar, buttons, sleeve and other details make that perfectly clear), but one's overall perception is clouded by the background, which has the same design of vertical stripes. The picture is an advertisement by

Elso Schiavo, an Italian graphic artist, who has intentionally incorporated elements of visual "noise" in order to intensify the effect of the photograph on whoever is looking at it.

Disturbances in the language of visual imagery can take many different forms. Just think, for example, of the use made of blurred colours, fuzzy outlines, the intentional distortion of parts of the face etc. But perhaps the most common devices are the use of darkness and mistiness: in the photograph on the top right-hand corner of the following page the car headlights blend in with the street lights and lose their definition. "Noise" can sometimes reach such a pitch that it prevents the efficient transmission of the visual message.

We would now like to suggest an unusual game, played by using photographic images broken up in such a way as to prevent a clear reading of the subject: the aim is to try and describe what they represent.

The photograph at the bottom of the next page was taken using a diffracting lens; can you tell what the mass of lights represents? The picture also shows how "noise" can be artificially recreated for purely aesthetic ends.

In the illustration on page 25 it is easy to make out the subject: the eyes, the mouth and the hair leave no doubt that it is a face, but what else can you tell about it? It is interesting to note that in this case "noise" has been created by reduplicating and splitting the image into small squares reminiscent of pieces of a jigsaw puzzle, which have then been arranged in such a way as to allow for a correct "reading" of the original

---

"A curious code" – answers to signs (opposite page)

1. *Fierce dog.* The drawing inside the rectangle obviously does not show the teeth of a rake: it is a schematic representation of the teeth of a snarling dog. The surrounding rectangle may mean that the dog in question is like a wild animal that has to be kept in a cage or at least tied up.
   Notice how in this case it is the meaning of the symbol which helps us interpret the image correctly.

2. *Dog.* The animal is denoted here by an inverted version of the preceding symbol, perhaps to indicate its docility and friendliness.

3. *Constantly patrolled by police.* This drawing recalls a picture of a watchful eye, the lid raised attentively.

4. *Rarely patrolled by police.* The position of the eyelid, the opposite of that shown in the preceding drawing, conveys the idea of a relaxed and downcast eye, one that is not watchful.

5. *Friends.* Two angles facing each other give the idea of two people opening up to each other: two people who meet and confide in one another. Hence the idea of friendship and not hostility.

6. *Very good.* A circle always gives the idea of something regular and perfect; if it contains another smaller circle inside, it means that the perfection is in some way related to what is inside. It is not hard to imagine what "very good because of what's inside" would mean to a tramp.

7. *Stop.* A line going horizontally, but broken at the end by a vertical line, seems to be saying do not proceed beyond this point.

8. *Rest easy.* Two geometrical shapes, as equal and regular as these two diamonds, when placed side by side convey a feeling of peace and quiet.

9. *Beware.* "Keep your eyes skinned" seems to be the message contained in these two circles, in which it is not hard to detect the shape of two open eyes.

10. *A long-winded tale.* This is rather a curious symbol: a series of triangles of ever-decreasing size suggest something being drawn out, perhaps a long drawn-out story.

11. *Nobody.* A rectangle that can be entered and left through an opening suggests the idea of not encountering anybody or, more generally, "here you will not find anybody or anything."

These symbols clearly show an uncommon degree of subtlety and a rare capacity for communicating information. It should be remembered that beyond the confines of the code these diagrams mean nothing: it is, in other words, their conventional meanings that allow images to be correctly interpreted.

image. A similar technique has been used in the pictures on page 26, with the difference that here they are the result of two different photographs being cut into strips and then rearranged in layers. The two photographs interfere with each other, but without entirely preventing communication of the visual message. Try to describe what they portray. The answers are on page 27.

Solutions to illustrations (pages 24–25)

The picture at the bottom of page 24 shows a city at night, Brasilia to be exact. The photograph below shows the same panorama taken without any artificial distortion.

The photograph reproduced on page 25 and again below left is a portrait of a Japanese model taken by the famous photographer Hideki Fuji. A cursory comparison with the broken-up version shows us what changes visual "noise" has made to our perceptive experience.

The picture on the left of the page opposite is the result of the breaking-up into strips (then re-mounting in alternating layers) of two photographs, one showing ordinary walnuts (this page, above right) and the other an exotic tree, a papaya (below right).

The photomontage shown on the right of the page opposite has been obtained by cutting the photographs on the left into strips, but with an added element of complication. Whereas by scanning the first, third, fifth and seventh strips we can easily make out New York's famous Brooklyn Bridge, it is not so easy to discern the same subject, viewed from a different angle, in the intervening strips (the second, fourth etc.), because we have to turn the page 90 degrees.

Word or image?

Images certainly pervade our everyday lives in greater numbers and with greater persistence than they ever have before. There are even some people who speak of the supremacy of the image over the written word, and it cannot be denied that hundreds of messages and items of information that until recently were transmitted mainly verbally are now entrusted to the evocative powers of pictures and visual communication in general.

There are, however, certain subjective aspects of life and abstract reality in which the use of images is inadequate or problematical, and verbal language will prove more suitable. States of mind, simple individual statements such as ''I am tired,'' ''I am bored and sleepy'' and complex situations such as ''I was unable to make the appointment because there was no public transport'' or social, artistic, literary and other prob-

'Ambler Music Festival/Institute of Temple University

lems can be more effectively described in words. As a general rule, we can say that in terms of the three main *functions* that any language has to fulfil, those of *description*, *evocation* and *expression*, the language of images lacks the descriptive and explanatory powers of the word. You doubt this? Then try to illustrate, using images, your doubt or, better still, the statement that you doubt.

Verbal language has a capacity for abstraction that its visual counterpart does not possess. Take, for example, a phrase like "the dog is on guard," and imagine that beside it there is the image of a dog doing precisely that. Straightaway we can see that the image is not necessarily the equivalent of the phrase expressed verbally. To begin with, it is not possible to tell with an image whether it refers to dogs in general or to one particular dog out of many. The most important element, though, is that the image accompanying the statement "the dog is on guard" may be interpreted visually in a variety of different ways. Countless other phrases could be formed to describe the image: for example, "here is a watchful dog," "a dog seen from the front," "the dog is looking around" and so on. The words can be changed virtually at will, whereas the image remains the same.

Man needs all sorts of languages with which to communicate, and just as he cannot manage to do this satisfactorily without words, neither can he do without images. Here, however, we are dealing with the capacity for description, in which verbal language displays an unparalleled degree of flexibility and conciseness.

In order to understand which particular role visual language fulfils more efficiently than its verbal equivalent, try reading the phrase about the dog to a small child and he will remain more or less indifferent. But if we show him the picture of the dog on guard, then he will undoubtedly display greater curiosity and greater interest, a sign that visual images, particularly of an animal like a dog, are a great attraction. If we then give him a toy dog, with ears pricked and wide-open eyes, he will stroke it, cuddle it and perhaps even take it to bed with him at night.

The picture of the dog, and then the toy substitute, both stir up strong emotions in the mind of the child, successfully creating the sort of reactions and behaviour that the phrase could never have done. In these circumstances images show themselves able to reach areas where words cannot penetrate: they have the ability to stir up strong and vivid human emotions.

Allies – not rivals

If, after all we have said so far, we have given the impression that there is some sort of rivalry between visual and verbal communication, it has been for reasons of clarity. There is no antagonism between image and word, whether written or spoken; they merely represent two different languages by which man is able to express himself. Man is a unitary being and there is therefore no sense in treating images and words as two opposing means of communication. They are, rather, tools to be used in conjunction with each other. There are frequent cases where the written word enhances the image's ability to inform, or conversely where the communicative capacity of an image is transmitted to the word. Let us consider two examples, one relating to the first case, the other to the second.

The advertising industry has long adopted the following tactic: a picture of a mouth-watering piece of fruit, a beautiful

Opposite page: the poster on the left was originally conceived by Milton Glaser to publicize a forthcoming musical festival; right: the advertising industry advertising itself. These three posters appeared in Paris in 1981: the first says "On September 2 I'll take off my top"; the second "On September 4 I'll take off the bottoms." And, as we can see from the third poster, that is exactly what happened. The series was intended to persuade people to trust advertising posters because they tell the truth.
Right: a highly original poster created by Bill Atherton, using a photograph by Alan Brooking, for the British Family Planning Association.

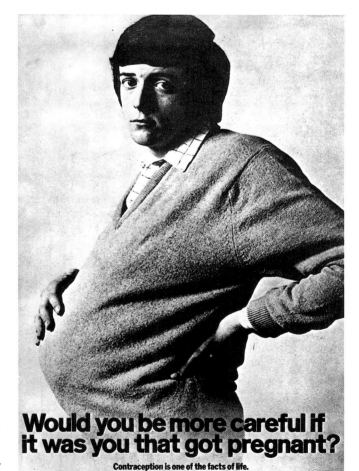

Would you be more careful if it was you that got pregnant?

Contraception is one of the facts of life.
Anyone married or single can get advice on contraception from the Family Planning Association.
Margaret Pyke House, 25-35 Mortimer Street, London W1 N 8BQ. Tel. 01-636 9135.

girl or a cartoon is first used to catch our eye, and the message is then spontaneously completed by the accompanying wording. If, however, we use a phrase like "the man is an ass," the utterance gains in expressive power through the image it conjures up and the meaning becomes clearer. Later on we shall deal with advertising at greater length; here we will merely investigate, sometimes using games, the second way in which words and images relate to each other.

From words to images

The word "muscle" comes from the Latin *musculus*, meaning "little mouse." But muscles have as much to do with mice

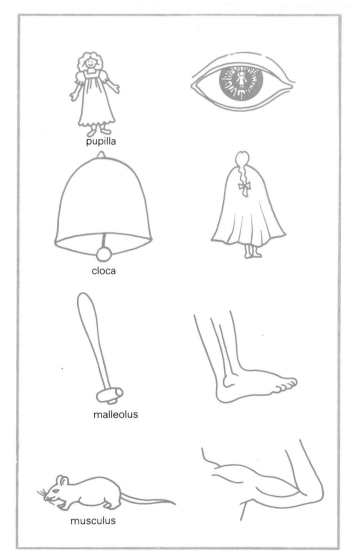

pupilla

cloca

malleolus

musculus

as chalk has to do with cheese. What, then, is the connection? Look at the drawings of muscles on this page: with a swollen central section and tapering ends, in constant movement, they may well be reminiscent of mice. *Musculus* is, in fact, a diminutive of the Latin *mus* ("mouse").

Any medical student knows that the malleolus is part of the ankle bone (the word comes from the Latin *malleolus* meaning "little hammer"). Clearly, in formation, it recalls the shape of the latter object. Similarly the word "cloak" derives from the medieval Latin word *cloca* meaning bell, obviously a reflection of the bell-like shape of this garment. The origin of the word "pupil," when applied to the eye, is also curious. It derives from the Latin diminutive of the word *pupa*, meaning "doll," and indeed if we look into another person's pupils we see our own reflection, reduced to the dimensions of a small doll.

We have cited only a few examples of a special branch of verbal language known as *figurative*, because it frequently makes use of images or figures.

In order to understand how this language is used, we have to turn briefly to philosophy. The individual and society are like two poles of the same reality, which is characterized by an intricate and complex network of relationships, information and messages. The majority of these are entrusted to words and, as we have already seen, increasingly to images. Rather than there being any antipathy between these two methods of communication, there is integration and mutual assistance. Thus words, either as an adjunct to the image or as an explanation of it, help to clarify the meaning.

There is, however, one particular way in which verbal language exploits the capacity of an image to transmit information quickly and concisely. We are referring here to the use of *metaphors*, rhetorical figures that play an important role in our literary tradition. A metaphor consists of the replacement of a word or phrase by a figurative image that is closely associated with some physical phenomenon or material object. When we speak of "freezing salaries" we are clearly using an image derived from the physical phenomenon of freezing, but transferring it to the realms of socio-economics. The figurative element is provided by the image of freezing, which could be replaced by the phrase "suspending any increase in . . ." The point we are trying to emphasize is that the creation of metaphors relies on images: to be more precise, it involves a transposition of images. Consider, for example, the phrase "a rippling cornfield." The image of a rippling sea has been transferred to a cornfield. The word "metaphor" itself comes from the Greek *metaphora*, meaning to transfer, or carry from one place to another.

Spot the metaphor

The word "delirium" was originally a metaphor (from the Latin *de*, meaning "out of," and *lira*, meaning "furrow"; hence its meaning of "to deviate from a straight line"). This is just one example, but language is so full of metaphors that, if we were to remove them from everyday speech, our ability to communicate would be drastically curtailed. The fact of the matter is that we are not even aware of the constant use we make of expressions such as "the heart of the country," "to be on tenterhooks," "to hit the nail on the head." Newspapers and magazines continually use metaphors, particularly for brief, effective and eye-catching headlines. It could be said that there is no area of human activity in which metaphor is not used to get a message across.

In the world of economics people speak of "fluctuations in the dollar"; to what image does this metaphor refer? Take your time before answering this simple question and then try to do the tests that follow. These may help you to understand and master the versatility of language. The test consists of discovering the metaphorical uses of a series of words. If, for example, the word is "neck," then one of its metaphorical uses would be "the neck of a bottle." Now see if you can work out metaphors using the following words: wing, tail, pillar, finger, fly, stool, moon, rake, iron, ashes, clouds, ear, water, nose, bag, needle.

Solutions: take someone under your *wing*; the *tail* of a speech; a *pillar* of the community; have a *finger* in the pie; *fly* in the ointment; to fall between two *stools*; once in a blue *moon*; to *rake* in money; *iron* out a problem; the *ashes* of love; head in the *clouds*; an *ear* of corn; to hold *water*; poke your *nose* into someone else's business; let the cat out of the *bag*; look for a *needle* in a haystack.

From images to words

There is one game of words and images that has become so much a part of our daily lives that most people have forgotten its noble origins. We are referring to the *rebus*, a word that some believe derives from the Latin phrase *De rebus quae geruntur* ("concerning the matters of the day"). The origins of the rebus may go as far back as rock paintings, the hieroglyphs of ancient Egypt and even to Chinese ideograms. The name of the god Osiris, for example, was represented in the form of a rebus by the image of a throne (*'usr*) and an eye (*'iri*), to which was added the image of the divine scepter to indicate that it was the name of a god (the hieroglyph is illustrated on this page).

The story of the rebus is thus a very ancient one and much more profound than its modern role as a brainteaser would suggest. It seems that the patrician families of ancient Rome delighted in creating coats of arms that recalled their names in the form of a rebus. The Colonna family, for example, used a section of a column shaft, echoing the way that their name derived from the Latin *columna* ("column"). During the Renaissance, Leonardo da Vinci loved playing around with rebuses, as can be seen in a manuscript now preserved in the Royal Collection, Windsor. Over the centuries, these games continued to be played by artists and intellectuals, who used them to find new juxtapositions of words and images. In modern times, following the rapid growth in magazines and books of puzzles, the solving of rebuses has become one of the most popular pastimes.

Here we shall deal mainly with the modern rebus, which is essentially based on one principle: the use of homophones to create abstract words. Homophones consist of words similar in sound but different in meaning. An example of homophones would be the words "fair," in the sense of "blonde," and "fair," in the sense of "market." Visually, a rebus is composed of several figures generally with one or more letters above them. The solution normally takes the form of a short phrase, a proverb, a common or widely-understood expression, or one single word of several syllables. The number of words making up the phrase and the number of letters in each word are given beneath each puzzle. It should, however, be remembered that the letters attached to the figures can come either before or after the hidden words, or may even come in the middle of them.

Like everything else in life, rebuses can vary greatly in complexity. A simple rebus will contain an assemblage of totally disparate objects bearing no relation to each other: for example, the drawing of a pine tree and an apple, to represent the word "pineapple." A more complex and more satisfactory rebus is one in which the individual elements depicted possess a certain coherence. Rebuses should ideally retain a feeling of unity, meaning that the figures of which they are composed should together represent a scene that has some overall sense.

We now invite the reader to tackle the small group of rebuses presented below, some of which are more difficult to solve than others. They take the form of four pictures that already make sense in themselves. In trying to unravel them, you should bear in mind the conventional devices used in creating a rebus. These will be explained in the solutions.

We should add one further piece of information concerning the rebus: the final result is normally an easily comprehensible word or expression, but one whose meaning relates either to concrete objects or abstract realities, with no direct bearing on the individual elements that go to make up the scenes in the pictures. You should also take into consideration the fact that not all the elements depicted are necessarily relevant to the solution of the puzzle. It is, therefore, up to you to work out which ones to include in your answer.

Rebus 3 (2 words: 11, 4 letters)

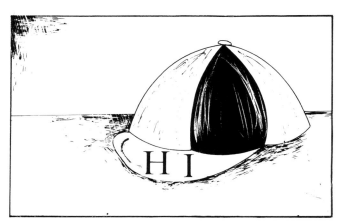

Rebus 4 (1 word: 8 letters)

Rebus 1 (1 word: 7 letters)

Rebus 2 (1 word: 8 letters)

Solutions

Rebus 1: on the left is the *core* of an apple with the *e* crossed out, and on the right is a telephone *dial*. The solution is therefore *cordial*.

Rebus 2: *top* O *log* Y = *topology*. In this one it was necessary to insert the letters O and Y to make sense of the spinning *top* and the *log*.

Rebus 3: this picture shows a *comb in a tin*, a letter O and a *lock*. If you include the O in the word *tin* it becomes *tion*, giving the solution to the puzzle: *combination lock*.

Rebus 4: the picture of a *cap*, preceded by the letters H *and* I gives the answer *handicap*. Notice how in this one the conjunction *and* is used as part of the puzzle.

Symbol or image?

There is no need for us to turn images into some sort of all-powerful myth: they cannot be used for communicating every sort of message. There are some significant aspects of subjective reality, as well as certain elements of daily life (the uniquely casual nature of events, for example), which can either not be figuratively expressed at all or only with great difficulty.

Although this is a fact, it is not our intention to dwell too long on abstract problems and so let us therefore consider something as concrete as the arrow, one of the most straightforward and widely used signs. People are not always aware of just how many messages this symbol can convey or how many meanings can be read into it.

First of all, is an arrow a symbol or an image? Try to answer this question yourself before reading on. The image of an arrow can bring to mind the weapon of the same name that has been used since prehistoric times, consisting of a thin wooden shaft equipped with a pointed tip at one end and a notch at the other into which the bowstring is fitted for firing. In this sense it is a concrete object with its own peculiar characteristics. An arrow may, however, be used as a sign, a conventionally accepted symbol: in the highway code, for example, it is frequently used to indicate the direction in which the traffic is moving, to indicate a detour, or to warn drivers of a bend in the road. In the abstract, formal language of mathematical logic an arrow indicates implication; in chem-

istry it is used to point to the direction of a reaction, while in physics, used above a letter, it signifies a vector. On a meteorological map the position of an arrow indicates wind direction; by varying the thickness of the shaft it is possible to give an indication of the strength of the wind.

In the first example, the arrow is to all intents and purposes an image or a picture, whereas in the second it is a symbol, a sign.

What is the difference? As an image it communicates an immediate message (the weapon associated with a bow), while as a symbol it requires a code to be understood. In other words, one needs to define the range of conventional meanings that it can possess. The arrow is a vital figurative device, occupying an area midway between image and symbol. It could be said that nowadays it is used predominantly as a conventional sign which, in its simplicity, is capable of expressing not only many different facets of external reality, but also abstract ideas or psychological experiences that form part of the individual's subjective world.

The reader may be forgiven for feeling slightly puzzled by what has been said so far. Let us therefore try to solve the problems laid out overleaf, all of which deal with the arrow as a symbol rather than an image. These will make you aware of the many different ideas that can be expressed by means of an ordinary arrow and also of how, once a certain meaning has been attributed to the arrangement of one or more arrows, its range of meanings can be notably extended by certain stylistic modifications.

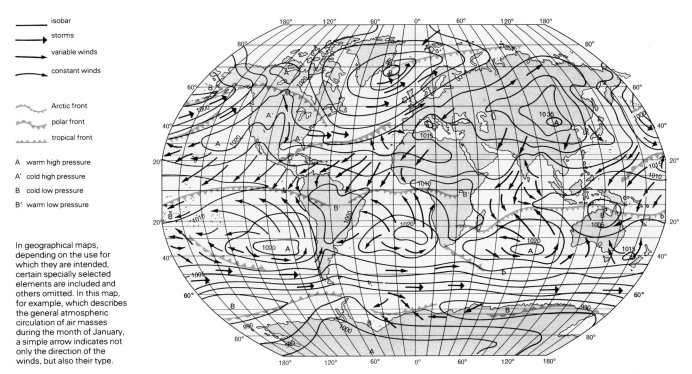

isobar
storms
variable winds
constant winds

Arctic front
polar front
tropical front

A warm high pressure
A' cold high pressure
B cold low pressure
B' warm low pressure

In geographical maps, depending on the use for which they are intended, certain specially selected elements are included and others omitted. In this map, for example, which describes the general atmospheric circulation of air masses during the month of January, a simple arrow indicates not only the direction of the winds, but also their type.

Playing games with an arrow

These exercises are arranged in the form of individual tests of logic, at the end of which the reader has to choose between three alternative solutions. The first tests can be solved without much difficulty, but they gradually become more abstract and more complex. There is no time limit: the tests are intended merely to stimulate the imagination. We start with two sample solutions to show readers how to tackle the other tests. The answers are on page 36.

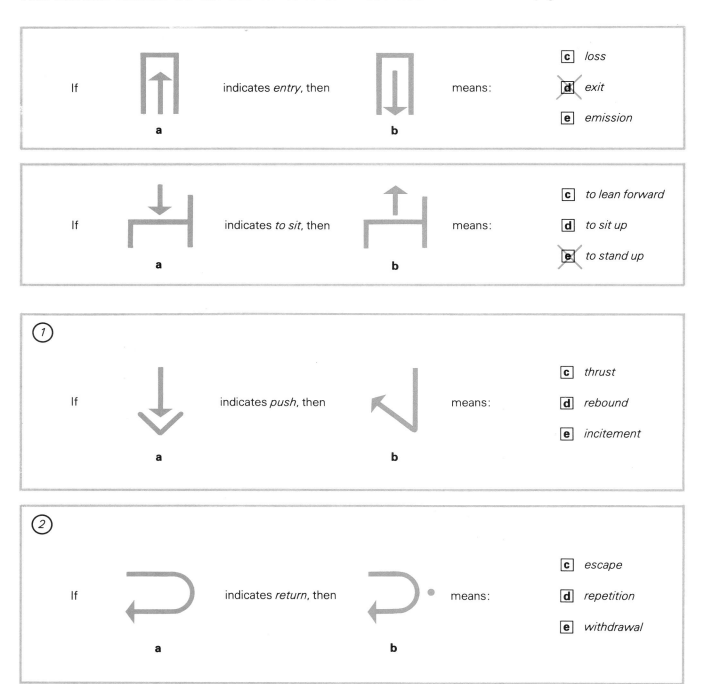

If [up arrow] **a** indicates *entry*, then [down arrow] **b** means:

- [c] loss
- [d] exit (crossed out)
- [e] emission

If [down arrow into line] **a** indicates *to sit*, then [up arrow from line] **b** means:

- [c] to lean forward
- [d] to sit up
- [e] to stand up (crossed out)

① If [down arrow] **a** indicates *push*, then [bent arrow up-left] **b** means:

- [c] thrust
- [d] rebound
- [e] incitement

② If [curved arrow] **a** indicates *return*, then [curved arrow with dot] **b** means:

- [c] escape
- [d] repetition
- [e] withdrawal

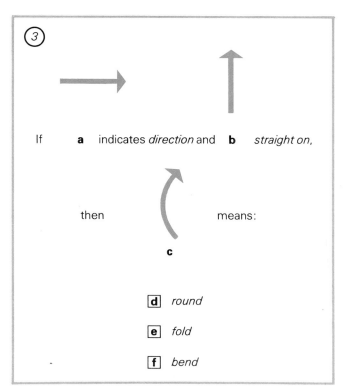

If **a** indicates *direction* and **b** *straight on*, then means:

c

d | round

e | fold

f | bend

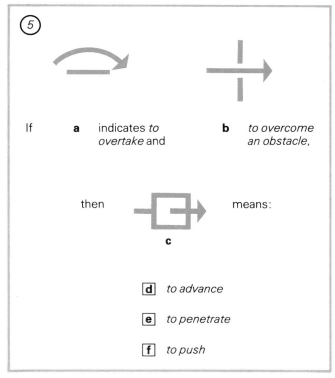

If **a** indicates *to overtake* and **b** *to overcome an obstacle*, then means:

c

d | to advance

e | to penetrate

f | to push

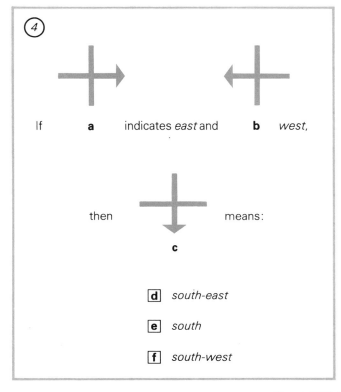

If **a** indicates *east* and **b** *west*, then means:

c

d | south-east

e | south

f | south-west

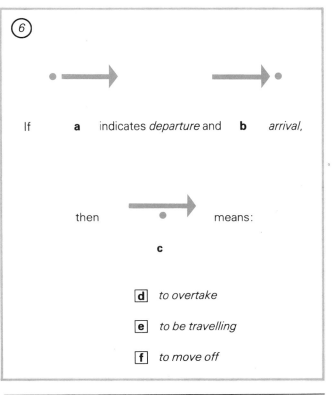

If **a** indicates *departure* and **b** *arrival*, then means:

c

d | to overtake

e | to be travelling

f | to move off

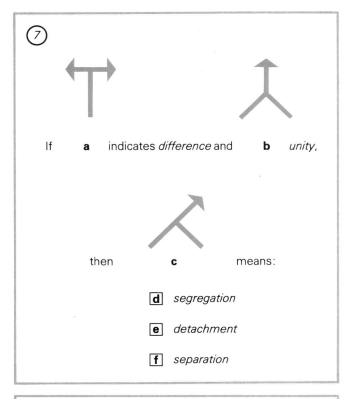

⑦

If **a** indicates *difference* and **b** *unity*,

then **c** means:

- d segregation
- e detachment
- f separation

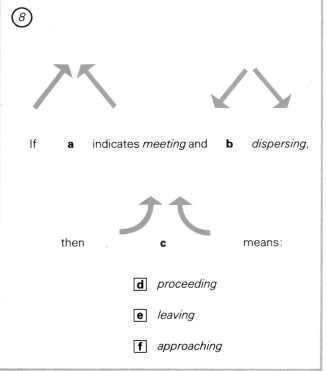

⑧

If **a** indicates *meeting* and **b** *dispersing*,

then **c** means:

- d proceeding
- e leaving
- f approaching

"Playing games with an arrow" – solutions to drawings (pages 34–36)

We will first give the correct solution to the individual tests and then provide a brief explanation as to why one answer is preferable to the others.

1. Answer *d*: if *a* indicates a thrust, then *b* indicates an abrupt change of direction, a *rebound*.

2. Answer *c*: if *a* gives the idea of returning, then the way in which the arrow in *b* veers away from the dot can only represent flight or *escape*.

3. Answer *f*: *a* and *b* show clearly that we are dealing here with the highway code, and so *c* must also be interpreted in this context; out of *d*, *e* and *f*, the only term that fits in with the shape of *c* is *bend* and certainly not either "fold" or "round."

4. Answer *e*: in this test, too, it is easy to see the context to which *a*, *b* and *c* belong; they represent the four cardinal points, which are determined by the meeting of the horizon with the meridian (the *north* and *south*) and the horizontal plane (*east* and *west*) and act as a means of determining direction. They are also found on compasses. *c* can therefore only represent the *south*.

5. Answer *e*: strictly speaking, we are not dealing here with the highway code, but with a more general context in which the arrow indicates movement in relation to some fixed object, represented in *a* by a horizontal segment, in *b* by a vertical line and in *c* by a small square which the arrow has penetrated, but without emerging completely; it thus becomes clear that *c* indicates the process of *penetration*.

6. Answer *e*: here, too, the green dot represents some generic sort of object, and so, if as in *a*, the arrow is placed in front of it, it indicates that something has been left behind, while in *b* it indicates approach; in *c* it represents passing something by without halting; it does not mean either moving off (*f*) or even overtaking (*d*), a term that would narrow the context to the highway code, but a general idea of continuing onwards, of *travelling*.

7. Answer *f*: the two arrows diverging in *a* give the idea of a parting of the ways, a differential split, whereas in *b* the conjunction of the two sections into a single arrow clearly conveys the idea of union; in *c* this conjunction does not occur in a regular way, but in one that indicates *separation* rather than detachment (there is no break in the figure); "segregation" implies a context that is too restricted to be appropriate here.

8. Answer *f*: we are here venturing into the realms of the abstract; thus if *a* is a generic indication of meeting and *b* of dispersing, then *c* can only indicate *approaching* (*f*), because the symbolic representation of "proceeding" or "leaving" would have been completely different.

Games with a psychological background

The subjective reality of the individual represents a boundless world of personal experience: feelings, hopes, expectations etc, whether conscious or unconscious, and mental processes: perception, memory, intelligence etc. Psychology is still in its infancy, which explains why science has only recently begun to tackle the study of the inner life of the individual, seen, not in isolation, but within the framework of social relationships. It should also be noted that inner reality can only be explained by means of constant reference to the world outside, to other individuals and to society.

The figuratively abstract symbol of the arrow can also be adapted to represent certain tendencies, mental processes and inner experiences of the individual.

In the following tests, based on psychology, the reader will reencounter symbols that had completely different meanings in the preceding exercises. This further illustrates the fact that the signs we use are conventional: their meaning varies according to the contexts within which they are used. We invite readers to tackle these problems which, like the earlier examples, are intended solely to act as informative games. In addition, you will be able to reflect on just what the symbols represent and on how they achieve their aim.

You will doubtless find it helpful to compare your conclusions with the solutions suggested by us on page 39 which are also explained in a rational manner.

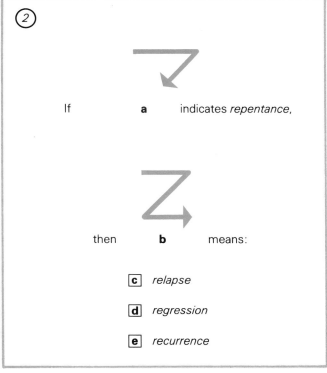

② If **a** indicates *repentance*,

then **b** means:

[c] *relapse*

[d] *regression*

[e] *recurrence*

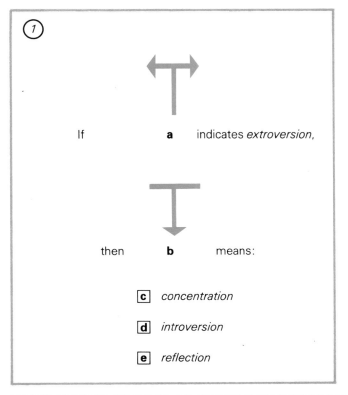

① If **a** indicates *extroversion*,

then **b** means:

[c] *concentration*

[d] *introversion*

[e] *reflection*

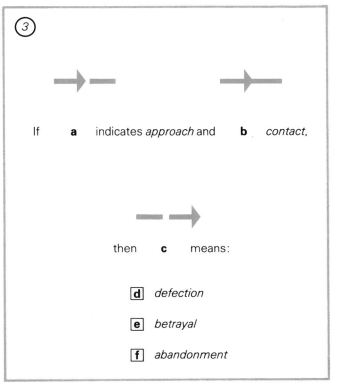

③ If **a** indicates *approach* and **b** *contact*,

then **c** means:

[d] *defection*

[e] *betrayal*

[f] *abandonment*

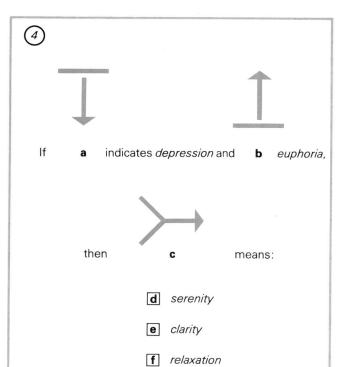

④

If **a** indicates *depression* and **b** *euphoria*,

then **c** means:

d serenity

e clarity

f relaxation

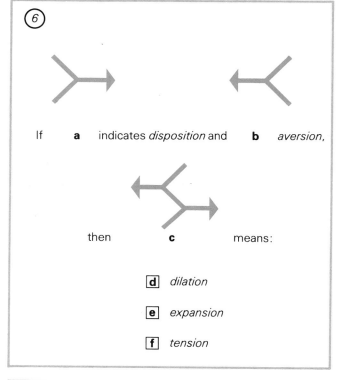

⑥

If **a** indicates *disposition* and **b** *aversion*,

then **c** means:

d dilation

e expansion

f tension

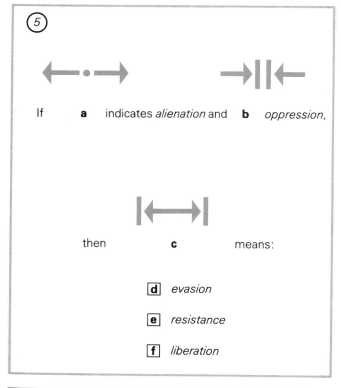

⑤

If **a** indicates *alienation* and **b** *oppression*,

then **c** means:

d evasion

e resistance

f liberation

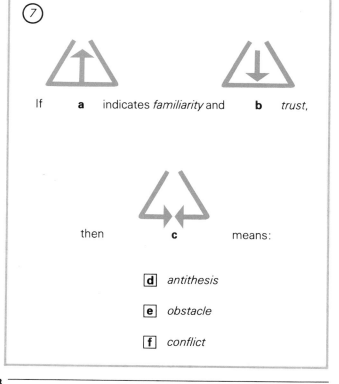

⑦

If **a** indicates *familiarity* and **b** *trust*,

then **c** means:

d antithesis

e obstacle

f conflict

"Games with a psychological background" – solutions to drawings (pages 37–38)

1. Answer *d*: the two arrows recall the idea of a person reaching outward, an extrovert character; in *b*, on the other hand, the arrow points in an opposite direction, inward; it therefore designates an introvert. Readers will notice that *b* could also indicate concentration and reflection, but it is meaning *a* which links in with *d*. Hence *introversion*.

2. Answer *c*: the term "repentance," represented by a sudden change of direction, brings us into the realm of individual moral and religious values; the z-shaped figure *b* suggests just such a zig-zag progress, which graphically represents the unstable behaviour of a person who cannot stay on the straight and narrow, but falls back into error after having repented. The correct solution can thus only be *c*, *relapse*, because neither regression nor recurrence have the same predominantly moral significance.

3. Answer *f*: approach (*a*) and contact (*b*) give a very precise human connotation to the two figures; of the three possible solutions, "defection" is unsuitable because it is an inappropriate description of human relationships; betrayal has too strong an emotional content within the context of *a* and *b*; all that is left is *abandonment*. The three images therefore describe the experience of approach (*a*), contact and almost merging (*b*) and finally of abandonment (*f*).

4. Answer *d*: if an arrow pointing downwards (*a*) indicates the lowering of mood from a condition of stability (the line above, from which the arrow seems to descend), an exactly opposing figure (*b*) will indicate the psychological reverse, meaning a state of euphoria; image *c*, formed of a horizontal arrow turning to the right in perfect balance, meaning that it veers neither up or down, will evoke the idea of inner equilibrium, in other words *serenity*.

5. Answer *e*: from a psychological point of view, alienation is a painful situation of inner conflict in which the individual, represented abstractly by the dot (*a*), feels he is a stranger to himself. A variety of different factors can create this condition, whether internal or external, but it manifests itself in a feeling of oppression (*b*). If this is what is meant by *a* and *b*, then *c* can only represent an individual's reaction against such a state of mind, hence the meaning of *resistance* (*e*).

6. Answer *f*: the result of combining an aversion (*b*) with a propensity, in other words an inclination toward someone or something (*a*), is a state of *tension* which seems to us to be very eloquently portrayed in *f*, not only by the opposing directions of the arrows, but also by the zig-zag course that they appear to be adopting.

7. Answer *f*: compared to the preceding test, the meanings of *a* and *b* here severely curtail the solution to *c*; familiarity and trust can, for example, refer to stages in a male–female relationship; *c* therefore clearly indicates a state of *conflict* between two people.

The illustrations, right, show examples of the "multiple language" of strip cartoons; above: stars around a head indicate pain, generally resulting from a blow (a cartoon by F. Verissimo and M. Paiva); below: brush lines are usually used to intimate speed (*Asterix*, by Goscinny-Uderzo).

A language with many uses

Until now, we have discussed the arrow and its role in visual communication, presenting it to the reader as a highly idiosyncratic graphic sign, midway between image and symbol. In addition, we have shown how nowadays it is used mainly as a conventional sign in a wide variety of contexts. There is, however, another type of language, very popular with the young, that also makes extensive use of these conventions: the strip cartoon. Strip cartoons are an area in which not only words and images come together, but also other codes such as those showing movement. For this reason cartoons represent a *multiple language*, made up from the harmonious juxtaposition of several different codes.

Strip cartoons contain numerous examples of conventional signs, the history of which remains, as far as we know, largely unexplored. There is, for example, the jumble of stars that appears around characters who have received a blow on the head, an idea which is also conveyed by their rolling eyes; the stars are a visual indication that the subject is metaphorically "seeing stars" as a result of being hit. Note how the metaphor (see page 30) is a means of communication that can also be expressed visually. Other very frequently used conventions are "speed lines," to give the idea of fast movement, or "sight lines," to show which way a character is looking.

The strip cartoon is basically an "illustrated" story, presented in the form of a strip or series of images, in which only the most important features of the action are portrayed.

The word "cartoon" itself comes from the Latin *charta*, meaning "something written on paper," while the word "strip" indicates the way in which the story is arranged. The words are contained in balloons which have a *tail* or *indicator* that points toward the mouth of the character who is speaking. It is important to note how the *outline* of these balloons, and also their tails, provide further information to the reader. If, for example, they have an unbroken outline, it means that the character is speaking in a normal voice, but a broken outline means that the words are either emerging from a distance or they are being spoken in a low voice. A wavy outline, however, with a tail looking like a series of small puffs of smoke, represents thoughts, dreams or memories. A jagged outline signifies an almost metallic voice emerging from some mechanical device such as a loudspeaker, radio or

Extracts from various cartoon strips. In the first (above left), the broken line of the "bubble" indicates that someone is speaking in a low voice to Mickey Mouse; in the second (taken from one of Asterix's adventures) the heavy print makes us realize that the figure is shouting, whereas the last one in the top series tells us that Donald Duck is talking to himself. We leave it up to the reader to identify the most important descriptive elements present in the lower series of images (the first two by Milo Manara, the third by G. Herriman). Then see how many symbols are used

in the frame opposite (by Guido Crepax) to convey a feeling of unbearable tension to the reader: the noises and screams in heavy black, the twisted posture of the figure, who covers his face. Strip cartoons are basically a series of visual messages, which are conveyed through figures accompanied by certain conventional signs and also, but not invariably, by words.

Their popularity depends on the fact that they are a synthesis of several different languages (visual, verbal, gestural etc.), which makes them very efficient communicators of ideas.

telephone. Even the different way in which the words are written out acts as a means of allowing us to understand their "weight"; if, for example, they appear in very heavy, bold type, they express the idea of a shout or of some strong emotion.

Other common conventional signs in cartoons are hair standing on end to indicate fear or terror, or wildly staring eyes to show shock or astonishment. Nor should we forget the question mark, one of the most widely used symbols conveying confusion, embarrassment, indecision. Finally, there are the different forms in which the words appear in cartoon language: as direct intervention by the characters (dialogue or monologue), as a narrative link, or as onomatopoeic sound effects. In this context the range of possibilities has been noticeably broadened. Should you have any doubt as to the truth of this statement, you may try solving the test on the next page.

From sound to image: onomatopoeia

The following game, which we hope will amuse the reader and will certainly pose no problems for regular readers of strip cartoons, can also be played by those who are less familiar with the genre. All they need do is rely on personal experience and stretch their imaginations a little. We shall now explain just what is involved and also provide the necessary background information. Onomatopoeia is the imitation, using vowels or consonants, of voices, sounds and thus also of actions and material objects. In the multiple language of cartoons it represents one of the most efficient forms of expression. The examples illustrated in the box above are some of the most commonly used; the game consists of conjuring up the relevant image (which may be an action, a scene or an object) by means of the onomatopoeic sound. The answers are on page 46.

The three circles

As with novels and films, there are many different types of strip cartoon. The most popular ones with children are obviously comics or adventure cartoons, but there are also erotic, detective, science fiction, and surrealist cartoons, as well as those dealing with subjects such as war.

On the following pages, we present a short and special type of strip cartoon, in which the action unfolds through a series of images, without the assistance of words. The reader's understanding of it is thus completely dependent upon the efficiency of its graphic portrayal. The tale it tells is a somewhat surrealistic one, and each reader will undoubtedly draw different conclusions from it. Whatever the case, however, we invite you to provide your own interpretation of the story and then turn to page 46 to read our explanation, which matches the one intended by the cartoon's creator.

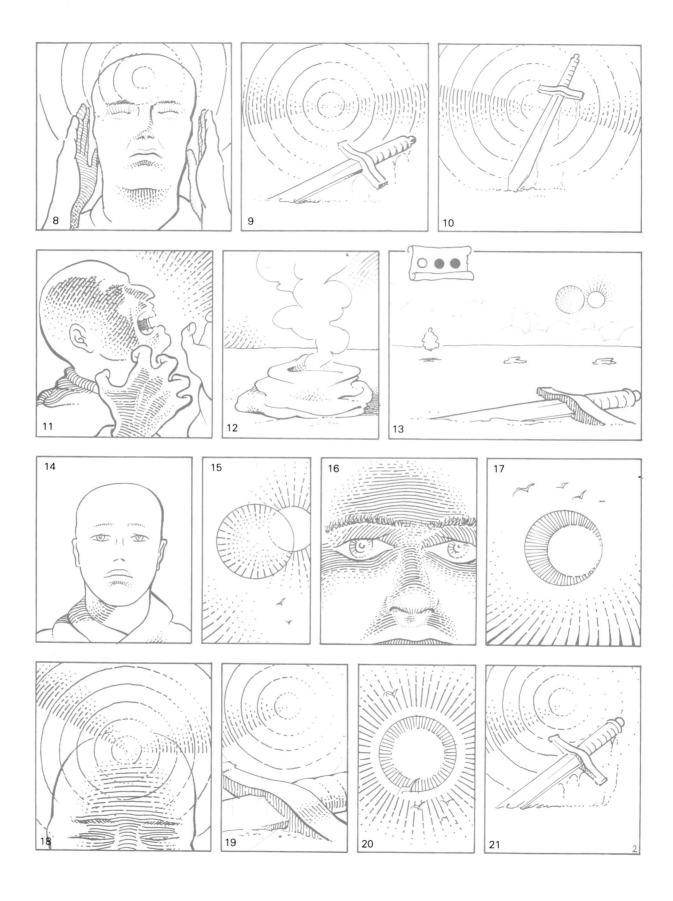

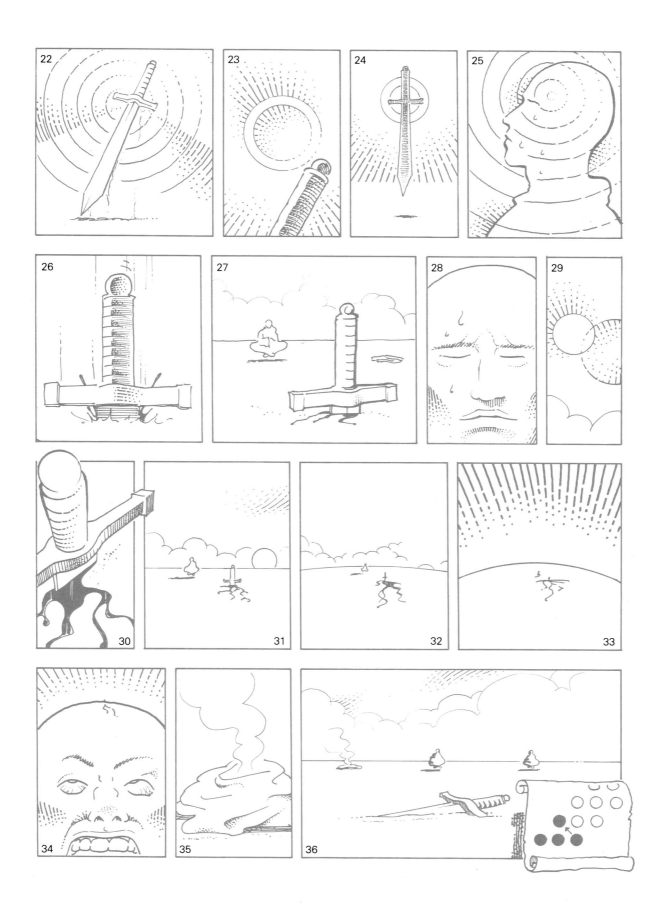

"From sound to image: onomatopoeia" – Answers

1. The sudden sound of a gun going off.

2. A bomb or dynamite exploding.

3. The sound of something bouncing on a spring, such as a jack-in-the-box jumping out.

4. A cowbell or the sound made by an old-fashioned fire engine on the move.

5. One or more people applauding.

6. A switch being turned on or off.

7. The noise of a wooden bridge or staircase breaking up or a bough breaking off a large tree.

8. A rider urging on his horse.

9. A person or animal swallowing hard.

10. Someone laughing.

11. The sound of someone being punched in a fight.

12. The sound made by a steam engine.

13. A sports or racing car, or even an aeroplane, moving off; it may also be the roar of a lion.

14. A sharp blow or smack with the open hand like someone being hit across the face.

15. Unlike CRRAACK, this noise recalls the breaking of a twig or something thin and brittle.

16. The noise made by tyres when the brakes are suddenly applied.

17. A big loud kiss probably on the cheek.

18. A dog sniffing, but also a person sniffing, perhaps because they have been crying.

19. A person or an object falling into water.

20. The sound made by a snake or by steam forced through a small opening such as a saucepan lid.

21. A rocket taking off or a vehicle moving at a very high speed.

22. The dull sound of someone beating something with a thick and heavy instrument, or the sound of heavy footsteps.

23. A clock ticking.

24. A cry of fright or pain.

25. The sound of someone knocking on a door.

26. A police car (or an ambulance) with its siren blaring.

27. Someone jumping for joy.

28. The sharp singing noise of a bullet passing through the air.

29. A vehicle speeding past.

30. The buzz of a mosquito searching for a victim, or an animal deep in sleep.

Explanation of the cartoon tale of "The three circles"

The three "circles" at the top of the cartoon represent the name of the story; an early clue is given by the fact that they match the three figures which appear immediately below. A sword also figures prominently in the first "frame." From the very first moment therefore we know that the story concerns three people and their relationship with the sword. Our attention is then drawn to just one of the three (the one on the left? on the right? at the center?), who is in a state of intense concentration: so much so, that waves emerge from his mind, reaching out toward the sword (3) and even trying to lift it (4). But the powers of the first character's mind are not enough to carry out this feat (5) and so, frustrated, he vanishes (6). Now that we see it is the one on the right that has been eliminated (7), the field is left clear for the two other protagonists. The second one, the man in the middle, then tries, but suffers the same fate (8–13). Finally, it is the turn of the third man, who brings even more psychic effort to bear (14–21) and finally manages to raise the sword (22–25), which plunges itself into the ground (26–27). He is now exhausted (28–29). But a strange liquid begins to flow out of the gash in the ground (30). Then the scene fades gradually into the distance (31–33), finally revealing that what we believed to be the ground is in fact the skull of a larger person (34) who, because of the wound he has suffered, vanishes into nothingness, taking with him the man responsible for his death (35). But the latter, as revealed by the final frame, was just one inhabitant of a larger system, identical to the earlier one, and his disappearance has started up the same sequence all over again, which could repeat itself until infinity.

Opposite: left, the Chinese "monad" is an eloquent example of a figure with a particularly strong significance. Some figures and symbols retain to this day their power to convey deep philosophical and religious meanings. Heraldic devices (opposite, right) also possess the same ability to convey a variety of meanings. They are composed of several symbolic images which together form the official emblem of a noble family or individual, of an organization or even an entire country. The heraldic devices shown here are taken from Diderot and d'Alembert's *Dictionnaire Encyclopédique*.

Special symbols

In comparing words and images we have already mentioned that words possess an unparalleled ability to describe and explain, whereas images are more efficient at conveying emotions and feelings. We cannot help but mention, albeit only in passing, the particular evocative powers possessed by certain symbols. We have already seen how the use of symbols has increased in relation to the growth of visual communication in modern society; the more social relationships increase, the more communication grows; the more communication grows, the greater the use made of images to convey information. In both the most distant and most recent past we find that images, figures and symbols can produce particularly strong emotional reactions in people. Think, for example, of what the cross has come to mean over the centuries to both Christians and non-Christians alike. There are also countless other religious or mystical symbols. The Chinese "monad" represents one of the main constituent elements of the universe: the balance between the female principle (*yin*) and the masculine (*yang*). There are, moreover, other more homely images: the four-leaf clover, which means good luck, or the skull and crossbones that often appears on electricity pylons to indicate danger.

National flags and coats of arms also possess specially evocative powers. The fascination that some symbols have exerted on certain individuals or even, as recent history has shown, on vast masses of people, seems to be in some way linked to religious and mystical meanings. Sigmund Freud, the inventor of psychoanalysis, and his follower Jung both sought to link the ability of certain emblems, such as the swastika, to excite obedience, loyalty or hostility, with the subconscious motivations of the individual.

A symbolic image conveying a feeling of something ancient, strange and incomprehensible will make people think in terms of some sort of hidden mystery and will endow its significance with a sacred, exotic flavour, too important to be revealed to the uninitiated. No words or rational discourse can transmit feelings, meanings and underlying values more successfully than such symbols.

It is not uncommon, during meetings of old war veterans from almost any country in the world, for individuals to show great emotion, often being moved to tears, on seeing their national flag, or the insignia of their old regiment.

"Your stepmother's second cousin's son"

This is not a tongue-twister or a riddle, but the definition of a specific degree of kinship. What conclusions can you draw from it: that some situations become even more complicated when expressed in words? Sometimes, all it needs is a diagram composed of simple geometric shapes, their relationship established by interlinking lines of different lengths, to provide information in a clear, synthetic way. In the case of complicated relationships, a family tree is an example of such a graphic representation. In the past, particularly during the Middle Ages, the legitimacy of a succession or of an inheritance was linked to the degree of relationship. Family trees are a clear illustration of the advantages of visual presentation: trying to reconstruct a degree of kinship verbally could create so much confusion that the reality would be obscured, whereas a genealogical representation would make it clear immediately.

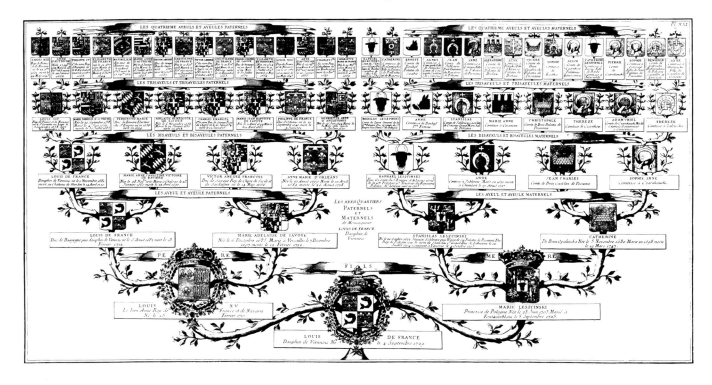

A family tree is nothing more than an ancient form of *diagram* or graphic representation. We shall now proceed to deal more comprehensively and extensively with this vital form of visual language.

Maps, anatomical drawings, diagrams . . .

Anyone who has ever taught will know that a figure, a sketch or a drawing is often enough to attract the attention of students. They will also know that some arguments, which are in themselves rather boring or particularly complex, can be made clearer and more interesting if they are explained with the help of illustrations.

There are certain images which seem particularly suitable for conveying special types of information, like geographical and topographical maps, for example. In these, a highly selective code represents some, but not all, of the characteristics of the subject under examination. Continuous lines link points of equal height: these are isometric lines. Different areas of green shading tell us what is cultivated land and what is forest. Other devices can show national boundaries, population density, natural resources or any other information required. A selective code, such as the group of signs and rules used for compiling maps, allows us to eliminate some items of information and convey only the data required by the user.

Another example of the informative, all-embracing image of the genealogical tree, in this instance the royal house of France (from Diderot and d'Alembert's *Dictionnaire Encyclopédique*).

One thinks of the anatomical drawings of Leonardo da Vinci, which leave out some details in order to communicate others more clearly. Many of these drawings do not give the impression of being merely artistic representations, and are, in fact, models by means of which this great artist/scientist sought to explain his theories on the structure of the body. If you have ever picked up a medical publication and looked at an anatomical drawing of a part of the body, you will have noticed that such pictures have none of the crude and gory realism of a surgical dissection. A photograph will never be as informative as a drawing which highlights certain details and ignores others.

A typical example of an image constructed using a selective code is the diagram. Teachers know that certain logical or temporal relationships and certain abstract concepts will be more readily assimilated if illustrated by means of diagrams. Anyone with even a smattering of scientific experience will already be familiar with the efficacy of using a combination of text and illustration to explain certain phenomena. Diagrams provide us with an abstract and efficient means of representing a reality, an idea or a concept.

There are some more complex areas, such as economic progress, growth in population, resources and trade, where it is important, not solely for experts, but also for ordinary people, to have immediate access to data. To convey exact and concise information on such data (and on countless other statistics), words alone prove inadequate and what is required are diagrams or tables made up of a combination of numerals and symbols. Graphs, diagrams, and charts allow for the precise and rapid comparative study of phenomena that might otherwise be poorly understood.

The advantage of using a diagram to describe a complex situation, whether it be a national education survey, a collection of logical relationships or the structure of a large business concern, is immediate and concise. Concepts that in words would have to be expressed by means of a series of phrases, gradually losing in preciseness and significance, will be clearly and coherently illustrated in a diagram.

To show what we mean, we have included a graph showing the growth in the world's population from prehistoric times up until the present day (see right).

Because of its simplicity, this graph gives an immediate idea of what has happened to the human race in relation to its environment: the gently rising line, which at certain points climbs steeply (toward the end almost vertically), embraces the whole time span of human history. The first part of the line, which rises slowly from left to right, represents the period in which man was a hunter, gatherer and fisherman and in which the resources available were not enough to feed even ten million people (indicated by the vertical lines). But about ten thousand years ago (indicated by the horizontal lines), at the end of the Neolithic era, man graduated from being a nomad to a farmer and cultivator. This historical event, which has come to be known as the Agrarian Revolution, resulted in an unprecedented rise in available food resources which brought about a sharp rise in population. A few millennia later, during the Iron Age, the population of the world passed the hundred million mark.

Toward the end of the eighteenth century the resources of farming appeared to have become inadequate, and so began the Industrial Revolution, very different from its agricultural counterpart, much swifter and more continuous, in which we are still involved today. It is to the Industrial Revolution that we owe the explosion of the world's population, indicated in the diagram by the almost vertical climb. In fact, on July 7, 1986, the total number of people in the world passed the five thousand million mark.

A world of images

Man has always made use of images to communicate certain types of message, and not only aesthetic ones, even when the written or spoken word was the prevailing system of communication. The moment in history when visual information really began to be disseminated on a massive scale can be identified with the invention of printing. The ability to produce multiple copies of a book encouraged man to see the image or picture as a tool of information with endless possibilities. And so herbals, books on costume, newspapers and

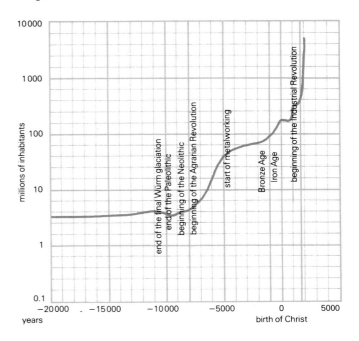

A graph is a diagram designed to express the progress of a particular phenomenon in a concise, synthetic fashion. The graph reproduced above represents the demographic development of the human race (the vertical coordinate) from prehistory up until the present day (the horizontal coordinate).

maps became a vital source of knowledge giving information on plants, important events and distant, unknown lands. The illustrations in Diderot's *Dictionnaire Encyclopédique*, published in Paris between 1751 and 1772, provide immediate and eloquent testimony to the standards reached in science and technology in Europe before the Industrial Revolution.

Since the introduction of printing, the role of the image has become increasingly important for communication, even at times transcending words or combining with them, frequently complementing and enhancing the ability of the latter to inform and to transmit messages. Today, almost any message that is aimed at the general public will be conveyed by visual means. The advertising hoardings along the roads in our cities, and in public places attract our attention because they are, quite literally, eye-catching, while their constant repetition means that their shape and colour become engraved on our memory. The persuasive force of posters undoubtedly lies not only in the way they are constantly being brought to our attention, but also in their use of easily comprehensible images to catch the eye, if only for a split second, of even those who do not have time to stop and read them. It is no accident that advertising hoardings rely for their impact on clear, self-contained designs that do not require any written explanation. Their presence everywhere and the increasingly efficient way in which they communicate their message help to strengthen the power of visual language.

Laughing with images

Visual language enters into many different areas of our lives. Pictures do not just have the ability to explain, inform and stimulate; they can also make us laugh. There is one particular form of visual message that reveals the full capacity of the human imagination. This takes the form of the quick humorous sketches of famous political or media figures known as

"caricatures." These represent an entertainingly objective way of reflecting and of highlighting real problems by dramatizing them in a thought-provoking manner: a few lively strokes of the pen can here convey much more than words.

The illustration on the opposite page shows a number of caricatures drawn to considerable expressive effect by Leonardo da Vinci.

The first example, in the top left-hand corner, shows the face of a man laughing mockingly at someone else's expense. Note how the feeling of malice and shyness is so skilfully portrayed by the features: the hooked nose, the small, sunken eyes, the wrinkled face and the open mouth, the pointed chin. With a simplicity of detail the artist has captured an image of a thin, mean-spirited character.

The face (shown top right-hand corner) conveys a completely different impression: hauteur, complacency? even an element of disquiet.

The caricature in the bottom left-hand corner is the face of an old woman, her hair combed back untidily, the nose snub

Examples of political satire.
Below: a French cartoon depicting the attempt on the life of the French president Sadi Carnot by an Italian

anarchist, 1894 (*Silhouette* magazine).
Right: a cartoon by Ron Cobb protesting against the proliferation of nuclear weapons.

MAN DEMONSTRATING HIS SUPERIORITY OVER ANIMALS.

and misshapen. The most outstanding feature, however, is the mouth, with its thick, protruding lips and teeth bared as though the woman were snarling at someone. What does it convey? Perhaps ferocity or rage, but certainly revulsion.

Brutish characteristics are also a feature of the three faces on the bottom right, evidenced by the animal-like features, particularly the one in the middle, with a snout rather than a mouth. Note how the nose and chin of the right face of this group seems to meet, obscuring the ugly sunken mouth.

The power of advertising

We live in a frenetic world, in which time is governed by the hectic pace of the day's activities. Now, more than ever, it is true that "time is money."

We seem always to be in a hurry: we travel by car to save time, live life in the fast lane. We never stop. We buy newspapers but never get around to reading them; we may open them but only have time to take in the headlines, pausing maybe slightly longer over the pictures. If we pick up a magazine, the sight of a full-page colour advertisement amid

Left: Krinski, *A temple for machine worshippers* (c. 1917).
Above: A cartoon by Siné from *The Guardian* newspaper (1969).

Below: the difference between these two images (Napoleon as seen by the French, left and English, right) clearly reflects the diversity of their message.

dense columns of print will capture our attention and infuse a feeling of well-being which becomes associated in our minds with the image of the product being advertised. We live in a society in which the influence and invasiveness of advertising is all-powerful. Advertising is a necessary prerequisite for the development of modern industrial society, which has to maintain a constant balance between production and consumption. We have to produce more and more, and so we must also consume more and more. And when the basic needs have been satisfied, new, artificial ones have to be created to encourage further consumption.

Advertising is the main tool used by manufacturing industry and nowadays it operates principally through visual communication. To make the public familiar with consumer products and to ensure their popularity, modern advertising experts rely on the evocative powers of certain images, using these to convey a skilful and subtle message which appeals to our emotions, our imagination and our hidden desires. There is good reason for people to speak in terms of "creating a need from nothing." Advertising has a power of which the man in the street is generally unaware; in fact, he almost invariably finds himself in a passive role.

As the production and the number of different consumer goods rise, so the advertising industry increases and perfects its powers of persuasion, sharpening its wits on the findings of market research, studies in mass psychology, the analysis of perceptual phenomena and research into the longevity of memory. It exploits these findings and these techniques to make the image of its products more attractive and more acceptable. Mindful of the need to capture our imagination and to exert some sort of influence over the consumer, advertisers have realized that these images need not necessarily be beautiful. Sometimes, in fact, the more ugly or strange the better, at all events one that is different, which will stand out and be noticed; it may be bizarre or even provocative and a little shocking, the all-important thing is that the image be noticed, that it attract the onlooker's attention, if only for a few seconds, and, the *sine qua non*, that it be as communicative as possible.

It could be said that advertising images in all their different aspects have invaded the very fabric of our daily lives. It is our opinion that being able to decipher their messages and know how to control their powers of persuasion will enable us to live a happier, simpler and less artificial life.

Having fun with images

The language of images has vast areas of application. In previous pages we have talked about visual communication in general, referring to some of these areas (drawings, symbols, road signs, posters, graphics, advertising etc). There are, however, countless other forms of language based on images: the art of painting, for instance, sculpture, architecture, carving, bas-relief, mosaic and inlay. When it comes to more

modern examples, we cannot avoid mentioning the language of photography, the cinema, collage etc. Even certain forms of music and dance have links with figures and images. The activities that can be carried out through the medium of image are thus many and varied. One of the most noteworthy of these are games, in which the image appears to have found one of its most suitably expressive applications. This book itself provides ample evidence of this: images can be a great way of having fun. Look at the photograph above and see what can be done with a hand, a bit of paint and a ping-pong ball: it certainly looks like a real flesh-and-blood giraffe!

Meanwhile, we invite our readers to have fun with the games in the next section.

Shadow games

Paris fully deserves its reputation as the city of light and entertainment. From the nineteenth century onward, it has preserved its unique reputation as the world's most famous pleasure center. Even modern tourists do not visit Paris solely for its monuments, churches and museums which have quite rightly made the city famous. They know that when night falls, Paris will surround them in its own unique atmosphere of magic and excitement, and the anticipation of its neon-lit bars and clubs excites a frisson of pleasure. The city's cabarets and music halls provide a worthy adjunct to its civilisation and culture. Most people, when they think of cabarets or floor shows, think of the *Folies Bergère* and the striptease shows that still draw crowds of spectators. All this is a genuine part of the Parisian scene. But few people know that during the last century one of the most popular Parisian entertainments was the shadow picture show, the creation of images by use of the hands. By placing the hands in front of a stream of light and giving full rein to the imagination, shadow shapes of all descriptions could be projected on to any receptive surface.

The origins of this curious game of images are unknown. It is, however, a very ancient skill, especially popular and widespread among children, and one which captured the imagin-ation of nineteenth-century France. The most famous and best-attended Parisian cabarets organized shadow shows which attracted vast numbers of people. It was in Paris, in 1892, that one of the few books on this subject was published, containing no fewer than a thousand suggestions. We now offer (below) our readers some examples of these "handmade" images. The first shows a profile of the devil; the subjects of the others are self-evident.

Look around!

Perceiving and thinking
are not independent: "I see what you mean"
is not a puerile pun,
but indicates a connection which is very real.
(Richard Gregory)

Images as a tool of knowledge

Man has always used images for his own purposes, not only as a means of communication, but also for the storing or imparting of knowledge. The caves of Lascaux, in France, for example, bear witness to man's primeval need to see and to create images, probably in order to communicate religious or ritual messages. But such a realistic representation of animals also reveals a need to codify specific information relating to them.

In more recent times, we can see how the development of certain scientific disciplines has been accompanied by images. Medicine has used, and still uses, familiar images to describe certain parts of the anatomy that are not externally visible. If someone talks about the "stirrup bone," the "anvil" and the "drum," it makes it easier for us to visualize parts of the human ear. This is because they bring to mind images of objects that form part of our daily experience. Most people know what an anvil and a stirrup look like, and there can be few who have not seen a drum.

Scientists, when faced with concepts that are too abstract to be conveyed verbally, will often create visual images and models. As an example of this we could cite chemistry, but we should also make special mention of the way in which Albert Einstein, inventor of the theory of relativity, made extensive use of familiar images such as trains, cars and even lifts to explain difficult concepts that lay outside the range of common experience.

Knowledge and imagery have always existed side by side,

the one assisting the other; this is particularly true in the case of anatomy, in which imagery appears to have almost developed a language of its own to describe parts and organs of the human body. Even an elementary knowledge of the structure and function of the eye, which we shall endeavour to explain overleaf, will confirm the truth of what has just been said.

A hole in the eye

Turn the page and look at the upper part of the top illustration. Cover your right eye and, from a distance of about 30 centimeters (c. 12 inches), focus your left eye on the cross to the right. Do this carefully and then wait. What happens? The disc on the left vanishes. In your case it doesn't? Then try moving the book (still at the same distance) very slowly backwards and forwards. You will notice that sooner or later the disc disappears from your field of vision. Now do the same with the lower part of the illustration. Either close or cover your right eye, and focus your left eye, still holding the book about 30 centimeters (c. 12 inches) away, on the cross in the bottom right-hand corner. At a certain point the thick line will appear to be no longer broken, but continuous, as though the break had disappeared.

As you will already have guessed, this is no ordinary game, there is no trickery involved. In order to understand the reasons for this effect we have to know how the eye is made

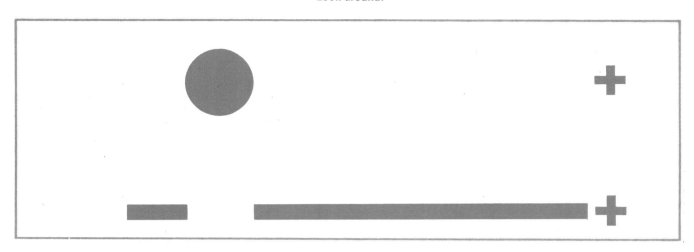

up and how the sense that we call "sight" is achieved, and in order to satisfy the reader's quite legitimate curiosity we shall try to provide an answer. You will understand the phenomenon much better after you have become more familiar with the functional structure of the human organ of sight. The explanation is as follows. In the inner part of the eye there is a point at which the nerve-endings of the light-sensitive cells come together to form the optic nerve. At this point we can see nothing. By inviting you to stare at the cross from a distance of 30 centimeters (c. 12 inches), all we did was to make the image of the disc coincide with this point, the so-called *blind spot*.

The second exercise is more interesting; here nothing ought to disappear, for the simple reason that no image is actually being projected. All there is before our eyes is a blank space. But what happens? We see the thick line join up; in fact, we see something where nothing exists. The most important lesson to be learned from this phenomenon is that when we see the world we are not conscious of this blind spot: objects appear to be continuous, with no visibly empty gaps. This tells us that our visual apparatus intervenes in the images that it receives, correcting errors and filling in any gaps even where this gives a misrepresentation of what the eye is actually seeing.

The world turned upside-down

A knowledge of the structures of the eye and the way in which these work is necessary for us to be able to understand perceptual phenomena that would otherwise be inexplicable. The multiplicity and complexity of the intervening physiological mechanisms are an indirect demonstration that sight is not just a straightforward reflection of images, but a constructive process, the result of the elaboration of visual stimuli.

Would you like to prove this for yourself? Then take an empty can, of the sort used for canned fruit. Make a hole in the

end, of a diameter no greater than that of an ordinary nail, and, using adhesive tape, cover the open end with a piece of semi-transparent paper. If there is no such paper available, use a piece of white paper smeared with cooking oil to make it semi-transparent. Then take a piece of black cloth and put it over your head, just like old-fashioned photographers used to do. Put the can up to your eye, with the papered end against your face. Then point it, as though it were a camera, at some brightly-lit object (the best thing would be to stand indoors and aim it through a window). You will now see the images of the objects at which the can is pointing, but upside-down. Why, then, do we not see everything inverted? Why do we not seem to be living in a topsy-turvy world? It is because our brain upends the images formed in the innermost layer of the eye and allows us to see them correctly.

The time has now come for us to examine the anatomy of this basic sensory organ in a little more detail.

Images on the retina

The layer of the eye on which the inverted images of the outside world are reflected is the *retina*, a word derived from the Latin meaning "little net." In fact, if we examine it closely using a special instrument known as an ophthalmoscope, we can indeed see a dense network of blood vessels. The retina is the most light-sensitive part of the eye; from it there radiate large numbers of nerve endings, which, as we have already mentioned, come together at the blind spot to form the optic nerve.

The eye has often been compared to a camera, and up to a certain point this is a valid analogy: the light-sensitive film corresponds to the retina. A detailed study of the eye, however, reveals a structure and an operative function that is much more complex and sophisticated than one would imagine.

The face of murder

Kate was found face down on the carpet, showing clear signs of having been strangled. The disorder in the room indicated that a struggle had taken place: the chairs by the desk were overturned, the carpet rumpled and there was a handkerchief lying on the floor. It was clear that the victim had either had no time to react or had reacted too late because she knew her murderer. The members of the homicide squad discreetly covered the body with a sheet and began their meticulous investigation. There were no marks, however, and no clues, the murderer had skilfully removed all fingerprints and any other evidence, however small. Outside, the ambulance had already arrived to take the corpse to the morgue. The inspector ushered in the doctor and nurses and gave the order for the victim's eyes to be removed immediately and preserved in a special saline solution for later examination. He then gave permission for the autopsy to be carried out, which is obligatory in such cases, and for the funeral to be held.

All the members of Kate's family were interviewed, together with anyone else who had been in contact with her on the day in question. Everyone had a cast-iron alibi, and her husband, a decent man, appeared distraught. The police seemed to have drawn a complete blank. They had made enquiries into the victim's life and had reconstructed her final moments down to the last detail, but there was not a single shred of evidence for them to work on. Kate had been a quiet-living woman, leading an ordinary life: there seemed to be no explanation for the crime.

It was then that the inspector ordered a strange operation to be performed on the victim's eyes: he had them dissected and the two retinas examined under a microscope. It came as no surprise to him to see the image of the murderer still clearly preserved, as though printed on a photographic plate.

This reads like the plot of some gripping film or detective novel, in which the murderer is finally unmasked and justice triumphs. In fact, large numbers of plots, whether in films or books, have drawn inspiration from the age-old belief that the final image remains engraved on the retina of the deceased. Even in the strangest beliefs, in the most outlandish films or novels, there is always a grain of truth.

Similarly, the belief that the murderer's face can be found imprinted on the victim's retina does contain a hint of truth. However, we shall not dwell here on detailed descriptions of specialist theories concerning neurophysiology and biochemistry. We shall merely point out that recent studies of Alzheimer's disease, a sort of senile dementia affecting the central nervous system, demonstrate that in certain conditions, using special chemical treatment, it is possible to identify the final image seen by a dead person on their retina.

The structure of the eye: a few explanatory notes

The external part of the eye contains three layers: the *sclera*, the *choroid layer* and the *retina*. We have already referred to the latter and we shall return to it later when dealing with the eye's light receptors.

The sclera is the outermost covering, which serves to protect the more delicate, inner layers. The word was chosen with good reason: it comes from the Greek *sklerós* meaning "hard," a clear indication of the relationship between its name and its function. Loosely attached to the sclera is the *choroid*,

---

Opposite page: below, a large *camera obscura* of the 17th century, within which the painter could trace his drawing by following the shapes projected upside-down on to the canvas.
Right: a cross-section of the eye.

1. cornea; 2. iris; 3. ciliary body; 4. *ora serrata*; 5. sclera; 6. choroid layer; 7. retina; 8. central fovea; 9. anterior and posterior chamber containing aqueous humour; 10. *zonula*; 11. crystalline lens; 12. vitreous humour; 13. blind spot; 14. optic nerve.

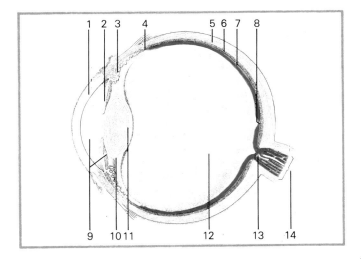

another term derived from the Greek, meaning "like a membrane": if we examine it under a microscope it appears to be formed mainly of blood vessels. This layer is modified in its central part to form the *iris*. When we say that someone has blue, brown or black eyes, we are referring to the colour of the iris, which is formed mainly of muscular tissue. The iris fulfils a very important role; just as the shutter of a camera acts as a means of regulating the amount of light striking the light-sensitive film, so the iris controls the amount of light falling on the retina. It is shaped like a ring and, being a muscle, it can contract and dilate in order to control the aperture of the central opening, the *pupil*. The latter looks like a hole, which widens and narrows according to the amount of light striking the retina. When too much light enters, the pupil immediately contracts until its diameter is less than 2 millimeters (c. 1/12 inches). If there is too little light, however, it will dilate, thus maximizing the amount of light entering the eye, achieving a diameter of 8 millimeters (c. 1/3 inches). The constrictive and dilatory muscles of the iris respond very rapidly, which means that the eye is able to adapt instantaneously to changes in light intensity.

It is interesting to note that when we see eyes of blue, green, brown etc, which are in fact the colours of the outer surface of the iris, it is because the latter is opaque, meaning that it does not allow light to pass through. Light therefore enters solely through the pupil.

The lens of the eye

Behind the pupil, and contained within a membranous capsule, is the *crystalline lens*, a bi-convex lens in the shape of a large lentil. It can alter its shape to concentrate rays of direct, reflected or refracted light on to the retina. These rays are subjected to a change in shape according to the degree of curvature of the crystalline lens. If the objects are nearby, the lens will curve slightly; if they are in the distance, it will distend.

When, after climbing a mountain, we arrive at the top and sit down to admire the countryside stretching out beneath us, the lens takes on a very flattened shape. Suppose, however, that the eye, from that position, alights on a nearby object; if the crystalline lens were to fail to adapt, the image would develop behind the retina and its outline would end up hazy and out of focus.

How then does the crystalline lens regulate itself? It curves so that the rays concentrate shortly before they reach the retina and thus create the correct image, thereby allowing us to see the outline of shapes. The fact that the mechanism which puts things into focus in the eye works automatically makes it very difficult for us to follow the stages involved in this process. A device very similar to that of the eye, known as "auto focus," can also be found in the latest generation of cameras.

There are some very common sight defects relating to the crystalline lens: if it is loose and you aim your gaze at some distant object, your vision may become blurred. This means that the images are being formed either shortly before or after the retina. In the first case the phenomenon is known as *myopia* or "short sightedness," in the second, *hypermetropia* or "long sightedness."

The front part of the eye is covered by the *cornea*, a name which reflects its hardness; it is, in fact, short for the Latin *cornea tunica* meaning "horny covering." It consists of a rigid, transparent structure, held taut by the *aqueous humour*. It possesses no blood vessels and receives nourishment directly from the aqueous humour, which makes it in a way independent of the organism. This means that in cases where the cornea becomes cloudy it is possible to replace it with one from a donor, without incurring any problems of rejection. This is because antibodies cannot reach it through the blood supply and then destroy it, as can happen in the case of other organ transplants.

Cold, soft and warm eyes

It cannot really be said that pupils are just holes, as this implies that there is something missing: in fact, they play a fundamental role in non-verbal communication between people. When we say that someone has warm, cold or soft eyes, we are generally referring to the diameter of the pupil, even without being aware of it.

It is widely believed that the eyes reveal a person's feelings, emotions and even changes in mood. And this is true. Research, however, has shown that the part of the eye linked closely to the emotions and mental activity in general is the pupil. You can prove this for yourself. If you are a man, look at the two photographs at the top of the opposite page. Which of the two girls do you find most attractive, most friendly looking, most feminine? If you are a woman, on the other hand, look at the two photographs below. Which of the two men seems to you most open, most welcoming, kindliest and also happiest? The vast majority of people given this test, whether male or female, indicated that they found such positive characteristics in faces with large pupils, and not in those with small pupils.

In times past, and perhaps even today, women used drops of belladonna to dilate their pupils, a sign of the awareness of the role of the eye pupil in communication. Nor is that all. Some psychologists, in trying to discover why large pupils make a person more attractive, have discovered that babies have appreciably larger pupils than adults. Clearly, this trait makes them even more attractive, and for a baby, which has to rely on grown-ups for care, it becomes a definite advantage. Some cartoon characters, such as Mickey Mouse, appear to have childish physical characteristics, particularly large eyes and pupils. It is these, according to psychologists, which subconsciously make us view such characters in a favourable light.

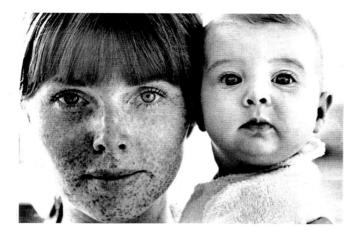

The physiological mechanisms of sight

The mechanism that produces sight is a very complicated one and here, too, we will try to provide as much help as possible with pictures. To begin with, we should say that the retina, like every other organ in the body is made up of cells. But these are no ordinary cells; they have the ability to convert light into nervous impulses, which are then transmitted to the brain through the optic nerve in order to be processed and transformed into the sensation of sight. The retina of just one eye contains some 131 million of these cells. Specialists have given a name to these retinal receptors: *cones* and *rods*, which recall shapes with which we are already familiar. But, and this may come as something of a surprise, these receptors do not point, as one would expect, toward the light, but toward the choroid. It is for this reason that humans, like all other vertebrates, are said to have an "inverted retina." But if these structures, which are supposed to respond to light, turn their backs on it, how can we see? In fact, before reaching the rods and cones, the light passes through various transparent layers.

The cones number about 6½ million, whereas there are 125 million rods. This fact makes one realize that not only do they fulfil different functions, but that there is also good reason for their numerical disparity. The fact of the matter is that there is an exception in the orientation of the cones, at a point known as the *fovea*, where their terminals do point directly toward the light. Because they are as closely packed together as sardines, under the microscope they look like long, thin rods, but countless tests have been conducted which prove that they are indeed cones and so there can be no doubt that this is the case. The further away one goes from the fovea toward the periphery of the retina, the easier it becomes to distinguish the difference in shape between the cones and rods.

The cones need a lot of light in order to function, and it is to these we owe our colour vision, whereas the rods function when there is little light, to give us shaded vision. Our vision in daylight, which makes use of the cones, is called *photopic*,

whereas our twilight vision, achieved through using the rods, is called *scotopic*: etymologically, the two terms mean "vision of light" and "vision of darkness," respectively. We shall now try to understand how these rods and cones function by reminding the reader of a few phenomena from everyday life. Everyone will have at some time experienced entering a dark room during a sunny day, thus passing abruptly from brightness into gloom. This happens, for example, if we go into the cinema straight off the street during broad daylight. This is when we bump into other people as we grope our way towards a seat, because we cannot see anything. A few seconds later, however, our sight will have improved, showing that our eyes have adapted to the new conditions. Let us now examine what happens. The example is important because it illustrates an abrupt passage from photopic to scotopic vision. We owe our rapid adaptation to the cones, but when the rods come into play it means that our sight has stabilized. The latter always start working when the light is poor, at dusk, for example, when everything seems to take on the same grey colour. Drivers know that, as the daylight begins to fail, they have to pay more attention and sharpen their reflexes. In fact, the rods do not give such acute vision and so one's reflexes slow down.

Above left: the faces of a mother and child. The pupils of the child are visibly larger. According to psychologists, this feature represents a stimulus capable of triggering parental behaviour. Below: schematic representation of the structures and different nervous connections of the retina.

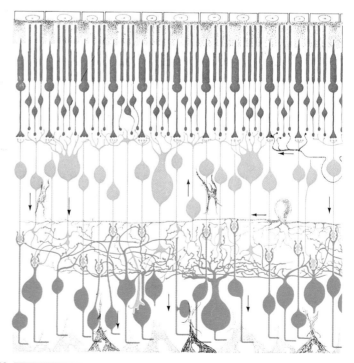

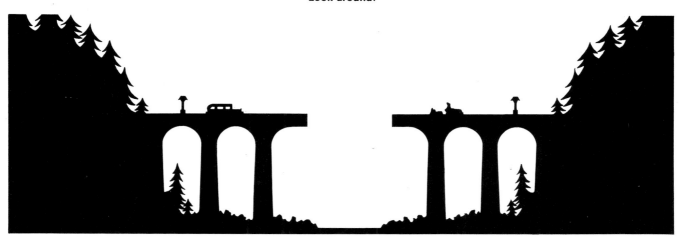

Joining up the bridge

The bridge in the illustration above has a gap in its central section. It is being crossed, judging by the silhouettes, by an old car (left) and a horse and cart (right).

What must we do to ensure that the two vehicles do not fall into the void? Try bringing the image toward your nose, keeping your eyes wide open and fixed on the two parts of the bridge as they draw closer. Doesn't it seem as though the two sections have come together, thus completing the bridge and allowing the image to be read correctly?

Before reading on, try to provide your own explanation for what has just happened. We will, however, give you a clue: the reason lies in the fact that we possess two eyes rather than one!

Two eyes are better than one!

Like cats and dogs and the majority of primates, humans possess *binocular vision*, meaning that we use two eyes which react together in perceiving the luminous stimuli emanating from the outside world. The anatomical arrangement of the human eyes, however, also plays an important functional role: man's eyes are, in fact, frontally situated. This means that they share virtually the same *field of vision* and both look in the same direction, overlapping considerably (about 170 degrees each). Many vertebrates, on the other hand, such as rabbits, pigeons, camels and others, have laterally-situated eyes and look out in opposite directions, thus permitting *panoramic vision*. The degree of overlap in an animal's field of vision depends on various factors, including how far toward the front its eyes are situated. In the figure on the right, for example, we can see that the rabbit (above) has only slight binocular overlap, whereas the cat (below) has much more. In humans it is almost complete.

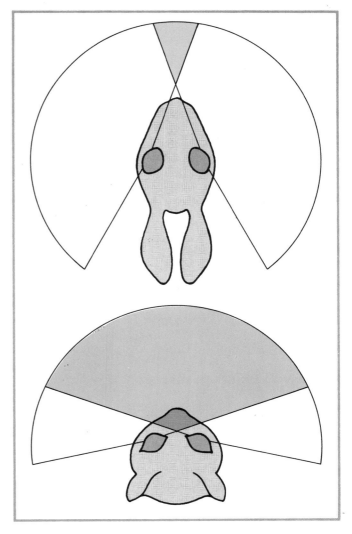

The gradual shifting of the eyes from a more lateral position to a frontal one has evolutionary overtones: it allows for precise judgement of the spatial positioning of objects through the assessment of distance, shape and size. When our earliest ancestors developed upper limbs capable of handling objects and of grasping branches in order to climb trees, it became vital for them to be able to make a rapid and accurate assessment of distance. It was at this stage of human development, the arboreal stage, that binocular vision became notably more highly evolved and more sophisticated.

In order to grasp the functional importance of binocular vision, all we need do is carry out a simple test: take a needle and cotton and try to thread the needle with one eye closed. You will immediately realize how much the judging of distance depends on both eyes and not just on one.

As we have already seen, two-dimensional images of objects form on our retina, but we see them as three-dimensional. This is the result of binocular or *stereoscopic* vision: our visual system succeeds in merging the images from our two eyes into a single, three-dimensional one.

Any explanation of what sort of information our visual system uses to achieve three-dimensional perception would involve knowledge of rather complex and still not fully-understood neurophysiological mechanisms. Let us just say that stereoscopic vision is, in general terms, the result of a process of comparison and inference that we shall now try to explain briefly. The two-dimensional images which, so to speak, become imprinted on the retina, are not identical. Between the center of one eye and the other there is a distance of 6–7 centimeters (c. 2¾ inches), which is the reason why both eyes do not see things at the same angle and, although the two images blend perfectly together (we do not see double), they still remain distinct. Our visual system exploits the differences between these two images in order to give substance, angularity and depth to shapes: in other words, they give them a three-dimensional quality.

Having said all this, it now becomes easy to explain the reason for the bridge-mending effect that we saw on the preceding page: by bringing the image of the broken bridge close to our nose, we restricted each eye's field of vision and made the two converge until the detached sections joined together.

An easy-to-build stereoscope

Photography, the cinema and television give us two-dimensional images, in which an impression of depth is achieved by the corrective mechanisms of our visual system acting on the basis of certain data: the relative size of objects, linear and structural perspective, spatial intervention, shading, position and movement etc. These are the same premises used to assess distance by those who see in only one eye. As we have already mentioned, however, when we see an object our eyes normally see two slightly different images.

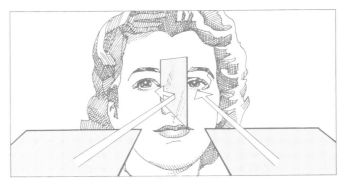

Our brain fuses the two, thus producing stereoscopic vision.

It is also possible to achieve the same effect with the two-dimensional cinematic and photographic images. Three-dimensional cinematography, in which the images, if seen with the naked eye, seem double, because they have been

taken separately (but simultaneously) with two lenses and then superimposed during projection, is no longer a novelty. If, however, the viewer uses special spectacles that reproduce the separation of the images, so that the right eye sees only what was filmed with the right-hand lens and the left eye what was filmed by the left-hand one, the outcome is not only the unification of the double images, but also stereoscopic vision.

People have been aware for some time now of the effects that can be achieved with matched photographs called *stereograms* which, using a similar technique, reproduce the same scene taken from different positions that correspond to the distance from the center of one eye to the other. During World War II stereograms were used widely for aerial reconnaissance photography to identify particular installations (factories, aerodromes, railway stations and military objectives) in enemy territory. It appears that it was one of these photographs that revealed the presence, in a German aerodrome, of

the famous V-2 rocket, to British intelligence. What is certain is that if their presence had been detected merely on an ordinary photograph, their identification as rockets on a launching pad would have been very difficult, if not impossible.

The instrument for viewing stereograms is called a *stereoscope*, which has been a very common parlour toy since the end of the last century. It succeeds in creating a very lifelike three-dimensional effect. The pictures below and on the opposite page, show two pairs of stereograms, each a mirror image of the other. If you want to experience the full three-dimensional effect, get a small mirror and place it to the right of your nose, as in the illustration at the top of the opposite page, keeping your eyes about 15 centimeters (c. 6 inches) from the two photographs. In this way your right eye will see the reflection of the right-hand image, while your left eye will focus directly on the one to the left. Adjust the mirror until the reflection of the right-hand image merges with the one on the left.

The three-dimensional effect will be particularly striking in the aerial view of Manhattan, in which the marked disparity between the two images produces a strange stereoscopic effect, bringing the viewer closer to the scene and giving him the mistaken impression that he is looking down at a model.

As far as we know, there are as yet no three-dimensional television sets on the market, even though 3-D television has been achieved experimentally. Research in this field is well underway among major electronics companies, particularly in Japan and the United States.

The tendency toward three-dimensionalism

Unexpected problems and questions can result from the examination of figures whose structure would, on the face of it, seem very straightforward. This is further proof, if further proof were needed, that visual perception cannot be taken for granted: all it needs is for the observer to adopt a slightly more analytical attitude, and an image, a figurative arrangement, will suddenly reveal hidden and unexpected depths. Coming to terms with this complexity is not just a scientific or philosophical exercise, it can also be of practical use. For example, knowing how to achieve a correct and, more importantly, an unambiguous perception of distance is a matter of vital importance for road safety specialists. On more than one occasion the reasons for seemingly inexplicable traffic accidents have been revealed by computer simulation, which recreates the degree of visual depth and three-dimensionality prevailing at the time; in other words, it shows the perceptive conditions in which the drivers found themselves.

Think also of theatrical designers, whose stage sets have to create three-dimensional effects and an illusion of depth in a relatively restricted environment. Of the countless other examples, we should mention the advances made in painting, when the mastery of perspective, and thus also the successful portrayal of three-dimensional space, resulted in a vast increase in its representational and expressive potential.

However, the fact that we tend to see the world in three rather than two dimensions does pose another problem, and one that is not easy to solve. We have already noted how the images of the world around us are received in upside-down form by the retina, that is to say by a two-dimensional structure; how then is it possible for us to perceive distance and the third dimension correctly?

This phenomenon has led psychologists to conduct research into the basic laws of spatial perception. In this book, however, we shall deal only with those that throw further light on the subject in hand. Above all, it should be noted that we have a natural tendency to place shapes in a "background," even when the two elements possess the same visual force: this is undoubtedly the result of our tendency to "three-dimensionalize." We shall now clarify what we mean with an easy example. Look at the illustration below: all it needs is a simple break in the visual homogeneity existing in the design on the left, a break achieved in the central design by a dark area bounded by an outline that we perceive as a figure, for our field of vision to arrange itself into two distinct parts, one of which, the nearer, comprises the "figure," while the other is its "background."

A continual puzzle

A jigsaw puzzle normally consists of large numbers of different pieces, all jumbled together, which convey no meaningful image, but which, when arranged in a predetermined order, reveal the shape of a familiar object or a scene filled with detail and colour. It is a pastime that calls for patience and concentration, but one that appeals to children, probably because they feel a sense of achievement when they have finally managed to piece the picture together and can admire it in its entirety. It is basically the same feeling of satisfaction that must have been experienced by those bygone artists who,

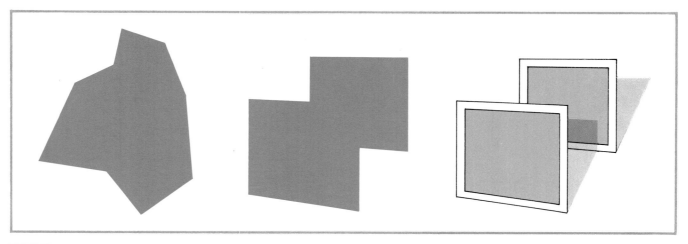

piece by piece, patiently created the mosaics which can now be admired in Byzantine churches. Jigsaw puzzles closely parallel the process of *visual perception.*

As a rule, the objects around us emit a variety of different stimuli and are contained within a context from which there also emanate other meaningful stimuli. Thus when a house, a tree or a person sends us different stimuli, we do not see varying shades and intensities of light in a completely disjointed form: we see recognizable shapes. This is because perception is not a purely passive process; it involves more than the simple reception of sensory stimuli. Just as the different pieces of a jigsaw, when arranged in the correct order, acquire a new sense of colour and form, so the stimuli transmitted by objects are organized in accordance with certain rules within a context that itself emits other, supplementary stimuli. It therefore becomes important to familiarize ourselves with the rules that govern the coordination of these stimuli, because it is on this that our understanding of the phenomenon of perception depends. It has been discovered that these rules generally work in the same direction, alternately assisting and enhancing each other, or they may work in different directions, mutually hindering and cancelling each other. Everything we have said so far applies mainly to our sense of sight, which, together with our sense of hearing, provides the most complex, but also the most rewarding examples of perceptive models.

Our lives are led within an intricate system of relationships with objects and people. Individuals satisfy their own needs, communicate with others and enjoy their surroundings because they are capable of perception. In general therefore perception is the process whereby man receives stimuli from the environment and then reacts to them. On a conceptual level, it thus involves a much broader range of experience than just sight alone. By its very nature, however, sight is the predominant element within the much vaster phenomenon of perception. Sight is the spatial sense *par excellence*: it provides us with images three-dimensional in both shape and colour, but it is also a temporal sense in that it provides us with information on movement and allows us to understand the changes undergone by objects.

An active process

From the few puzzles and brainteasers we have included so far, the reader will already have grasped one fundamental truth: sensory perception in general, and vision in particular, is not just a reflection of the world, but a very real intellectual process. When our eyes see something we instinctively try to make sense of it, even if we are unaware of the perceptive mechanisms involved. The physical world sends information to our sensory organs, which recognize, examine, select and convert it into meaningful structures and shapes through a serial process that can occur almost instantaneously. To be more precise, it is our organs of sense which gather the data

and send them to the brain, and it is the brain that carries out the process of selection, analysis and logical restructuring which gives us the sensation of "perception." This active computation of sensory stimuli is so comprehensive that sometimes, when the data reaching us from the outside world is incomplete, the perceptive process assumes elements that are not actually present. In doing this it is either making use of knowledge acquired from past experience or exploiting its intellectual capacity. We have already seen an example of this in the way that our visual system compensates for the gaps left by the blind spot (see page 56).

A world of stable objects

After all the toils and tribulations of the journey we have finally reached the seaside. We enter our hotel room, put our luggage on the floor, open the window and admire the view which is to be the scene of our holidays for the next fortnight or so. Our gaze is drawn to a series of different elements: the blue sea, the beach, the fishing boats moored in the harbour, the grey rocks, the umbrellas on the sand, the streets filled with cars and people.

At this point, if anyone were to ask what had caught our eye, it is highly unlikely that we would declare it to be a matter of luminous dots and shadows. More to the point, we would probably say that we had noticed a variety of different sights. This is because our perception is geared toward physical objects, toward an overall view of things rather than to the different qualities that characterize them. Of course, the different properties of objects also attract our attention, but we do not see them in isolation. What we see is blue sea, not "blueness" as a quality divorced from the sea; we see white boats, not "whiteness." We sink into soft cushions, not just "softness" *per se*, and so on. Our perceptual experiences are thus not isolated; they represent the overall sensation of the surroundings in which we live.

If we turn round and physically move away, we know that objects will remain, complete with their qualitative characteristics, in the same place as where we first saw them. And if we return to the same spot, we will see them all over again. This phenomenon, which to many people may seem obvious, is known in psychology as *constancy of perception* and represents a sort of intellectual acquisition. It can be more properly defined as the tendency to qualitative invariability, within certain limits, of objects, despite the variability of conditional stimuli.

The identification and definition of these limits falls within the realm of perceptual psychology.

Light and colour

From the moment that an object is taken to be a stable and permanent element of our perceptive experience, we come to see it as such regardless of its lighting. The phenomenon whereby we tend to see objects with their normal colour, independent of the prevailing conditions of light and shade, has come to be known as *constancy of light* and *constancy of colour*.

There are, however, circumstances in which the perceptive consistency of colour can be gravely compromised: this occurs when objects are bathed in a coloured light. We can all recall theatrical scenes in which the protagonists of a drama or tragedy are suddenly lit by, for example, a greenish light, which makes them change from their normal colour and produces an immediate reaction in the minds of the audience. People enjoy discothèques not just because of the dancing and the beat of the music, but because of the bright lights and colours that every now and then flash across the floor. Here, too, excitement is generated by breaking the chromatic consistency and making people appear to change colour.

There are therefore special circumstances in which objects can assume different colours from the ones they possess in the clear light of day. On a general level, it can also be said that when objects are bathed in a light restricted to a narrow range of the spectrum (see page 156), even though the light may appear to be white, the colour of the objects will change. There are different ways of proving this: something yellow may be perceived as red, if bathed in a light composed solely of red and blue-green, while something grey may appear green if bathed in a green light. It has also been discovered that a fluorescent object will radiate light waves of a different length from those which illuminate it.

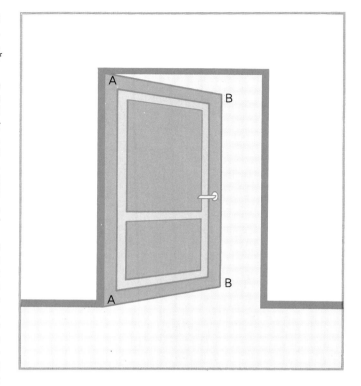

Constancy of shape

In the figure above right, which represents an open door, the outer edge indicated by *B* seems farther away than the one indicated by *A*. And yet on paper the two edges are the same distance away from the viewer. This phenomenon occurs because we perceive the image as a sign that a specific movement has taken place: the opening of a door that was previously shut. For this reason we perceive edge *B* as having moved away from us. In addition, edge *B* has become shorter than edge *A* in the picture. We sense, however, that the door has remained the same and has not altered either its shape or its size. When a door is opened, its rectangular shape, as seen by someone who always keeps the same distance away from it, undergoes a series of changes: it becomes a sort of trapezium, the base of which, represented by the outer edge, will become continually foreshortened until it blends in with the hinged edge and thus becomes a vertical line of the same thickness as the door. And yet, we still sense that the door has remained the same and that its rectangular shape has undergone no changes. Instead, we perceive the distortions that occur when it turns on its hinges as movement. This phenomenon is known in perceptual psychology as *constancy of shape*.

Constancy of dimensions

Anyone who has travelled either by car or train will undoubtedly have experienced going through a long tunnel. No sooner has one entered it than one starts looking for the exit, as though searching for reassurance. If the tunnel is fairly long, but not too long to obscure the exit, the latter will appear as a dot of light; although the size of this dot may vary, it will always be noticeably smaller than the entrance. If, however, someone were to ask us whether the tunnel's exit really was smaller than its entrance, we would certainly reply that this was not the case. The world might be full of jokers, but it would be carrying things too far to imagine such a thing. The phenomenon becomes even clearer if we stop to observe, from a particular angle, the arched structure of a church or cloister. Each arch is, so to speak, framed by the preceding one (see photograph, opposite page), with the result that the last one appears to be less than half the size (it all depends on the distance) of the one nearest us. Nevertheless, if we were asked which of the arches were the larger and which the smaller, we would unhesitatingly reply that they were all of the same size. We may, paradoxically, see the arches as different, but we "perceive" them to be the same size because we make an unconscious mental adjustment to the bare facts as received by our senses. Our capacity to see a distant object as being of the same size as one close-by is known in perceptual psychology as *size constancy*.

A compromise

The phenomenon known as size constancy reveals, perhaps more than any other perceptual experience, the way in which the mind is actively brought to bear on the visual stimuli received from objects. We have already noted how we unconsciously carry out a process of intellectual correction on the data received from our senses and we should not delude ourselves into thinking that our senses reflect the world as it is. They provide only some of the many pieces of information concerning the world about us: those on which they are

Below: although, in accordance with the laws of perspective, we see the arches of this church as being of different sizes, we perceive them as identical. Similarly, in the photographs on the right, which show the sculptor Alexander Calder, we perceive the dome in the background more or less in its real dimensions, even though in both the photographs they are those of a hat.

already predisposed to operate. Thus vision does not provide us with information on all the electromagnetic waves that envelop us, only those within the spectral range. We will deal with this phenomenon in a later chapter.

Psychological research has thrown some light on the processes involved in the perception of an object's dimensions. We do not perceive the real size of an object situated a certain distance away from us, according to the laws of perspective. What happens is a sort of compromise between the perspective dimensions and the real ones. It naturally falls to perceptual psychology to define the nature, rules and principles of such compromises. One general law, however, applies here: the dimensions that we perceive relate to the real ones in direct ratio to the amount of information available. The more incomplete and ambiguous the information, the more the perceived dimensions will tend to match the perspective ones. To sum up, it can be said that the compromise between real and perspective dimensions depends on the context within which one's perceptual judgement operates.

Constancy of position

If you want to carry out a very interesting experiment, go to a specialist laboratory and obtain a pair of prismatic lenses mounted on a support, of the kind that turn one's vision upside-down, and ask a friend to try them on. Then ask him to walk toward some familiar, prearranged object. Because he is seeing the world the wrong way up, he will initially feel disorientated and, as he moves, everything will seem to rotate. But gradually, as though he were trying to reorganize his surroundings by establishing fixed points of reference, he will reduce his head movements and finally reach his goal. This shows how the individual, when faced with disorder in his surroundings, creates stable points of reference in the form of objects that he will later use to orientate himself. The phenomenon whereby an individual perceives objects as stable, despite the variety and amount of information emanating from the latter, is known in psychology as *constancy of position*. The reason that we see the world around us as possessing an inherent stability is perhaps linked to our experience of its continuity: this attitude towards our surroundings is determined to a large extent by learning, in other words, by the influence of all the occasions on which our perception of objects as stable has been confirmed.

This constancy seems so natural to us that we are unaware of the problems connected to it. It is a subject with which we will deal only briefly, however.

One of the fundamental differences that exist between the animal and vegetable worlds is movement. Certainly, one of the reasons for the evolutionary success of the animal species is the fact that they are able to move from place to place in search of food. When we move, we perceive the world as stable and we know that it is we who are responsible for movement, and not inanimate objects. This also happens

 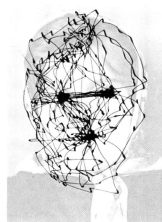

at crucial moments: when we whirl round like windmills and then stop, the world seems to be spinning round, inducing an unpleasant feeling of nausea. Effectively, we *see* the world going round, despite the fact that we *perceive* it as stable. We also experience a feeling of nausea when watching films that have been taken using a shaking camera. But why do we not feel the same effect when we turn our head rapidly? Primarily, because our eyes, when they move, quite literally jump from one point to the next and do not see everything that passes by during the movement and, secondly, because it depends on the constancy of position of objects and not on the way in which our eyes operate.

Compensatory mechanisms

The parallel between the eye and a camera does not hold good once one ventures slightly beyond the realm of common sense. After all, we are not immobile subjects in a static environment. Only in specialist laboratories is it possible to artificially recreate a situation in which the seeing subject and the seen object are completely motionless. Apart from anything else, in such circumstances the eye will still continue to move and make corrections to the image on the retina: the so-called *saccadic movements* (see illustration above). In everyday experience, movement is the norm.

Let us now try to discover what changes occur in our field of vision when we move about: the objects seem to move with us, albeit in different ways. If we draw close to an object it will seem to grow; when we pass in front of it the object rotates around us. If we bow our head or move it round and round, we change the orientation of our surroundings. We, however, are unaware of all these movements and perceive the world as being fundamentally stable. Is there a reason for this?

Our perceptual system possesses mechanisms that are able to correct and compensate for these movements. What happens is roughly as follows: the compensatory mechanisms compare the visual stimuli with the *proprioceptive* stimuli (the ones that provide us with information relating to bodily movement) and, if the visual and *proprioceptive* information coincide, then our surroundings are perceived as stable. Any deviation from this coincidence will result in a feeling of movement.

The phenomenon of perceptual constancy helps us to understand how we are able to negotiate our surroundings correctly, to handle objects and assess their shape and distance and also to judge whether they are static or moving. It can, however, deceive us into thinking that we are seeing things that correspond to reality. For example, take a pen or pencil in your hand and hold it in a vertical position in front of your eyes. Then bring it close to your nose and focus your gaze not on the pencil, but on one of the fingers of your other hand, which should be about 30 centimeters (c. 12 inches) away from your face. You will then see two pencils rather than the one that is really there.

Everybody knows that people who have one drink too many run the risk of "seeing double." An excessive intake of alcohol can make things seem to move or change shape, appear deformed, when in fact they are constant. There is also the strange phenomenon of *hallucination*, which can affect people in particular circumstances and make them imagine that they are seeing people, objects or strange shapes. A driver, if driving by himself at night in conditions of extreme tiredness, may see strange shapes and objects looking like cars or obstacles. There are also drugs, known as hallucinogens, which can induce hallucinations. These are certainly exceptional cases, but all it needs is a few examples to show that the correspondence between what we see and what actually exists cannot be taken for granted.

Now take a look at the figure above and try to describe what you see: a sort of candlestick, perhaps, with leaves sprouting out of it? Now try taking a closer look and see if you can detect

another image; imagine, for example, that those strange leaves are human eyes. Suddenly the leaves and the candlestick disappear, leaving in their place a sort of mirror-image of two human faces. We thus find ourselves in a situation that is

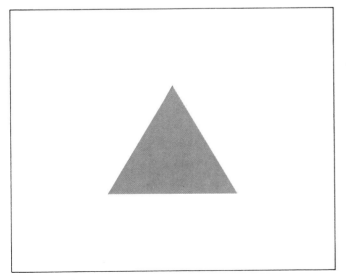

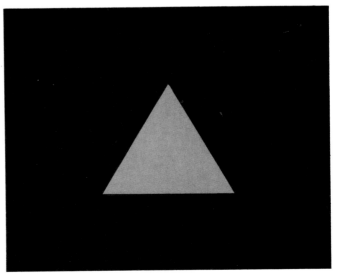

the direct opposite of those we have just described: here we were unable to detect a figure that was there the whole time. One immediately thinks in this context of the numerous cases of animal camouflage that occur in nature; only the trained eye can "see" certain animals or insects in the wild, let alone their nests or lairs, even when they have no covering.

Now examine the two illustrations at the bottom of page 69. The grey triangle on the left appears darker than the one on the right, despite the fact that the two figures are, from the physical point of view, two surfaces reflecting exactly the same amount of light. Why, then, do we see one as being darker than the other?

The discrepancy between the physical characteristics of objects and the way in which we see them involves a variety of different factors such as shape, colour, clarity and size. Yet again, we can see that the relationship between perception and the outside world cannot be taken too much for granted. Anyone naive enough to think that all our eyes do is to reflect reality, is mistaken. There are countless things that can be seen, but do not exist, and, conversely, there are things that exist, but which cannot be seen. Obviously there are also things that exist in the same way as they are seen. It is these which allow us to establish the correct relationship with the world about us.

It is not our intention to complicate things that are intrinsically simple, but just to encourage the reader toward a more critical and rational attitude to visual experience.

Upside-down letters

We now offer you a few simple games that are nothing more than amusing curiosities. They will, however, show how even

the simplest perceptual phenomena can hide problems of considerable importance. If you have a head and shoulders photograph of yourself to hand, of the sort used in passports, try placing it in front of you, but upside-down. It isn't so easy to recognize yourself, is it?

Now take a look at what is written in the box below and try to read the two sentences. It is difficult enough to read the printed letters, whereas the handwritten ones are almost impossible to decipher.

There is an explanation for this phenomenon: our difficulty in reading upside-down letters, whether typed or handwritten, derives from the fact that we are used to reading with our eyes moving from left to right. When the letters are turned upside-down, our eyes thus tend to move in the wrong direction. It seems that the same explanation can be applied to upside-down faces.

> *It is not easy reading upside-down*
>
> *reading upside-down*
>
> *It is not easy*

Upside-down faces

Don't turn the page round, the photographs have not been inverted in error. Just try and work out who they are. We will allow you thirty seconds. If you are not successful, then turn the page upside-down and you will instantly recognize Paul

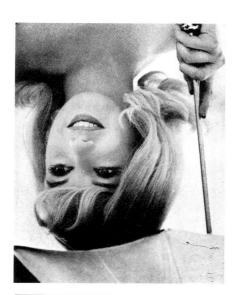

Newman, Elizabeth Taylor and Marilyn Monroe. But why was it so hard to recognize three such famous faces?

We will try to provide an answer, even though it is no easy matter. In the meantime, we suggest you try another game along the same lines. Take some out-of-date magazines, cut out a few photographs of famous people and show them upside-down to your friends, inviting them to identify the personalities. You will see that it is not that easy.

Now let us take a look at the figure, above left. Even though it is upside-down, we can see two eyes and a mouth, the unmistakable signs of a face. But what sort of expression does it have? Sad or happy? Then turn the page round to see. It is certainly not a happy expression; one would rather say that it was angry.

And now for another game of recognition. Try to identify the monuments in the photographs below, but again without turning the book round. In this game, one's memory also plays a very important role, but you will notice that it is much easier to recognize monuments (the Eiffel Tower in Paris, Tower Bridge in London, the dome of Florence Cathedral) than faces.

Two-faced images

The figure, above right, shows three faces. The first seems to belong to a rather jolly clown, the second to an old king with a crown on his head, while the lines of the third recall a round, smiling face. Now up-end the drawings: the clown is still a clown, albeit a little less smiling; the old king has taken on the appearance of a young girl, while the round, smiling face has become sad and seems to be almost crying.

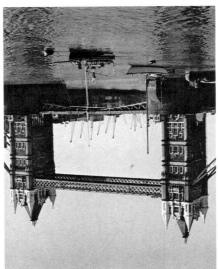

You can also play this game in another way. Look at the three illustrations while holding them in a vertical position at knee-level, with your head bowed down. The faces look the same as when you hold the book upside-down. In fact, what happened in this case was that you held the book upright, but the effect was the same as if, without realizing it, you had up-ended your head and with it the image that forms on the retina. This means that the orientation of the image on our retina plays a fundamental part in the recognition of figures such as faces.

An explanation

We shall now try to provide an explanation for these phenomena. When we see a figure at the wrong angle, upside-down for example, or when we look at something with our head bowed, a corrective mechanism intervenes in the perceptive process, compensating for the different movements on the basis of real environmental references. If, for example, we look at a distant object, its image on the retina will be small, and yet, we can tell that the object is not small by assessing its correct proportional relationship to reality. This perceptual phenomenon can be explained by stating that the retinal image is in some way compensated for by a mechanism that takes distance into account. And just as the correction of size is called "constancy of dimensions," so the process of vertical adjustment could be called *constancy of orientation.* How then can we explain our difficulty in recognizing upside-down faces?

It would seem that when looking at an upside-down face our compensatory mechanism is confronted by a problem with which it cannot cope. A face contains too many details, lines and features, each of which must be accurately interpreted for it to be recognized as such. When we concentrate our attention on making a correct identification of the eyes, for example, the other elements, such as the mouth and nose, remain unaltered and continue to be incorrectly perceived on the retina. Hence the confusion and the consequent difficulty in "seeing." If we then consider that, in recognizing a face, the relationship between its different features are of crucial importance and that, because these are too numerous to be taken in all at once, they cause our eyes considerable problems, the phenomenon is in itself hardly surprising.

Discover the meaning

Look at the figure, above right and ask yourself what you see. You will probably answer that all you can see is a strange, irregular shape. Now rotate it 90 degrees in a clockwise direction and look at it again. The shape will immediately bring to mind the characteristic outline of Africa. Return the book to its original position and examine the figure on the bottom

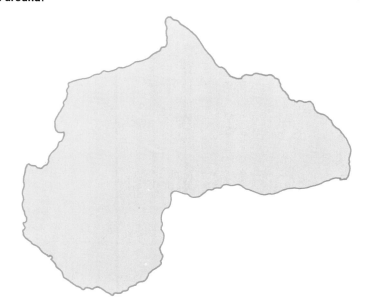

right. Although you will not recognize anything, the preceding figure will have given you a clue to what lies behind this apparently meaningless jumble of lines and shapes in relief. Turn the page upside-down and you can see that it is a small map of Europe. Does it not seem strange to you, this sudden loss of meaning by a figure as soon as it is inverted? If you take another look at the figure above, you will now recognize Africa, even on its side, whereas the figure below will still not look like an inverted relief map of Europe. Familiar figures at unusual angles will look different when their orientation has been altered.

In psychology, ordinary experiences, made familiar by everyday life, have often posed extremely interesting problems.

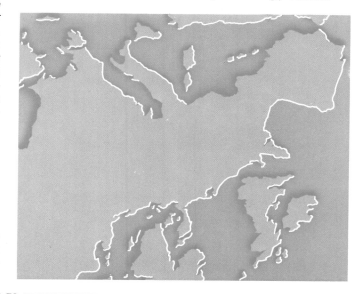

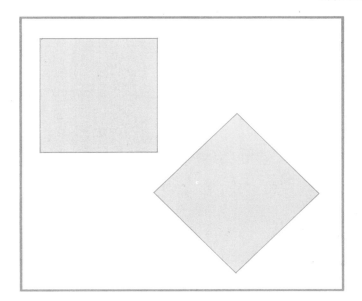

Phenomena such as these were already known in the past. In the last century Ernst Mach (1838–1916) noted that a simple square seems different when it is rotated 45 degrees. The figure on the left shows two identical squares: however, the one on the right looks more like a diamond than a square and, what is more, its corners do not appear to be right angles.

A game with maps

So far, we have spoken of maps only as specific images, capable of synthesizing and communicating a vast amount of information concerning the topography of a country, its latitude and longitude, its centers of population, climate etc. But it is also possible to play games with maps.

Those strange, irregular outlines in the illustration below are ten countries of Eastern and Western Europe (to the same scale), although clearly their position here does not correspond to their geographical location. Try to work out which countries are represented. The solution is overleaf.

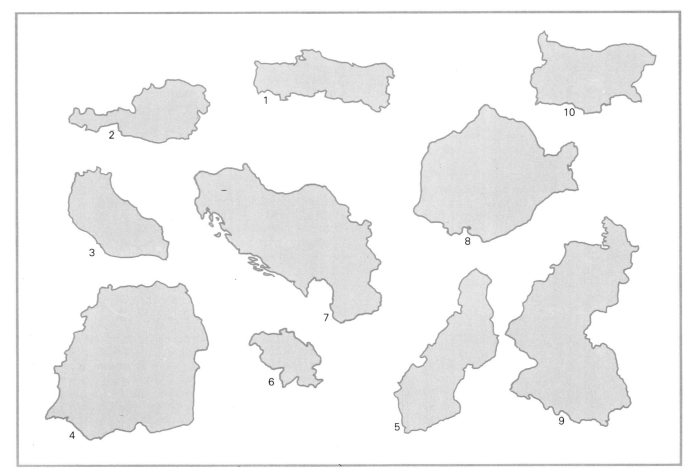

Strange phenomena

Take another look at the square at the top of page 73 and try tilting your head at an angle of 45 degrees. The square does not look like a diamond: it still looks like a square. And so if we rotate the figure 45 degrees the square changes shape, or rather it appears to change shape, but if it is we who tilt at an angle of 45 degrees the square still remains a square. How can this be? Now try another experiment: place the square in front of you, but rotated so that it looks like a diamond, and then tilt your head at an angle of 45 degrees. What do you think you see? A square, perhaps? On the contrary: you still see a diamond.

These simple experiments, which we hope have not confused you, mean only this: the thing that alters the apparent shape of a figure is not the change in orientation as received by the retina, but the change in orientation perceived in relation to the figure's surroundings. It was the *Gestalt* psychologists (see page 77) who first revealed the overriding importance of relationships, where absolute characteristics are concerned, in perception.

What we have presented as games are, in fact, proper experiments, which have caused considerable problems to perceptual psychologists. The perception of a figure's shape involves the automatic assignation of a "top," a "bottom" a "left side" and a "right side". It would thus seem that it is orientation in relation to the directional coordinates of the environment in which we live, and in which we see objects placed, that has a profound effect on our perception of shape; the latter does not therefore depend solely on the internal geometry of an object.

One very commonly-held view, not just among ordinary people, but among scholars as well, equates perception of shape with the identification of outline, with the latter being the result of sudden differences in light intensity. Shape would therefore be the perception of a succession of outlines. Outline is certainly one of the basic prerequisites for the perception of shape, but it is not the only factor involved: there are also certain cognitive processes in which the characteristics of figures are described and adjusted by our perceptual system.

Yet again, we can see how the analysis of apparently simple perceptual phenomena has revealed an altogether more problematical and complex reality.

Cross or square?

What do you see in the figure above? The tips of four arms of a cross, or four corners of a square perhaps? The significance of four dark dots arranged with a certain regularity depends on how the individual assembles them in his mind and then "sees" them. The most interesting point for us, however, is that when we see the four dots, we do not just look at them passively, but feel the need to give them some kind of meaning and group them together into a more complex structure (a cross, square, or some other figure) than the simple, equidistant regularity that they display.

This phenomenon provides further proof that perception is not just a passive registering of data, but a constructive and deductive process. It also shows how every act of perception is a subjective and personal experience.

Reversible figures

There are certain perceptual situations in which we can detect the active role played by the individual with much greater clarity. We are referring to cases of *figure-ground ambiguity*, in which images, if viewed for a length of time, seem to turn inside-out and back again, inverting their perspective.

One such image is reproduced on page 69 (above): people looking at it will say that they see a sort of dark candlestick with leaf-like appendages against a white, rectangular background. If, however, they are encouraged to take a closer look and identify other shapes, they will admit that the same lines

---

Solution to bottom illustration (page 73)

1. Portugal	6. Switzerland
2. Austria	7. Yugoslavia
3. Hungary	8. Romania
4. Poland	9. West Germany
5. Czechoslovakia	10. Bulgaria

can also be interpreted as the outline of two human faces. They will then notice how, once the two faces have appeared, the candlestick vanishes: what was originally the background has now become the figure and vice versa. This is not because we are unable to see two figures at a time, but because, by organizing the visual data to form two faces, the candlestick immediately loses its status as "figure" and becomes "ground," taking, so to speak, a back seat.

By using this example we become aware of what happens when we place an image in a background or, conversely, when we remove a figure from its background and turn it into a figure. We use our brain to create a sort of double presence: the "ground," in which we place a figure, plays a supporting role, but is always there, even when we are not aware of its existence because we are not seeing it.

Necker's cube

Figures that alter their appearance if gazed at for a certain length of time have always interested students of psychology and fascinated the layman. One classic example of this phenomenon is the cube shown below (Fig. 1), which, at first sight, is reminiscent of a transparent cube. In psychology it is known as *Necker's cube*, from the name of its discoverer Louis Albert Necker, who in 1832 referred to the phenomenon of perspective inversion spontaneously revealed by certain line-drawings.

If, in fact, we gaze at the figure for a long time, concentrating particularly on corners *A* and *B*, we can see that at a certain point they change places, so that the surface which at first appeared to be behind comes to the front and vice versa. The fact is that the two different orientations will subsequently alternate, with neither prevailing: we continue to see first one and then the other, but never both at the same time. How can we explain this sort of phenomenon, in view of the fact that Fig. 1 still remains the same and that our eye is therefore still receiving the same visual message? The explanation provided by psychology goes something like this: since perception is

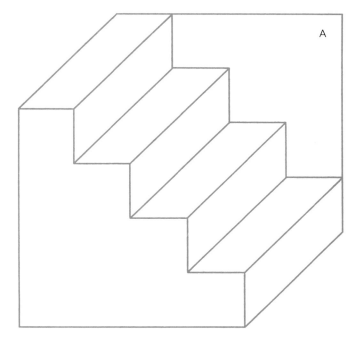

not a passive sensation, but a meaningful organization and restructuring of data, then "reversible" figures will transmit information that our perceptual system can arrange into more than one equally valid representation or description. As a result, it will accept either one or other of the images. In this case perception is not "unstable" but *multi-stable*. See further reference to Figs. 1, 2 and 3 (below) on page 77.

Schröder's staircase

Let us now consider another example of a multi-stable figure: the so-called *Schröder's staircase* (above).

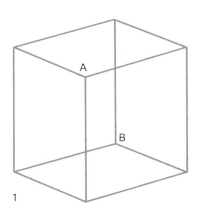

1

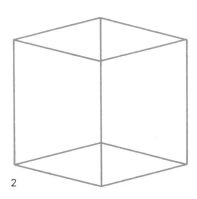

2

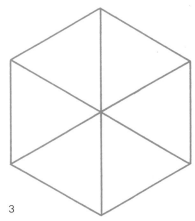

3

Here, the invertible perspective is less marked than in Necker's cube: if the staircase is rising up toward the left, then wall *A* is the background, but if the steps are seen as the underside of a staircase, then the wall comes into the foreground. In order to create this inversion, concentrate hard on the figure and try to organize the visual data along different lines.

The figure–ground phenomenon is one of the favourite subjects of psychological research in understanding the mechanisms of perceptual cognition.

Mach's dihedron

What does the figure on the right remind you of? A sheet of paper folded lengthwise in half and then placed half-open on a table, with the fold vertical as it rests on the angle formed by one of its two short sides? Or a piece of paper folded in the same way, but resting on its two long sides, with the entire length of the median fold clearly visible at the top? Or perhaps a roof seen from above? It could represent any of these things. Known as *Mach's dihedron*, this is another example of a reversible figure. Despite its simplicity, it is interesting because it shows how inversion can, in a manner of speaking, be created with an actual object and not just by means of its image.

Take a piece of fairly stiff card, fold it and place it on a table with the fold parallel to the surface of the table (as in the second explanation provided above), close one eye and look at the card from above so that the fold forms an angle of 45 degrees with the line of your gaze. Keep the card in the same position and continue to look at it, since that will tend to give the structure greater stability. If you continue doing this for a while, at a certain point you should experience an unexpected phenomenon: the card will suddenly appear to stand upright, rather like walls forming the corner of a room. The effect is undoubtedly entertaining, even though it does require a little patience to achieve.

Mach's dihedron and the other ambiguous figures are among the most thought-provoking and curious phenomena of perceptual psychology.

Figure-ground ambiguity

There are many factors determining the ambiguity of the figure-ground relationship. For example, in an image where one figure contains another, the vaster area is seen as the background and the smaller as the figure (below, first drawing on the left); in the second image the white and black cross are interchangeable as figure or ground, while in the third the white cross clearly stands out as a figure against the black ground, in the same way as the black cross stands out against the white ground of the fourth image. The ambiguity relates not only to the alternation between ground and figure, but to the image *per se*, in that, given a figure whose parts are structured in such a way as to create a visible image, this leaves the way clear for another image to be created by restructuring certain details into other meaningful layouts.

We offer the reader as an example the drawing "The wife and the mother-in-law" (opposite), conceived by the caricaturist W. H. Hill and first published in 1915: the chin of the young woman becomes the old woman's nose, the old woman's mouth is transformed into the girl's necklace and so on. Let us now try to understand how this happens.

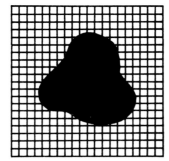 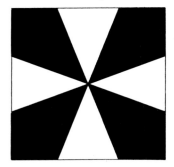 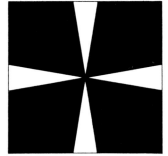 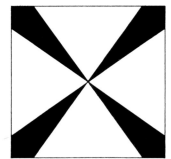

structure of our world. The games and various brainteasers we have introduced thus far, and which we shall continue to include, are based, both in their arrangement and in the explanation of their solutions, on the principles of Gestalt psychology (*Gestalt* meaning "shape" in German). It is to this branch of contemporary psychology, which deals with the conditions of our perceptual experience, that we owe the identification and clarification of the principal factors affecting perception. It would therefore seem appropriate to give a brief explanation of it. Its fundamental principle states that Gestalt is a configuration in which the function of the parts is determined by the organization of the whole; it is, therefore, a whole whose significance does not derive from the sum of its individual parts.

The birth of the theory is commonly dated to 1912, the year in which the Czech psychologist Max Wertheimer published his article *Experimental studies on the perception of movement*. Others who contributed to the formulation of the theory were Wolfgang Köhler and Kurt Koffka, who in 1921 founded the magazine *Psychologische Forschung* (Psychological Research). Amongst Köhler's most important works, there is one that particularly deserves to be mentioned: *Gestalt Psychology*, published in 1929 and still the most lucid and exhaustive exposition of the theory of this school of psychology. Koffka particularly distinguished himself by the long series of studies that he conducted in support of the Gestalt theory, whose sphere of influence and scope he greatly enlarged. His main work, *Principles of Gestalt Psychology*, was published in 1935 and remains a classic work of psychology.

The three founders of Gestalt psychology were all opponents of the Nazi régime and in 1938, after being forced to close down their magazine, they emigrated to the United States. From then on their research broadened and new discoveries were made. It was, above all, the theories of Gestalt psychologists on *structure*, on the priority of the whole over its parts and on the interdependent relationship of perceptive data, which allowed the theory to be extended to include the study of thought and intelligence.

Once a particular detail has been picked out and identified by means of some significant feature, such as an ear, there then immediately follows the attribution of meaning to other features, such as the young woman's chin and nose. Thus once one detail has been identified, this, together with the other lines, establishes a series of relationships which ultimately produce the girl's face and not the old woman's. The ambiguity originates in the fact that different, but equally valid, arrangements can be made of the same visual data.

Now turn back to the illustration at the bottom of page 75 and see what it represents: Figs. 1, 2 and 3 all show the same cube, but viewed from different angles. Fig. 1 is clearly three-dimensional even though the figure is reversible. In Fig. 2, the perception of depth is not as immediate as in Fig. 1, but still possible. In Fig. 3, however, it is very difficult to make out the third dimension, even though it is the same cube; it appears, to all intents and purposes, to be a flat figure.

A bit of history

The perception of an object as either figure or ground is governed by certain laws and depends on a number of different factors. The time has come to refer briefly to these factors since they are generally the same as those that determine the phenomenon of perception, in other words, the perceptive

Structure

The time has now come to provide further clarification of the concept of *structure* within perceptual psychology, by referring to some of its other contexts. When we listen to a piece of music, for example, we do not perceive a simple series of single elements (the notes), but a coherent, unitary harmony. Similarly, when we look at a painting or a statue we do not perceive a sum of parts, but a structured entity. What counts in a structure is the relationship between the parts: if one of these changes, then the others change too. The structure does not change, therefore, unless the relationship between the parts changes, just as a tune can be played in a different key and yet still sound the same.

The law of Prägnanz

Wertheimer places the law of *Prägnanz* (which in German means "pregnant with meaning") in sixth position, but we are introducing it first, not only because it is of such fundamental importance, but also because it gives a greater insight into Gestalt reasoning than any other theory. It deals with *good shape*, meaning the capacity of certain figures to be more readily perceived than others. "Good shapes" include circles, squares, hexagons and all other figures displaying a certain geometrical *regularity*.

Prägnanz can be expressed in certain specific forms that we shall now examine individually. It signifies regularity, but this can sometimes involve several meanings.

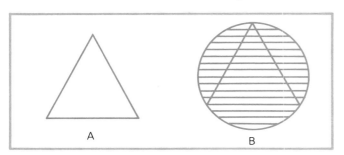

Look at the figure above: the triangle *A* has been inserted in circle *B*, but the regularity of the lines forms such a significant entity that we no longer perceive the base of the isosceles triangle, even though its other two equal sides can be clearly seen. In this case there is a conflict between two regular shapes, that of the triangle and that of the close parallel lines.

Good shape also signifies symmetry and simplicity, as in the figure below. We shall now try to describe figure *A*. It looks nothing like the composition of *B* and *C*, but more like a cross and a hexagon. This is because both the cross and the hexagon possess two axes of symmetry which *B* and *C* lack.

We have said that the law of *Prägnanz* would help us

understand the Gestalt point of view. This is because when a group of perceptual data is arranged into a figure, a meaningful image, the interpretation of the latter does not depend solely on the characteristics of the individual elements, but on the relationship established between them.

Proximity

In the figure below we can see groups of vertical lines, each group being formed of two lines. In this structure the elements appear to be grouped in twos simply because some are closer together than others. This is the principle of proximity,

according to which all the things that we perceive are grouped together on the basis of the distance between them. The lines in the illustration are seen as being in pairs because the distance between the two lines that compose them is less than the space separating them from the lines forming the adjacent pairs. By speaking of *pairs* we have introduced a new concept, on the basis of which we have formalized the figure above. If all the vertical lines were equally spaced, rather than some being closer together than others, we would simply say that they were a series of ten identical vertical lines, rather than five pairs of vertical lines. This law does not just affect our visual perception of objects, but also our acoustic perception (as in music, for example) and our tactile experiences.

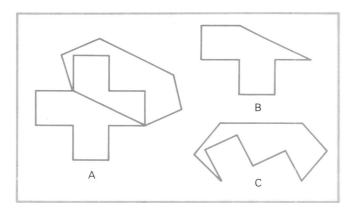

Equivalence

The figure shown immediately above represents a series of equidistant dots, but here, too, we tend to think in terms of pairs. The factor of proximity has been replaced in this structure by another one, that of *similarity*, which can be briefly expressed thus: elements of similar shape and colour tend to group together to form independent configurations. There are numerous perceptual experiences in which we tend to link several objects together to form a single element. When we see a long line of people by a ticket office, we say that they form a "queue." Similarly, a series of separate black and white stripes across a street form a "pedestrian crossing." Likewise when we see a meadow full of daisies we do not see only the daisies: we link the different visual data on the basis of the law of equivalence. It cannot be denied, however, that proximity also plays a part in these examples. On the other hand, perception is a coherent, unitary experience in which we have distinguished several elements only for the purposes of method and analysis.

are saying that our visual system tends to discourage sudden changes in direction by a rectilinear section, and so, at the points where it intersects other sections, we join it to the one continuing in the same direction.

In the figure below right, we see A as a square partially intersected by an oval, even though there is nothing to prevent us seeing the figure as being formed of a square (B) which has one side with a curved re-entrant, and an oval intersected at a certain point by a straight line (C).

These factors, which we have identified individually, come together in vision to form visual perception. It is not only in this field, however, that the analysis of a phenomenon imposes what appear to be artificial methodological distinctions.

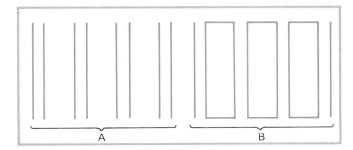

The law of the closed shape

In the illustration above, the vertical lines composing figure A also recur in figure B, and yet the latter appears radically different from A. All it needed was to join up the broader intervening spaces for the two figures to be very differently perceived. This phenomenon can be explained by the *law of closedness*, which says that a closed shape is more significant than an open one. When dealing with closed shapes, the most significant ones are the simplest: thus a circle is more significant than a square, a square more significant than a rectangle and so on. This perceptual tendency is so powerful that sometimes we see figures and shapes as closed when the enclosure is not complete.

The law of the good curve or shared direction

Look at the illustration above right. In A we see something resembling a thread passing behind two sails. If we focus our attention on B, we see a regular line (st) being vertically intersected by a less regular one (xy). We do not, however, see B as a figure composed of sx and yt (see fig. C).

Let us now try to understand the principles operating in A and B: both cases show a union of elements which, like the line passing behind the sails and like lines st and xy, appear to have a *shared direction* or a *good shape*. In other words, we

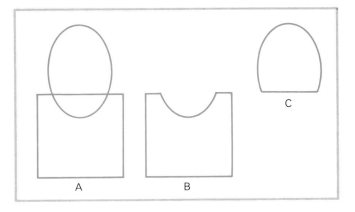

Maurits C. Escher: artist of visual ambiguity

One modern artist who proved particularly adept at exploiting recent psychological discoveries and at expressing in his works the general cultural trends of our century, is the Dutchman Maurits C. Escher. In his later works, in fact, it is not hard to recognize the influence of modern mathematics and crystallography, and often we can clearly see how his work is inspired by studies conducted into visual perception.

The early years of this century saw the spread of the theories and discoveries of Gestalt psychology (see page 77) which, by analyzing the conditions of our perception, had shaken the common-sense belief that "we see the world as it really is." In fact, we sometimes see things that are not there, while at other times we cannot see things that really are there, so great is the ambiguity and relativity of what we perceive. Some figures make sense if considered within a context, others appear to alternate figure and background and so on. Escher was able to translate this ambiguity in visual terms, as well as providing an artistic interpretation of what has come to be known as the loss of absolute certainties, a trend which characterizes contemporary culture. He himself stated that studies of visual perception lay at the base of his work. His reading of works by psychologists such as Koffka were basic to the development and elaboration of his art.

One of the discoveries of the Gestalt movement showed how, under certain conditions, lines and two-dimensional planes will transform themselves into three-dimensional elements. In the illustrations of Necker's cube (see page 75) we can see how psychologists dealing with shape and form noted that it is our natural tendency to simplify that organizes some formal arrangements into two-dimensional figures and others into three-dimensional ones.

Opposite: Maurits C. Escher, *Waterfall*, lithograph, 1961.

Above: Maurits C. Escher, *Sky and water 1*, woodcut, 1938.

Recognize the shapes

If we inhabit a world in which the language of images is becoming more and more dominant, then knowing how to read this instrument of communication and information means gaining a greater sense of awareness. The games illustrated on the following pages complement and, in a way, enhance what we have said so far. They are designed solely to entertain and exercise your visual capabilities.

In our everyday life, and at work, it is often important to be able to recognize a certain shape, to distinguish it from others and to assess its distance and dimensions.

Despite their simplicity, the tests that follow will force our imagination to identify certain formal characteristics. They are not intended to educate anyone in the reading of images; that would require a completely different exercise. They may, however, prove useful, partly because they have been conceived along similar lines to psychological tests designed to assess the visual aptitude of the individual. If nothing else, they will lead to a greater degree of self-awareness.

The games consist of choosing, from several figures of identical geometric shape, the one whose size will continue a certain series or which belongs at a precise point within it. You thus have to be able to "see" size correctly on the basis of a comparative study of smaller and larger dimensions. We have chosen the most common and familiar geometric shapes, such as circles, squares, triangles, ovals etc. The exercises are therefore very simple to perform: they are just an amusing way of testing yourself through a game composed of images. The answers are on page 94.

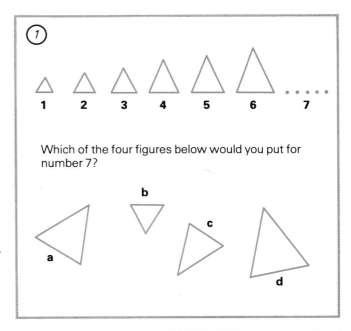

Which of the four figures below would you put for number 7?

②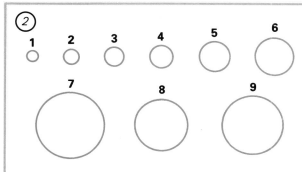

The nine circles are arranged in ascending order of size. Only number 7 is clearly out of place. Which of circles *a, b, c* or *d* would you replace it with in order to make the correct progression?

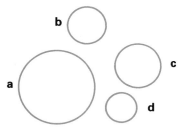

④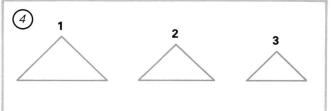

Which of triangles *a, b, c, d* or *e* should you place at the end of this series decreasing from left to right?

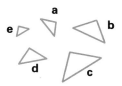

③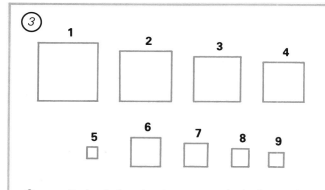

Square 5 clearly breaks the progressively decreasing order of the series. Which of squares *a, b, c* or *d* should you replace it with in order for the series to be arranged in the correct progressive order?

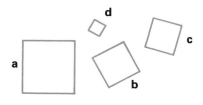

⑤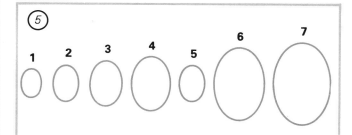

In this series of eggs, number 5 is out of place. Which of eggs *a, b, c, d, e* or *f* will correct the series?

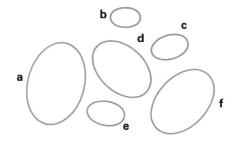

Find the figure

These games, like those you will have encountered earlier in the book are based on geometric shapes: they are, however, differently constructed. The individual images in each game represent the different stages in a reasoning process which, so to speak, ends in a conclusion.

The latter involves choosing from a number of figures whose peculiar characteristics complete the logical reasoning process.

The solutions of the individual tests, together with a rational explanation, are provided on page 94.

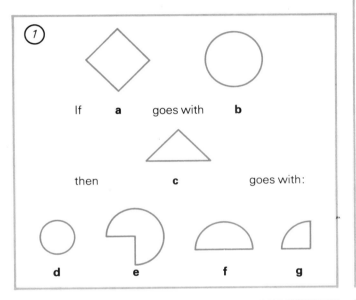

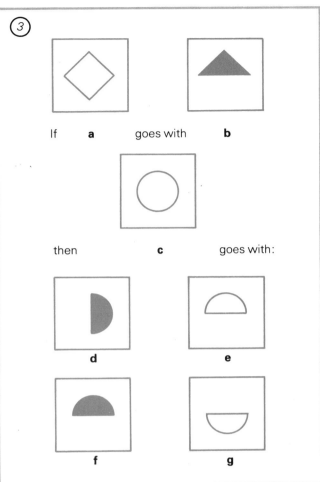

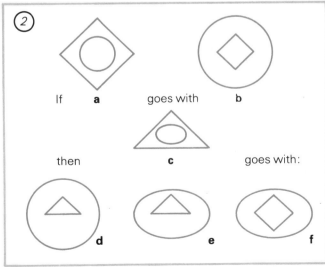

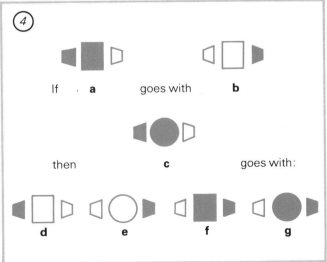

Composing figures

The following games consist of linking several shapes together to form a new one. In mathematical terms, one would say that, in order to complete these tests, one has to add up the different pieces in order to achieve the geometric figure shown beneath. All the pieces, which are identified by numbers, are needed to complete the game. Should you so wish, you can try using a pencil to reconstitute the figures by drawing the individual elements on to the shapes. Once you have finished, you can check the results on page 94. We would suggest, however, that the best method is to take a sheet of tracing paper, trace out the individual elements and then transfer them to something more substantial, such as a piece of stiff paper or card. Next, carefully cut out the individual pieces, following the outline exactly and then try to recreate the different geometric figures. In this way the game becomes more active, more involving and more entertaining. In addition, once you have cut out the pieces for each game, you can get your friends to play too.

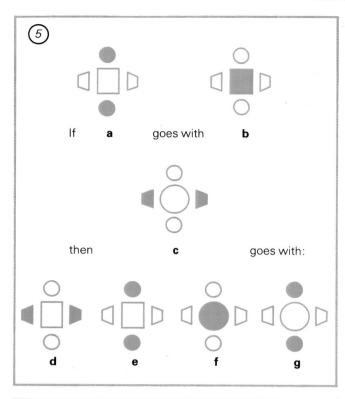

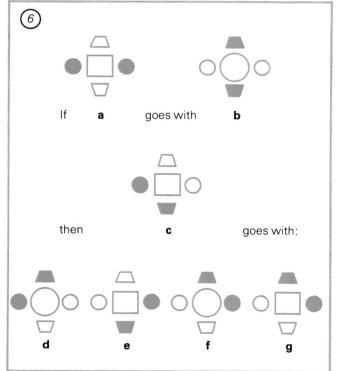

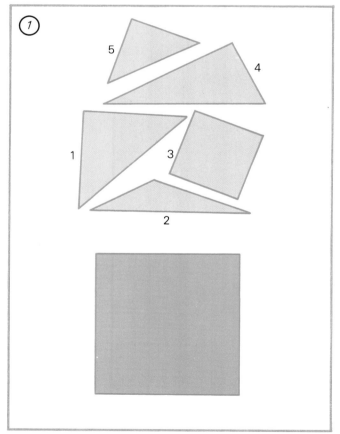

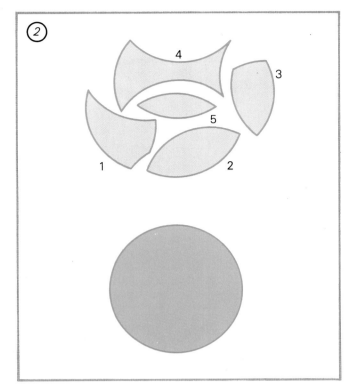

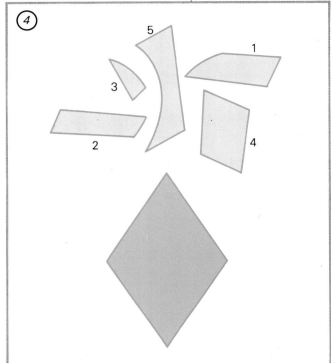

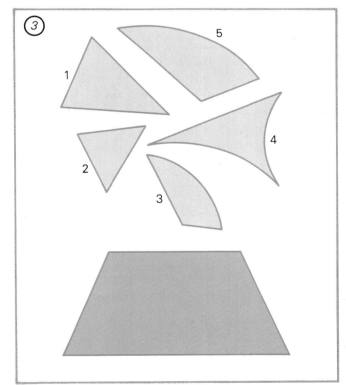

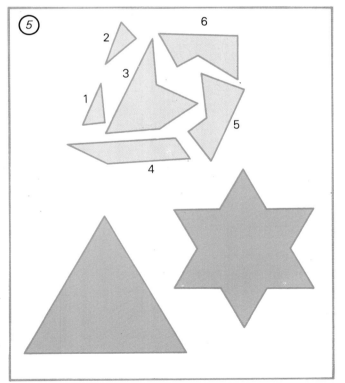

Superimposing figures

If you superimpose two figures, you will obtain another one with a very different outline. The game consists of identifying the new figure, while retaining a very clear mental image of the two original ones. You need a "good eye" to choose the correct shape from the several possible alternatives, having discarded the unacceptable ones purely on the grounds that they do not contain the characteristics present in the originals. And so, in the games that follow, if you superimpose *a* on *b* (or vice versa), which of the figures *c*, *d*, *e* or *f* will you obtain? The answers are on page 94.

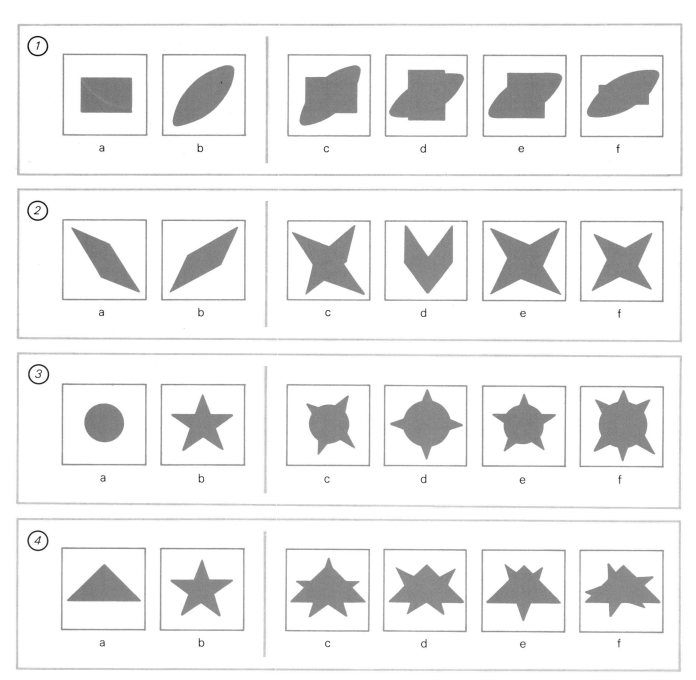

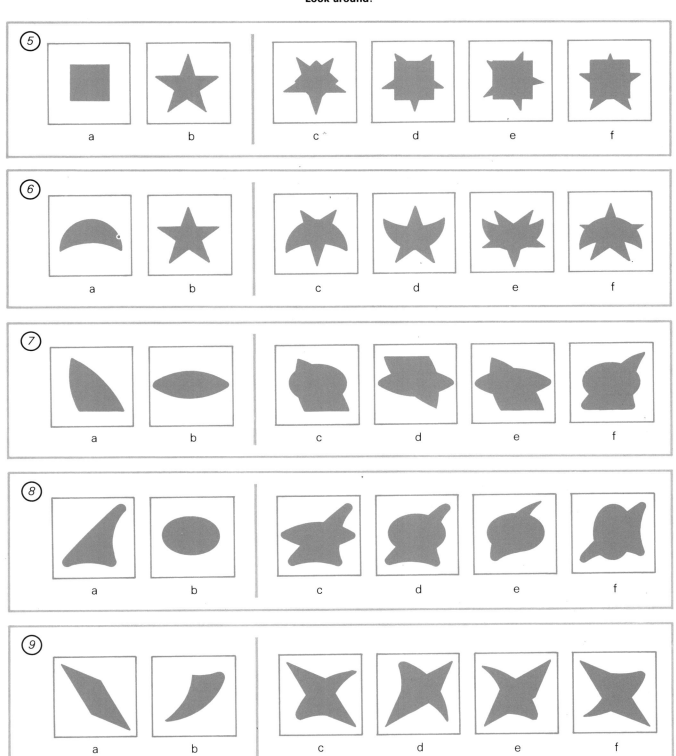

Discover the key

In this series, too, the main point is to identify the criterion whereby the figures relate to each other. In other words, you have to work out the rationale, linked to the figural characteristics, behind the different stages in the reasoning process. At first sight, the images will not always seem to have anything in common, but if you examine them carefully, particularly in the early tests, you will see how easy they are to solve. Once

you discover the key, you can use it to solve the other games, which will then fall easily into place. For this reason we are not going to reveal the key, but leave it for the reader to discover by completing all the games before looking at the solutions on page 94. One final observation before setting to work: the final series of tests (superimposition and composition of figures) is inspired by similar conjunctive operations (addition and intersection). Therefore the exercise may prove useful from this point of view as well.

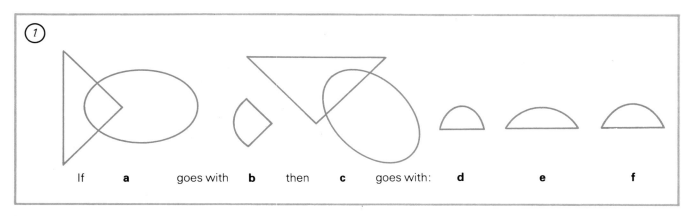

If   **a**   goes with   **b**   then   **c**   goes with: **d**   **e**   **f**

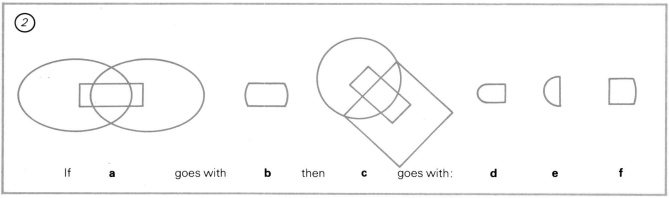

If   **a**   goes with   **b**   then   **c**   goes with: **d**   **e**   **f**

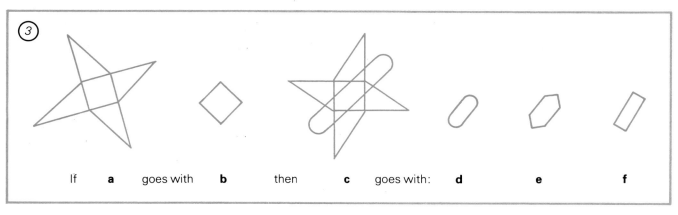

If   **a**   goes with   **b**   then   **c**   goes with: **d**   **e**   **f**

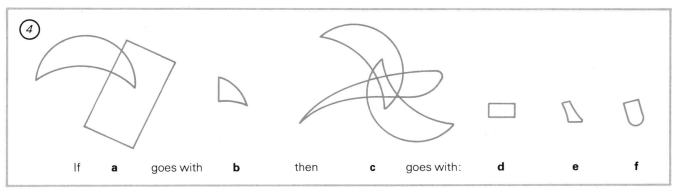

④ If   **a**   goes with   **b**   then   **c**   goes with: **d**   **e**   **f**

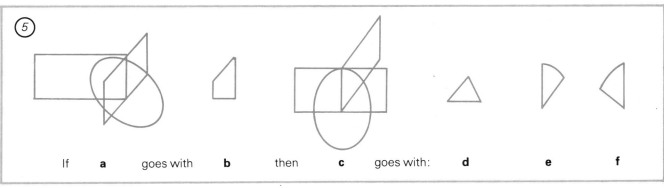

⑤ If   **a**   goes with   **b**   then   **c**   goes with: **d**   **e**   **f**

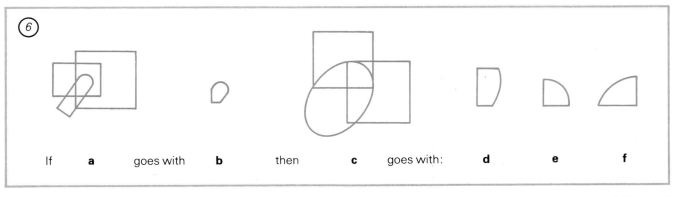

⑥ If   **a**   goes with   **b**   then   **c**   goes with: **d**   **e**   **f**

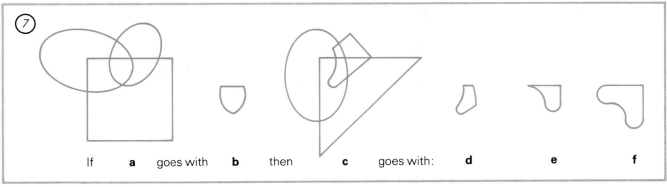

⑦ If   **a**   goes with   **b**   then   **c**   goes with: **d**   **e**   **f**

An old Eastern game

City buildings are often grey and uniform, especially those on the outskirts – in the industrial zones. They look alike in shape and colour, often instilling a sensation of monotony in the observer. But now and then the uniformity is broken by a light-hearted note, as one comes across a building where the windows are filled with coloured paper designs of every description – the work of children – their imaginations allowed to run riot. These, if readers have not already guessed, are the windows of any infants' school. Children, in fact, derive particular satisfaction from creating figures and objects out of pieces of folded paper, altogether unaware that their games have a very old cultural tradition, linked to the history of the Orient.

Origami: art or game?

It seems perfectly legitimate to ask this question when considering the famous Japanese game of *origami*. Its origins are lost in the mists of time, but down the years countless generations of Japanese have delighted in this pastime. It consists in the folding of paper to obtain different shapes and objects, but particularly animals (fish, birds, cats etc.). In the eighteenth century kimonos, the traditional robes of Japan, were decorated with folded-paper birds. In modern Japanese society origami is largely a game played by children, although adults do still play it too. It has been known in the West for many years and in the last two decades has attracted a large number of enthusiasts, both children and adults, particularly in Europe and South America.

The reasons for its success probably lies in the potential for creativeness – more art than game – it brings out among its followers: from a simple sheet of paper it is possible to create a whole new world of realism and imagination.

The technique of origami

A piece of paper is folded along predetermined straight lines in order to create, in stages, a somewhat stylized and geometrical shape resembling an inanimate object or, more often, an animal. One clearly needs a certain skill at folding the paper, but this comes with practice. In fact, a sheet of paper can be folded in countless different ways, but anyone playing the game must know which sequence of folds will ultimately create the desired effect.

In ancient origami it was not permissible to cut, glue or colour the paper. It was, in fact, a search for pure form. In modern origami, however, the use of scissors is permitted, albeit within certain limits. Sometimes a small nick or incision, a dab of colour here and there, will make the figures seem more attractive and life-like.

The average origami beginner generally starts with a few *basic shapes*, from which he will, in time, move on to more sophisticated figures. One of the most prolific, regarded by adepts as also the most refined and elegant, is undoubtedly the *bird-shape* (see illustrations below). This can act as the basis for creating many creatures: overleaf we show the

BASIC BIRD-SHAPE

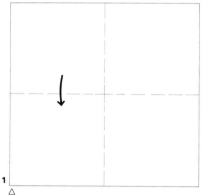

1
△
Mark the paper by making the appropriate folds along the median lines indicated. Then fold it over in half.

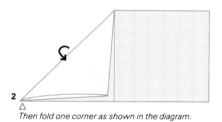

2
△
Then fold one corner as shown in the diagram.

3
△
Turn the paper over and fold the other corner as well.

standing crane and the flying bird, the first for its astonishing effect, the second for its movement. The reader should be able to follow the successive steps as illustrated in the drawings. Once a certain confidence has been instilled, new horizons open up.

In order to create the basic bird shape, as for any other origami shape, all you need is a piece of coloured paper, the size of which is up to the individual (for the example proposed we would suggest a square of at least 25 × 25 centimeters [c. 10 × 10 inches]). Then proceed as shown, bearing in mind that the unbroken lines in the diagrams represent the convex folds, while the broken lines are the concave folds.

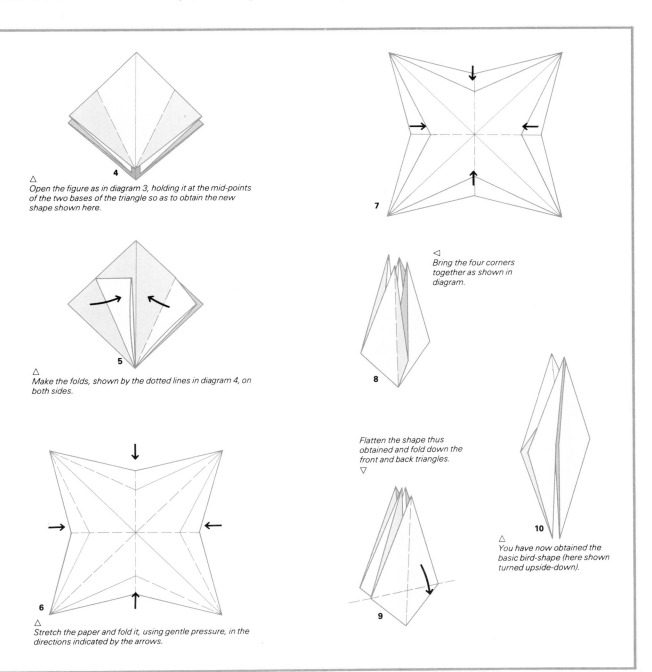

△
4
Open the figure as in diagram 3, holding it at the mid-points of the two bases of the triangle so as to obtain the new shape shown here.

△
5
Make the folds, shown by the dotted lines in diagram 4, on both sides.

6
△
Stretch the paper and fold it, using gentle pressure, in the directions indicated by the arrows.

7

◁
Bring the four corners together as shown in diagram.

8

Flatten the shape thus obtained and fold down the front and back triangles.
▽

9

10
△
You have now obtained the basic bird-shape (here shown turned upside-down).

STANDING CRANE

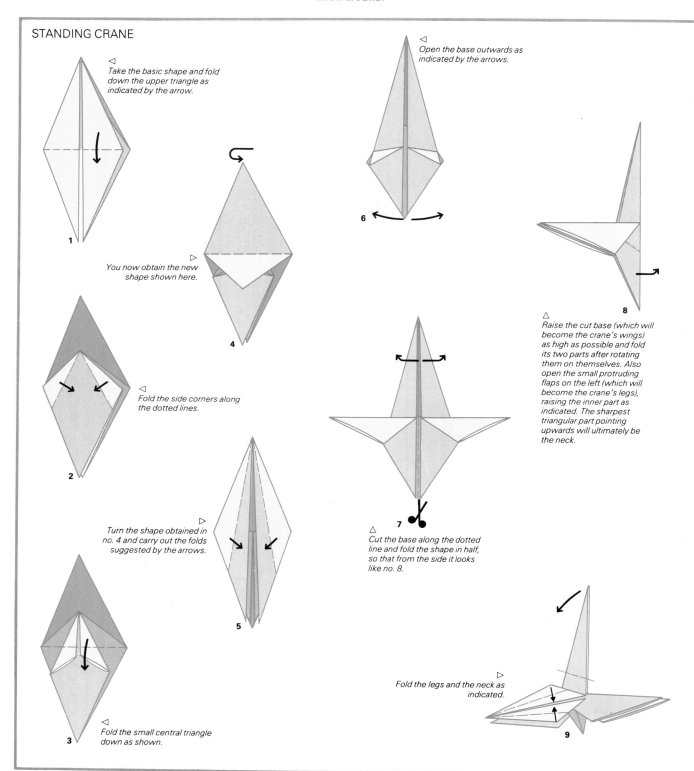

◁ *Take the basic shape and fold down the upper triangle as indicated by the arrow.*

1

▷ *You now obtain the new shape shown here.*

4

◁ *Fold the side corners along the dotted lines.*

2

▷ *Turn the shape obtained in no. 4 and carry out the folds suggested by the arrows.*

5

◁ *Fold the small central triangle down as shown.*

3

◁ *Open the base outwards as indicated by the arrows.*

6

8

△ *Raise the cut base (which will become the crane's wings) as high as possible and fold its two parts after rotating them on themselves. Also open the small protruding flaps on the left (which will become the crane's legs), raising the inner part as indicated. The sharpest triangular part pointing upwards will ultimately be the neck.*

7

△ *Cut the base along the dotted line and fold the shape in half, so that from the side it looks like no. 8.*

▷ *Fold the legs and the neck as indicated.*

9

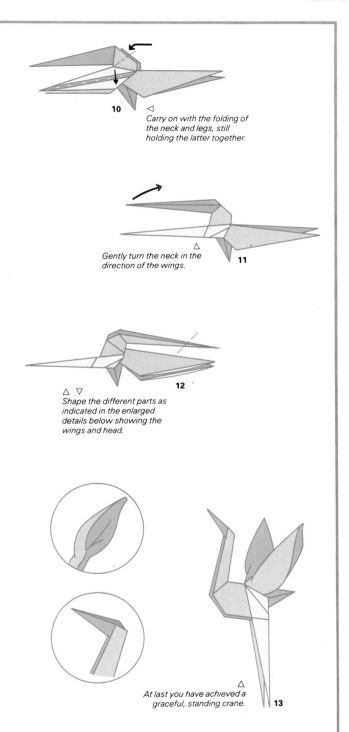

10

◁ Carry on with the folding of the neck and legs, still holding the latter together.

△ Gently turn the neck in the direction of the wings.

11

△ ▽
Shape the different parts as indicated in the enlarged details below showing the wings and head.

12

△
At last you have achieved a graceful, standing crane.

13

FLYING BIRD

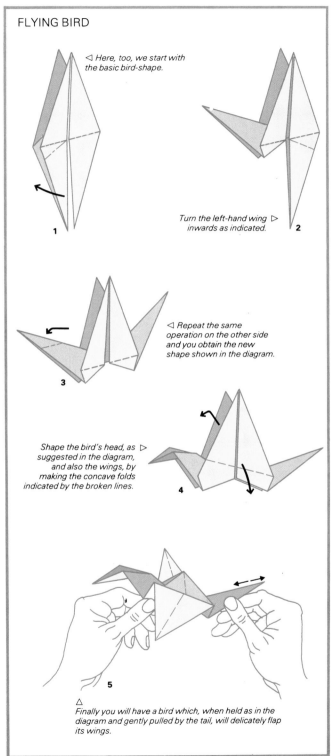

◁ Here, too, we start with the basic bird-shape.

1

Turn the left-hand wing ▷ inwards as indicated.

2

◁ Repeat the same operation on the other side and you obtain the new shape shown in the diagram.

3

Shape the bird's head, as ▷ suggested in the diagram, and also the wings, by making the concave folds indicated by the broken lines.

4

5

△
Finally you will have a bird which, when held as in the diagram and gently pulled by the tail, will delicately flap its wings.

"Recognize the shapes" – Solutions (page 81)

1. *c.*   2. *c.*   3. *b.*   4. *a.*   5. *d.*

"Find the figure" – Answers to drawings (pages 83–84)

1. Answer *f*; Fig. *c* is, in fact, exactly half of square *a*. And so if, in the reasoning process, square *a* is followed by circle *b*, then the exact half of square *a*, provided by triangle *c*, will be followed by the corresponding half of circle *b*, as represented by *f*.

2. Answer *e*; Fig. *b* is nothing more than an inversion of *a*, which represents a square containing a circle; thus if *c* is a triangle with an ellipse inside it, its figurative inversion will be an ellipse enclosing a triangle; hence Fig. *e*.

3. Answer *f*; Fig. *a* is a square containing another square which has been rotated so that its corners point towards the mid-point of the sides; in the second figure (*b*) two elements of the inner square have been modified: it has been halved and also filled in. The figure that follows *a* in the reasoning process (that is to say, *c*) takes the form of a square containing a circle; the one following *b*, therefore, will be a circle containing a coloured semi-circle. Hence the answer *f*. Note how very important the position of the figure also is. Fig. *d* is similarly composed of a square containing a coloured semi-circle, but the latter's position does not correspond to that of the triangle in *b*.

4. Answer *e*; in Fig. *b* the small trapezium, which was blank in *a*, has been filled in; the same must therefore apply to the figure following on from *c*, although the rectangle must be replaced by a circle. The only figure that fulfils these conditions is *e*.

5. Answer *f*; the transition from *a* to *b* involves the colouring of the central geometric shape; the same must occur in the figure following on from *c*, which can only be *f*.

6. Answer *f*.

"Superimposing figures" – Answers to drawings (pages 86–87)

1. Answer *c*; in *d* and *e* it is the position of the rectangle (and in *e* also its shape) which does not correspond to that of *a*, while in *f* it is the shape.

2. Answer *e*; Fig. *c*, *d* and *f* are too far removed from the original position and dimensions.

3. Answer *e*; all it needs here is to count the number of points of the star that project beyond the circle to make the correct choice: *c* and *d* have to be rejected because they show only four, while *f* shows six.

4. Answer *c*; the correct solution is reached here by following the arrangement of the points of the star.

5. Answer *f*; in all the alternatives the star shows its five points projecting beyond the square, but only in *f* does close examination reveal the same position as in *b*.

6. Answer *f*; a half-moon and a five-pointed star give way to a rather strange figure: in *c* it is the position of the star that does not correspond to the original, while in *d* and *e* it is the half-moon's position that is wrong. The only one left is *f*.

7. Answer *e*; in *c* the ellipse is too bulky, in *d* it is the sort of triangle with arching sides that has lost its original position; in *f* both elements are the wrong shape.

8. Answer *d*.

9. Answer *f*.

By their nature, these games recall the graphic representation of figural building processes. To be more precise, their shapes recall combinations of one or more entities, formed by joining together elements from individual bodies, bearing in mind, however, that the elements occurring in the superimposed areas are taken into account once and not twice in the building process.

"Discover the key" – Answers (pages 88–89)

These games are also based on the figural building process. The passage from Fig. *a* to Fig. *b* represents nothing more than the identification of the intersection of two or three overlapping figures. Anyone with the slightest knowledge of elemental structure will know that the intersection of one or more bodies is achieved by shared elements. Because we are here working with images, however, we have to reason in terms of surface and area. In this context the intersection of two or more figures represents nothing more than the area shared simultaneously by all of them. Once the criterion on which the tests have been organized is explained, you should not encounter too much difficulty in finding the correct solution.

1. *f.*   2. *f.*   3. *e.*   4. *e.*   5. *e.*   6. *e.*   7. *d.*

"Composing figures" – Solutions to drawings (pages 84–85)

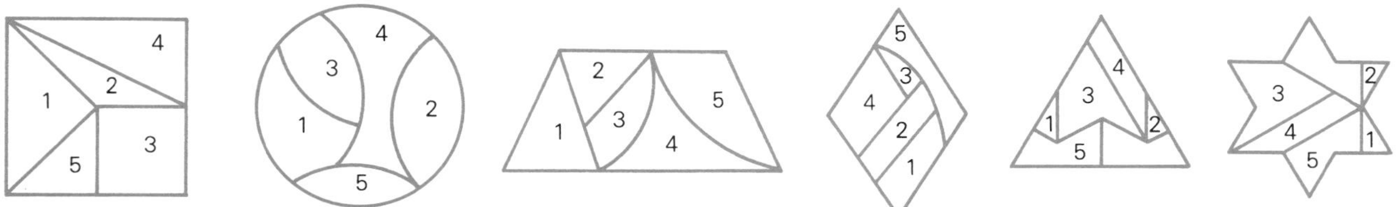

Seeing is believing

*Symmetry . . . . is one idea
by which man through the ages has tried to comprehend
and create order,
beauty, and perfection.*
(Hermann Weyl, *Symmetry*)

The many facets of symmetry

When we allude to the factors of perception, namely the structural principles within our perceptive system, we are really talking about the conditions and bases on which we build our knowledge. We know the outside world through our senses, and particularly through our sense of sight. One of the fundamental principles whereby we organize our perception of objects is *Prägnanz*, which we defined as "good shape" (page 78). But what precisely does this term mean?

Perhaps we can define the notion more clearly by resorting to ideas that are more straightforward and concrete. Let us say, then, that "good shape" means order, regularity, simplicity and symmetry, but also structural coherence between the whole and the parts. The perceptive data form themselves into meaningful objects, into figures characterized by balance and harmony, based on a principle whereby the various parts come together as one, appearing, as it were, to go well together. The qualities that distinguish "good shape" are relative, in the sense that they do not appertain to a single part but to the relationships between the various parts. Where symmetry exists, there is also order and regularity; where order exists, there is also simplicity. Nevertheless, the contrary is not always true: there can also be order and regularity in nonsymmetrical figures. By and large, however, when we talk of *symmetry*, we are implying the presence, too, of harmony, order and simplicity.

Furthermore, there are deep cultural reasons for giving symmetry a special measure of priority in comparison with other properties. In the history of culture it has been one of the most fruitful of all concepts and has played a fundamental role in the most varied fields of human activity: in scientific knowledge, for example, but equally so in the arts, especially painting, sculpture and music. Religious experience, too, has acknowledged the attraction of symmetry, attributing to it a certain sacred significance.

In everyday language the concept of symmetry has, for most people, two meanings: the word "symmetrical" means well proportioned and well balanced, and in this sense is synonymous with beauty, whereas the term "symmetry" is associated with our experience of symmetrical objects in the natural world. This latter interpretation, however, relates only to one particular and common form, known as bilateral symmetry.

Symmetry in the sense of good proportion and balance implies an inter-relationship of parts which come together to form a whole. This is especially applicable to works of art such as painting and sculpture. It is no mere chance that great masters of the past, seeking to explain the theoretical principles of their works, were much taken up with the subject of proportion, understanding it to be a measure between the whole and the various parts composing it.

Polyclitus, a sculptor of ancient Greece, wrote a treatise on proportion. Much later, during the Renaissance, Leonardo da Vinci studied the symmetry of the human body; and his contemporary, the German artist Albrecht Dürer, wrote the *Treatise on Proportion*.

Symmetry defined as the proportion of the parts is equally applicable to music, in which case we refer to it as "harmony."

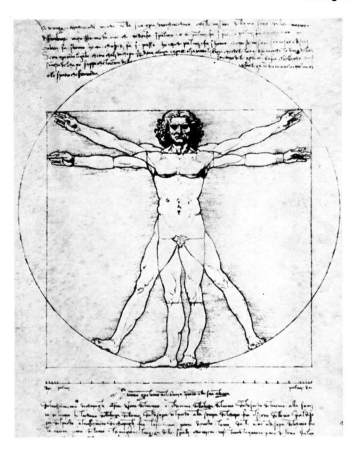

Left: Leonardo da Vinci, *Rule for the Proportion of the Human Figure* (Galleria dell'Accademia, Venice). Leonardo's studies of anatomy were based on the concept of symmetry.

Opposite page: below, Indian terracotta figure of Mother Goddess (third–second century BC), in which the symmetrical parts are clearly in evidence (Musée Guimet, Paris).

Historical developments

The word "symmetry" comes from the Greek *sýmmetros*, made up of two words meaning "with" and "measure" and literally means "commensurable" or "having a common measure," in the sense of two quantities of the same kind which have or do not have (if incommensurable) a common measure. The meaning of "symmetrical" or "asymmetrical" was therefore closely associated with that of "commensurate," "proportionate" etc. Subsequently the terms "symmetrical" and "asymmetrical" came to be applied in other technical contexts, especially with the growth of scientific knowledge.

The wide-ranging implications of this concept were evident, above all, in the field of natural observation, not only because it could be used to explain any regularities and likenesses, but also indirectly in the sense that the unexpected presence of asymmetry could stimulate enquiry for other explanations and reasons. For example, the lack of symmetry in chemistry, in crystallography and in the natural sciences has often been resolved with the discovery of new, more profound and more complex forms of symmetry. Thus the fairly simple and elementary notion of "bilateral sym-

metry" led to that of "multilateral symmetry," which is a feature of crystals, of certain periodic phenomena and of many everyday objects. In recent times the intuitive concept of symmetry has been defined and formally specified in mathematics.

An exact definition

We have no intention of boring the reader with mathematical formulas and symbols, even though patient and sensible use of logical symbols can be extremely valuable not only for understanding concepts and relationships, but also for grasping a method i.e. a way of tackling generalized and abstract notions. For present purposes, however, we will merely consider a few ideas and stress the importance of arriving at a formal definition of a concept like symmetry.

Confronted by nature, man has endeavoured to reconcile the infinitely varied appearance of objects by reference to principles such as order, regularity and homogeneity. Among these principles, that of symmetry has proved particularly fruitful; in arts, science and mathematics, it has constituted one of the most important guiding ideas, a scheme into which any number of phenomena can readily be fitted. As a further example, study of the infinitely small and basic constituents of matter reveals astonishing symmetries. It is worth emphasizing that science can only fully accept a theory when it is given a precise mathematical definition. Symmetry is one of those concepts which has been thus defined and as a result quantitatively measured; this is of no mean importance considering the vagueness and ambiguity of so many pseudoscientific notions.

The mathematical definition of symmetry is based on the theory of groups, one of the most recent developments of modern mathematics, which makes a formal study of the movements of a figure that mirrors itself. In this way various types of symmetry can be explained and precisely defined in this area of mathematics.

Buridan's ass

Buridan was a medieval French philosopher (c.1290–1358) and rector of the University of Paris, where he taught in the faculty of Arts until his death. He is remembered for his interesting demonstrations in logic, a subject he wrote about in his books, but his name is forever associated with the celebrated fable of the ass. If, Buridan argued, we take an ass and place it the same distance away from two equal piles of hay, the ass will eventually die of hunger because in such a situation it will be unable to choose between the two forces that attract it in equal measure.

There is no trace of this curious little tale in Buridan's published works, for it is part of the body of oral legend surrounding the philosopher. Probably he used the example to underline the difference between humans and animals; man alone is capable of exercising free will and self-determination, whereas an animal lacks this ability, its behaviour being determined by outside stimuli. When the stimuli are equal, as in the case of the ass in the fable, they exercise an attraction of equal intensity, but from opposite sides, thus cancelling each other out. The paradox of the situation is that although the ass has enough to eat, he still dies of hunger. What is really interesting about Buridan's fable, is that it illustrates the notion of bilateral symmetry.

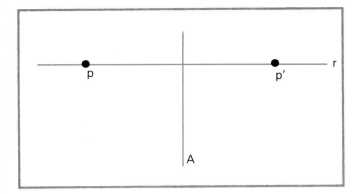

Indeed, a more famous contemporary, Dante, adapted the fable for his own narrative purposes in Canto IV of the *Paradiso*:

Intra due cibi, distanti e moventi
d'un modo, prima si morria di fame,
che liber'uom l'un recasse ai denti . . .

(It is said that if a man with free will were placed midway between two equally attractive foods, he'd rather starve than take a bite of either . . .)

Bilateral symmetry

The ancient balance of two scales or pans represents one of the earliest practical applications of bilateral symmetry. The term "balance" is, in fact, derived from the Latin *bis*, meaning "twice," and *lanx*, which means "plate." The image of the two plates or pans itself symbolizes the idea of equality: if there is to be symmetry, equal weights must be placed in both pans. If the weights are disparate the levels of the pans will be different, one of the two being lower than the other, thus breaking the symmetry.

It is easy for us to grasp the geometrical concept of bilateral symmetry by taking the simple structure of the balance as our example. Given a line of reference A, a figure is symmetrical in relation to this if, mirrored against it, it replicates itself. In the figure at the top of the page, we can create the pattern of the balance by drawing the line r at a right angle to A and placing the dot p' at any point on it which is the same distance as the dot p is from A, on the opposite side.

The concept of symmetry is often associated with that of *left* and *right*. On the basis of the above definition, it is not difficult to comprehend that left and right are purely relative to the posiition of the onlooker; if we stand in front of the balance, we have one pan on our left and the other on our right; but if we stand on the opposite side, the pan which was to our left is now to our right, while the one originally on the right is now on the left.

Discovering symmetry

Let us now play some games. Here and on the opposite page are some easy tests in which certain figures are paired together according to symmetrical properties.

What you have to do is decide, after carefully considering the relationship between two figures **a** and **b**, which of the three or four alternatives **d** to **g**, is symmetrical to figure **c**. There is no time limit, but you should try and complete each little test as quickly as you can. The correct answer will prove your ability to distinguish bilateral symmetry. The earlier examples are quite easy, the later ones slightly more difficult. The first two are already provided with answers to point you in the right direction. Solutions are on page 101.

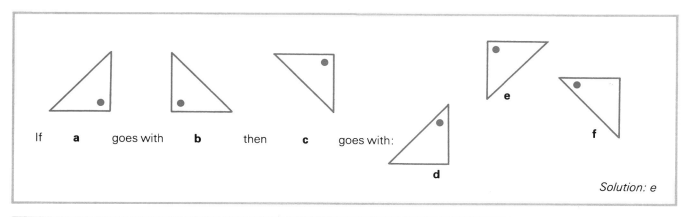

If **a** goes with **b** then **c** goes with:

Solution: e

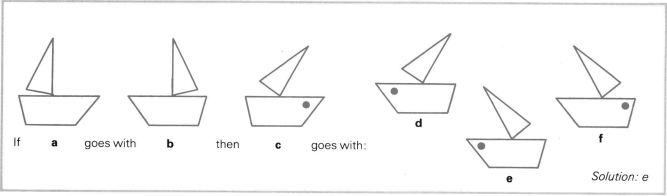

If **a** goes with **b** then **c** goes with:

Solution: e

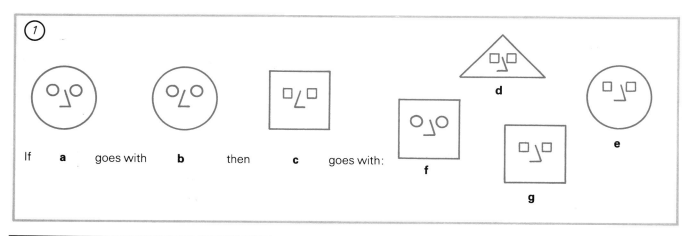

① If **a** goes with **b** then **c** goes with:

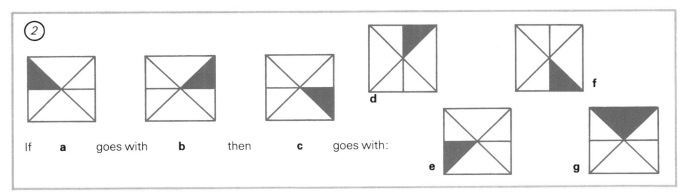

(2)

If **a** goes with **b** then **c** goes with:

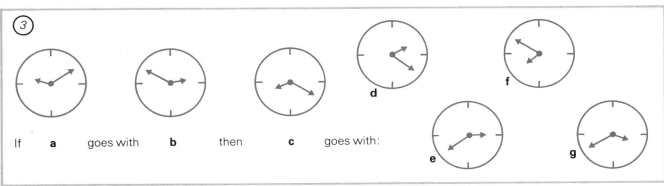

(3)

If **a** goes with **b** then **c** goes with:

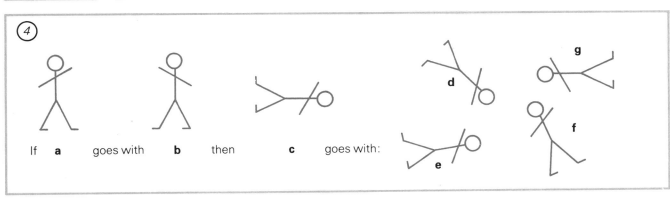

(4)

If **a** goes with **b** then **c** goes with:

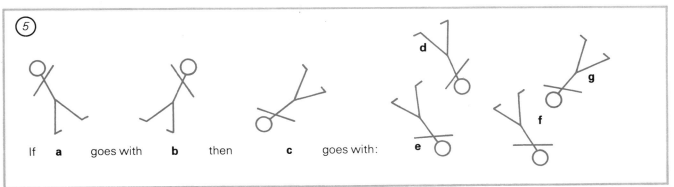

(5)

If **a** goes with **b** then **c** goes with:

Symmetrical boats

The tests on bilateral symmetry which appear on this and the following page all involve the figures of little boats, which differ from one another only in small details. The idea, as with the preceding game, is to examine the relationship between boats **a** and **b**, and then match boat **c** with its symmetrical figure among the four examples **d** to **g**. As before, the tests are arranged so as to be progressively more difficult. The solutions are at the foot of the opposite page.

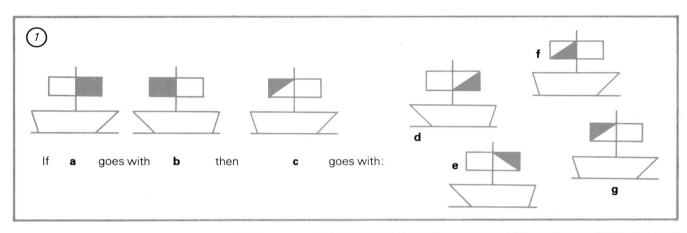

(1) If **a** goes with **b** then **c** goes with:

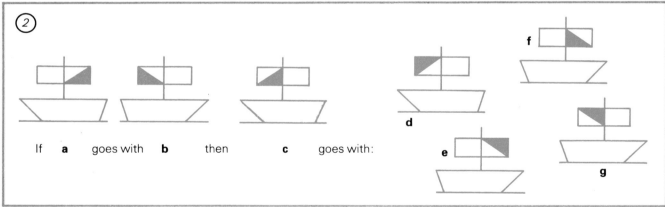

(2) If **a** goes with **b** then **c** goes with:

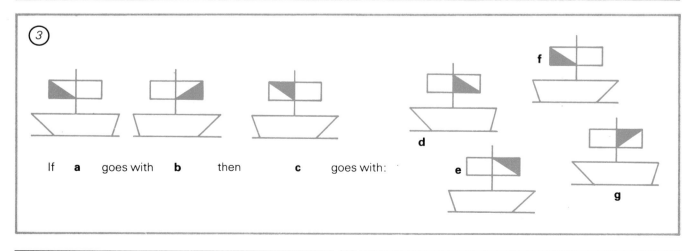

(3) If **a** goes with **b** then **c** goes with:

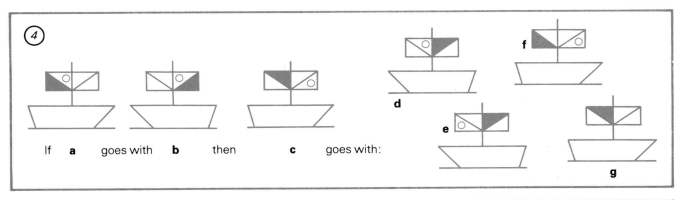

④ If **a** goes with **b** then **c** goes with:

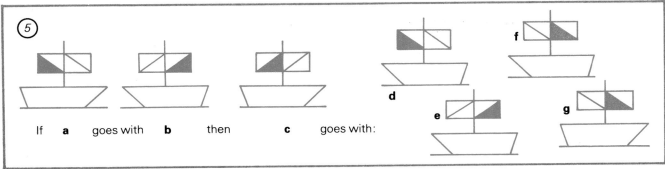

⑤ If **a** goes with **b** then **c** goes with:

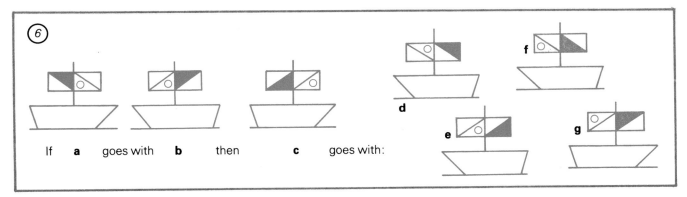

⑥ If **a** goes with **b** then **c** goes with:

"Discover the symmetry" – Solutions

1. *g* is the specular image of fig. *c*. It cannot be *f* because of the round eyes.

2. *e*.

3. *g*. *e* cannot be the specular image of *c* because the small hand points to three.

4. *g*.

5. *e*. This puzzle is more difficult because there is more than one detail to consider.

"The symmetrical boats" – Solutions

1. *e*.

2. *f*.

3. *g*.

4. *e*.

5. *f*.

6. *f*.

The wonders of nature

There are innumerable examples of bilateral symmetry in nature. Without delving into the doctrine of final causes, it would seem that this type of symmetry is one of the most common schemes in the general organization of living things, although we should not expect to find it perfectly represented in every existing organism. Nevertheless, it appears in a surprising variety of aspects. The different parts of the human body are distributed in accordance with geometrical relationships which obey the laws of bilateral symmetry: one eye is symmetrical to the other, and the same applies to the hand, the foot and so forth. All examples of asymmetry seem to occur mainly in the internal organs, the heart being the prime example of this. The same observations can also be extended to other living organisms, especially the vertebrates. Yet not all animals are symmetrical: certain protozoans cannot be divided into specularly (mirror-like) equal parts and have become asymmetrical as a result of adapting to their natural surroundings. This is also true of flat-fish such as the flounder and the sole which crawl upon or are fixed to the seabed. Apparently the most important element for these organisms is the direction of gravity. On the other hand, animals that can move freely on land, in water or in the air, do possess bilateral symmetry.

The bilateral formation of the organs of locomotion (limbs and muscles) has undoubtedly proved so advantageous that it has prevented the development of asymmetrical forms. Try to imagine what it would be like to move about on only one leg. In the course of geological time, the advantage to the individual of possessing bilaterally symmetrical limbs and external organs may explain why the internal organs (such as the heart, the liver and the stomach) have followed the laws of symmetry either to a lesser extent or not at all.

Why is it that the distribution of the various parts of a living organism so often appears to obey the geometrical laws of

bilateral symmetry? And why, in the general organization of the natural world, does such symmetry exist?

It is not easy to provide an immediate answer to these intriguing questions. Let us start by trying to define, in general terms, a living organism. It is a system which has established its own equilibrium or balance with the surroundings and which tends to maintain this equilibrium and indeed to make it even more stable. When we spoke earlier of the intuitive concept of symmetry, we said that it is closely associated with balance, equality and proportion. A system in equilibrium therefore has every chance of being symmetrical; or in other words, a system which tends toward a state of equilibrium finds its natural and ideal form in the symmetry of its parts.

Imagine a quantity of matter, even if it is not live: should no other forces and laws intervene in the way it realizes its state of equilibrium, it will tend to assume a rounded shape. This is why stars and planets are spherical; and possibly it is why many planktonic micro-organisms, suspended in the surface layers of the sea, also develop more or less spherical forms. Other protozoans, coelenterates and anthozoans exhibit so-called *radial symmetry* which, as the name suggests, is based on rays emanating from a central point.

The Earth too has its own symmetry, although it is not a perfect sphere. It rotates on an axis and this motion has gradually flattened it at the poles, giving it something nearer the shape of an orange.

It is interesting to note that the ancients regarded the sphere as the most perfect form of symmetry. The followers of Pythagoras, famous for their theories of numbers, claimed

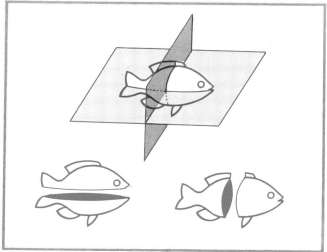

An ancient example of symmetry

In the civilization of ancient Crete the two-edged axe (below, upper illustration) was the symbol of Minoan power. Minos, according to legend, was the king who founded Crete and he was involved in the events featuring the Minotaur, Theseus and Ariadne. In Cretan art we also find various testimonies to the taste for regularity and symmetry. The double-edged axe, in addition to symbolizing royal power, was also the stylized representation of perfect bilateral symmetry. The handle may be seen as the axis of symmetry for two specularly symmetrical figures.

Symmetry is therefore a criterion which has fired human imagination from the beginning of time. Yet it is only one of the principles whereby man has come to recognize reality and indeed it has its limitations. Here is a concrete example. In the bottom illustration two axes are seen in positions that are perfectly symmetrical. But if we push them towards each other so that they touch and overlap, not only do they change shape and appear to be two different figures compared with the originals, but they also lose their symmetry.

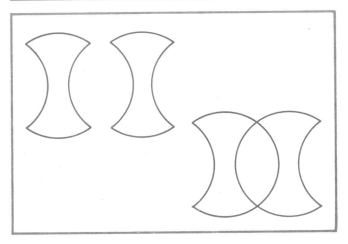

that the circle in the plane and the sphere in space were the most perfect geometrical figures, thanks to their perfect symmetry of rotation. The Greek philosopher Plato, for his part, derived bilateral symmetry from the sphere, which he understood to be the original form. To convey his thoughts, he frequently made use of legends and myths. In one myth he related how man, when time began, was as round as a sphere, so that his back and sides formed a kind of circle. Zeus, the father of the gods who dwelt on Mount Olympus, proceeded to cut him in two and commanded Apollo to expose the face and genital organs. Then he threatened to divide them in two again, remarking scathingly: "Thus, if they persist in their insolence, they will be made to walk on only one leg!"

The interesting point about this myth is that bilateralism is here described as an inferior form of symmetry, while the loss of spherical symmetry is felt to be shameful or, in terms of Christian religious belief, a punishment for sin.

Symmetry exists as well in the inorganic world, although this is not immediately apparent. Even if general laws cannot be applied, it is true to say that of all the possible geometrical systems of symmetry in crystals, the most numerous are those based on bilateralism.

Forms of symmetry

Bilateral symmetry is merely one instance of symmetry applicable to operations such as reflection and rotation. If an image is reflected in a mirror, it is repeated in identical fashion but inverted in relation to the original; this is a case of *specular* or *reflected symmetry*.

If, on the other hand, we think of such a figure revolving around an imaginary axis perpendicular to the plane in which it lies, we describe it as having *rotational symmetry*. To be more precise, given an axis, which we label *1*, we talk of a figure having rotational symmetry around *1* if with every rotation around this axis it replicates itself. Let us look at the illustra-

tions below: the hooked figure *a* represents the asymmetrical figure which is the departure point, the figure which generates the principal forms of symmetry. In *b* we see the specular image of the figure, obtained simply by reflection in a mirror placed at right angles to the sheet of paper. In *c* and *d*, however, rotational symmetry is generated by supposing that there is an axis perpendicular to the plane of the paper: obviously if rotation proceeds in two stages (*c*), the first half-turn will produce another hook; but if rotation is carried out in three stages (*d*), each of 120 degrees, then we get three hooks. Finally, there is another possible kind of symmetry (*e*), called *translatory symmetry*, obtained simply by moving the hook a certain distance, without reflecting or rotating it.

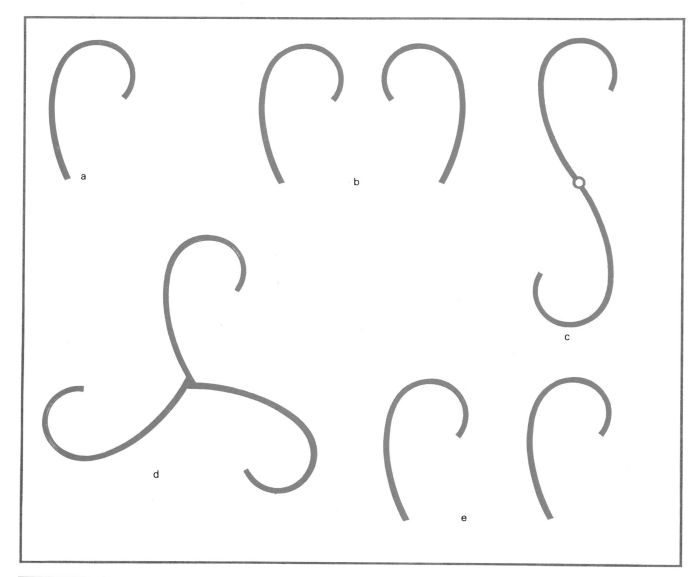

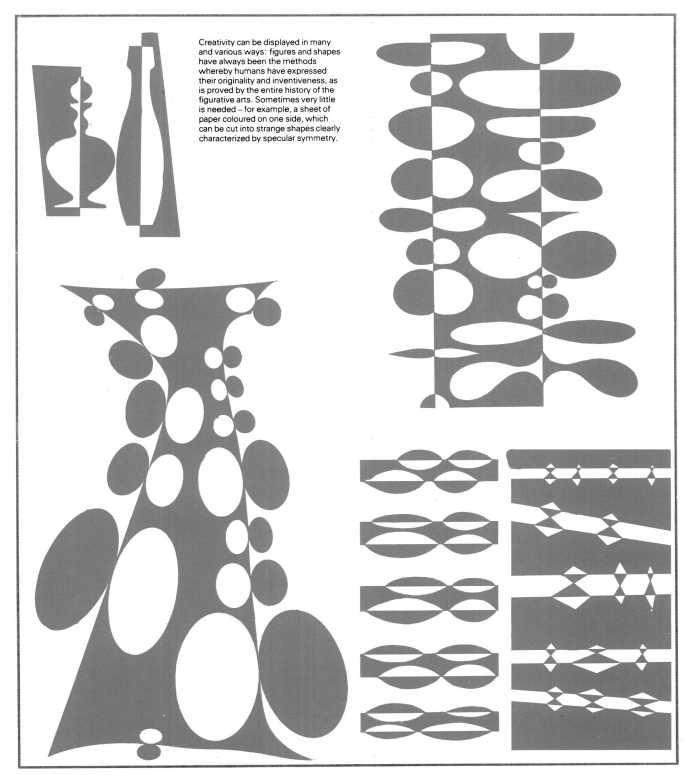

Creativity can be displayed in many and various ways: figures and shapes have always been the methods whereby humans have expressed their originality and inventiveness, as is proved by the entire history of the figurative arts. Sometimes very little is needed – for example, a sheet of paper coloured on one side, which can be cut into strange shapes clearly characterized by specular symmetry.

Other games with symmetry

Given the role played by symmetry in different types of cultural and artistic activity, we now invite you to exercise your capacities of perception in another series of tests. As previously, you have to choose from several alternatives the figure which symmetrically matches another. The tests are complicated by the fact that the correct matching figure is jumbled up haphazardly with others. Furthermore, in this series you must first identify the type of symmetry involved: you can find this out by examining the way the first two figures (**a** and **b**) in each test are arranged. Only after looking carefully at these will you be able to solve the test correctly. The games, as before, get increasingly difficult; the first tests present simple forms which are still recognizable as instances of bilateral symmetry, but the later ones contain figures in which the symmetry is determined by a rotating movement.

Remember, as you do these tests, to take into account what you have already learnt from the text and accompanying illustrations on page 104. Solving them correctly will require some imagination on your part, for you will need to carry out the appropriate movements in your mind. These tests are certainly harder than the last ones but probably more useful. The solutions are on page 109.

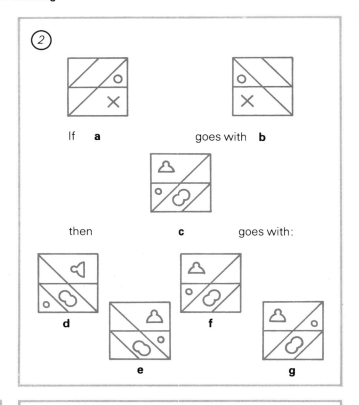

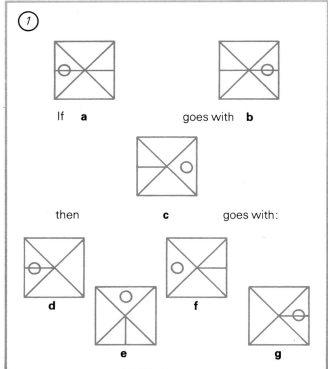

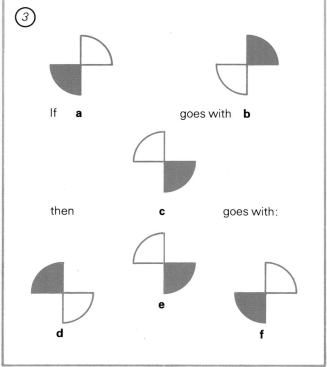

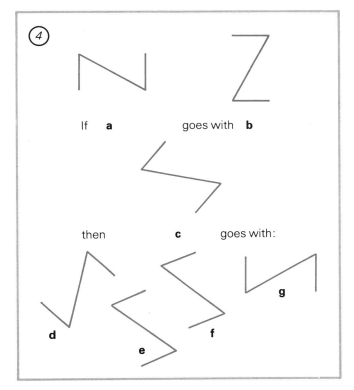

④

If   **a**   goes with   **b**

then   **c**   goes with:

d   **e**   **f**   **g**

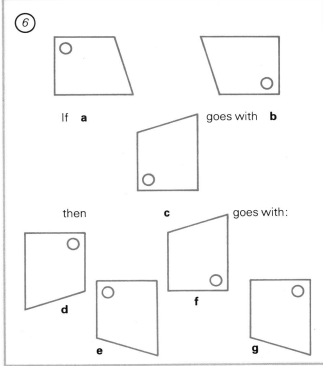

⑥

If   **a**   goes with   **b**

then   **c**   goes with:

d   **e**   **f**   **g**

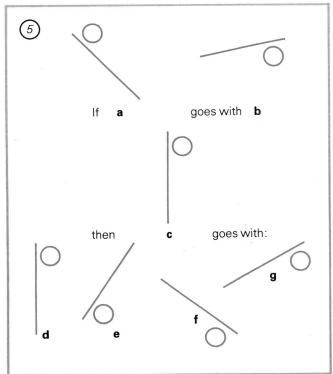

⑤

If   **a**   goes with   **b**

then   **c**   goes with:

d   **e**   **f**   **g**

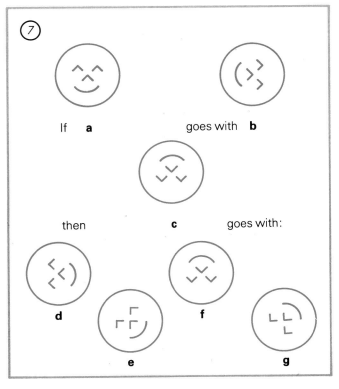

⑦

If   **a**   goes with   **b**

then   **c**   goes with:

d   **e**   **f**   **g**

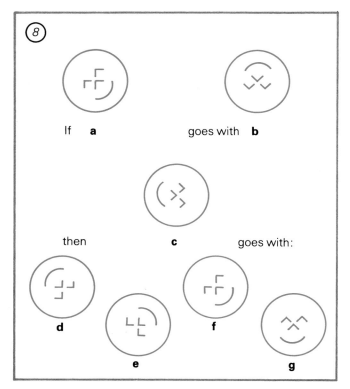

If **a** goes with **b**

then **c** goes with:

d e f g

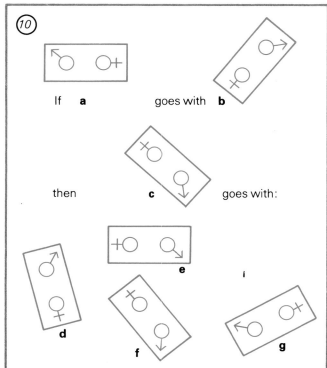

If **a** goes with **b**

then **c** goes with:

d e f g

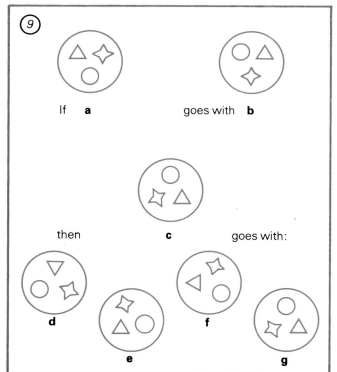

If **a** goes with **b**

then **c** goes with:

d e f g

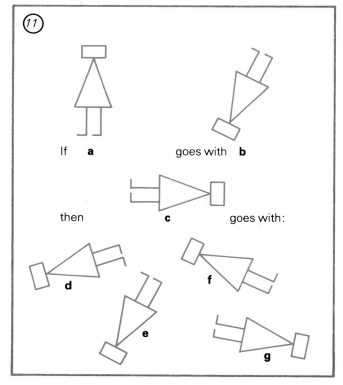

If **a** goes with **b**

then **c** goes with:

d e f g

"Other games with symmetry" – Solutions and explanations

In looking for the solutions bear in mind the following. As we said at the beginning, it is not hard to identify the type of symmetry involved, as may easily be deduced from the first two figures (*a* and *b*) in each puzzle. It is a little more difficult to choose the figure which correctly matches the other (*c*) symmetrically when rotated. This matching figure has been deliberately mixed in with the others to put you off. The puzzles require some degree of concentration and imagination on your part.

1. *f.* There is, in fact, a relationship of bilateral symmetry between *a* and *b*, and the only figure which has the same relationship to *c* is *f*.

2. *e. a* and *b* are specularly symmetrical and the only figure which is in this sense related to *c* is *e*.

3. *d.* There is a rotation of 180 degrees between *a* and *b*, so that the only figure to match *c* is *d*.

4. *d.* A rotation of 90 degrees is involved.

5. *f.* There is a rotation of 120 degrees between *a* and *b*; so the figure which matches *c* must be *f*.

6. *d. b* is the same as figure *a* but revolved through 180 degrees (take into account here the features of the circle and the oblique side of the rectangular trapezoid); so the only figure which can symmetrically match *c* in this way is *d*; *f*, in fact, has the oblique side in the right position, but the location of the circle inside makes it different from *c*.

7. *d.* There is a rotation of 90 degrees between *a* and *b*; the figure which matches *c* in this way is *d*.

8. *f. a*, to reach the position of *b*, must rotate through 210 degrees; by performing the same movement with *c* we get to the position of *f*.

9. *e.* Here too there is rotational symmetry; to work out the angle you have to look at the triangle, the star and the small circle inside the figure; they vary from one figure to another by 120 degrees; so the only figure to match *c* is *e*.

10. *g.* There is a rotation of 120 degrees between *a* and *b*; obviously there is the same relationship between *c* and *g*.

11. *f.* The measure of rotation is rather more difficult to identify in this last puzzle; but since it is around 210 degrees, the figure which matches *c* must be *f*.

A rude shock

"Trust you to walk straight into the glass!" yelled Jimmy's mother, giving him a good box around the ears. But on this occasion poor Jimmy hadn't done anything wrong. When his mother had told him that he would be accompanying her to a wedding reception that afternoon, he had been delighted. In his mind's eye he could already see the tables stacked with delicious cakes and drinks; he could almost taste them. The lobby of the restaurant was done up in grand style, with carpets, flowers, paintings and crystal chandeliers. As the other guests trooped into the main room, Jimmy, in his haste, failed to notice the heavy glass door and ran straight into it. The thump was so loud that people nearby turned in alarm, for the lad seemed to have hurt himself. His mother, in embarrassment, let fly instinctively with a slap on the ear. She was admittedly a bit too quick to hit him, but this is the way parents choose every now and then to show their children how worried they are. Jimmy didn't utter a sound; it wasn't the first time he had received such treatment. In any case, the attraction of all the cakes considerably outweighed any pain and humiliation. So he gave the glass a wide berth, not even casting a backward glance at the door which had been so clean as to be invisible.

We can laugh at what happened to Jimmy, which is a common enough event in comic films, where waiters carrying trays piled high with food suffer exactly the same fate. But such accidents do underline a problem which is of psychological interest. Panes of glass are transparent, and so is the air, which we cannot see; yet we say that a steamed-up window is also transparent. So what exactly is transparency or, to put it more plainly, when is an object transparent?

Transparency: seeing through things

Transparency, too, is one of those phenomena of perception which require precise definition in order to narrow down its possible meanings. As a rule, we say an object is transparent when we see not only the objects which lie beyond it but also the medium itself. In this strict sense crystals can be called transparent even if they contain impurities, however slight, which can be seen in the form of reflections, marks and so forth; and in the same way we describe the air as transparent when we are made aware of it by the presence, for example, of thin cloud. If you think this a trifle far-fetched, try the following experiment. Take a square of coloured, transparent plastic, similar to the colour filters used for cameras, and place it over a bigger piece of uniformly black or white paper; if you look carefully, the plastic loses its transparency. This shows that transparent objects are not always seen as such: the uniformly black or white piece of paper destroys the perception of transparency.

The opposite is also true, namely that what is not physically transparent is perceived to be so. If you put the pieces of black and white paper side by side and then place the square of coloured plastic so as to partly cover both of them, you will get a clear perception of transparency. This means that physical transparency and perceived transparency are quite different. Let us now examine the conditions whereby we see transparent objects. They have been studied both by psychologists and by physicists, such as Hermann von Helmholtz, since the nineteenth century.

A scientific approach

We have all had something to do with transparent objects and have formed some ideas as to what transparency is. Yet this is not as simple as might at first appear. A more thoughtful, painstaking approach to the subject will reveal aspects and problems that mere common sense and intuition would never have suspected could exist. This is not a matter of complicating issues or of creating difficulties out of situations which are in themselves simple and easy. It is never an advantage to be ignorant of problems: to be conscious of the way in which we perceive the world, to understand the conditions and limitations of our perception, is to increase our self-knowledge and self-mastery.

Transparency represents one aspect of the psychology of perception that helps us to appreciate better the difference between common sense and a scientific approach to problems. Once a given phenomenon has been established as the object of study, science seeks to ascertain, first and foremost, what conditions are necessary and sufficient for realizing such a phenomenon. Although the concept of "necessary and sufficient conditions" has a precise logical definition, we shall explain it very briefly in the light of experience. Thus necessary conditions are those without which the phenomenon cannot occur. Frequently, however, the necessary conditions, although fundamental, are not enough, and must therefore go hand in hand with sufficient conditions. In some cases the conditions are both necessary and sufficient; but occasionally we can separate them and determine which conditions are necessary and which sufficient.

Analysis of the phenomenon of transparency distinguishes three principal types of condition: topological, figurative and chromatic. Before describing the topological conditions, we must mention the minimal necessary condition: in order for the perception of transparency to occur, there must be "at least" (which in mathematical terms means "not less than") four surfaces in the field of vision, two of them uniting to form a single object which, being situated above or in front of the other two, thus appears transparent. Now we can more easily understand the meaning of *topological conditions*: each of the two areas which, coming in contact with one another, create the transparent surface, must be in in contact with one – and only one – of the other two areas. Look at figures *a* and *b* on this page: there is a clear impression of transparency.

If, however, we somehow remove this condition (figures *c*

and *d*), the perception of transparency disappears. The topological condition provides for necessary but not sufficient conditions. In order for there to be the impression of transparency, there must also be *figural unity*.

In *e* there is no perception of transparency: the part in black, the part in dark grey and the part in light grey are, in fact, perceived as three successive layers.

A non-transparent effect, due to an incorrect arrangement of layers, is also evident in *f*, whereas this does not happen in *g*. The effect of transparency seen in *g* vanishes, too, if we break up the circle along the line dividing the transparent figure from the opaque one underneath, a line which must be perceived as belonging to the opaque figure (cf. figures *h* and *i*). Finally, *j* shows how other modifications of shape do not eliminate the impression of transparency.

Colour and transparency

What are the relationships between colour and transparency? Have a look at the illustration below: at top left there is a clear impression of transparency, which becomes less pronounced as the intensity of the green is diminished (top center); but if the latter is increased, as in the figure at top right, the perception of transparency is likewise increased. When the two parts are identical, as in the figure at bottom left, there is no perception of transparency. If we continue our examination of the chromatic limits of transparency, it is evident that if the dark green part appears on the white background, and the light green on the black background, perception of trans-

parency is impossible. This same condition is even further accentuated in the figure at bottom right, where the difference between the light and dark green background colours is less than that of the colours in the central region, which is therefore not perceived as transparent.

We have described extreme instances of the phenomenon of transparency with very simple colours (white, black and green), but they hold true for any other combination of colours.

A theoretical explanation of transparency

We have somehow managed to transform a simple phenomenon such as transparency, which we normally take for granted, into a problem. So perhaps we ought now to try to explain it.

Let us start by asking in what sense transparency is a problem. To go back to the previous examples of looking at a transparent object, what we perceived as a single surface was replaced by a perception of two surfaces of differing shades, placed one behind the other. How can this be possible, given that the rays emitted by the transparent surface and by the surface placed behind it strike the same zone of our retina? How is it, in other words, that a single sensory process (the source of the stimuli is a single surface, namely the page of the book) is translated into the perception of two objects placed above each other, at different distances from the eye and with different constituent colours?

Various explanations have been attempted, but for the sake

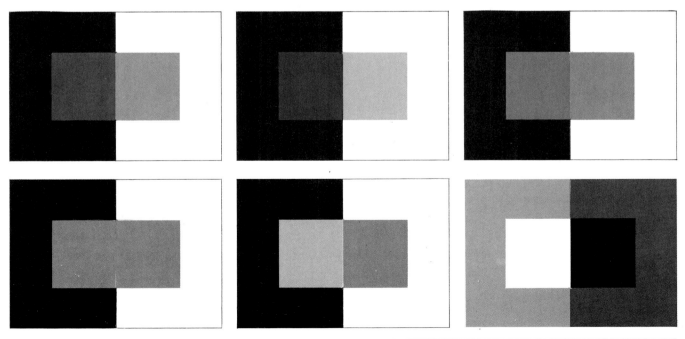

of convenience, and without going into technical details, we shall look briefly at the hypothesis formulated in 1933 by G. M. Heider. He postulated that the phenomenon of transparency was an example of *perceptive fission* or *colour fission*. As a rule, when we look at a coloured object, we do not see a pure colour but one combined with other colours. In chromatic perception there is normally a mixing of colours, a phenomenon which can be verified by rapidly rotating a disc of differently coloured sectors. According to Heider, the fission of colour, which causes transparency, works in the opposite manner to that of fusion. What happens is that in our perception of a single zone, a *stimulant colour* (in the examples we have just seen it was the original green), splits into two different colours which constitute respectively the transparent layer and the underlying surface as seen through transparency.

Black, white and grey are three colours which vary only in tone and which can therefore be defined very simply by the percentage of light that they reflect, that is to say by a single number known as *reflectance* or the *coefficient of reflection*. For this reason they are also described as achromatic colours. It is not a difficult idea to grasp, if we remember that every surface absorbs and reflects part of the light which strikes it; thus an ideal white which reflected 100% of the light it received, would have a reflectance of 100, while at the opposite extreme, a black which absorbed 100% of the light reaching it would have a reflectance of zero; a sheet of white paper generally has a reflectance of 80, and greys vary from 4 to 80. However, the principal qualities of the chromatic colours, like red, yellow, blue etc., vary in accordance with three coefficients (the so-called *trichromatic coefficients*) and thus require three numbers in order to be described. Application of the law which defines the mixing of colours, known as *Talbot's law*, although it was already familiar to Newton, makes it possible to predict what colours will be obtained by mixing with other colours. It is obvious that if the chromatic fission which causes the perception of transparency is the opposite of fusion, the same law can be employed to describe and predict the phenomena of transparency. It is therefore possible to determine precisely the nature of transparency by means of formulas and indices. When, in studying a phenomenon, certain laws can be formulated, it is then possible to deduce from them the necessary conditions.

Here we have only touched upon the problems associated with the perception of transparency. The curious reader who wants to know more is advised to consult the bibliography at the end of this book, which lists several works of varying degrees of complexity.

Paradoxical figures

Look at the figure at the top of this page and try to say which of the two objects is transparent: the knife or the light bulb?

Experience tells us that bulbs are usually transparent, while

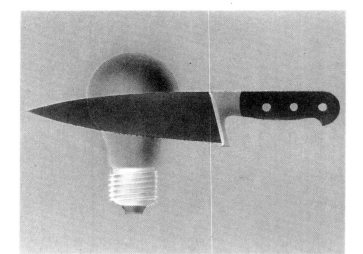

knives are opaque. But after looking carefully, you may decide that it is the knife which is transparent. And if you were asked which of the two objects is in front and which behind, you would probably say without hesitation that the knife is clearly in front and the bulb behind. This is a perceptive situation which poses a paradox: the organization of the field of vision causes us to see things as transparent which we know from long and established experience to be opaque. How is this contradiction to be explained?

Now look at the lower figure on the opposite page. Are the leaves transparent or is it the bottle? And again: are the leaves in front of or behind the bottle? Common experience persuades us that the bottle is transparent, but these leaves really seem to be in front of it. Confronted with this perceptive situation, many would say that the leaves are actually transparent and that the bottle is behind them, even though this contradicts the elementary rules of perspective. So this is the paradox: our eyes persuade us that the opaque object is in front whereas reason and logic argue that transparent objects must stand in front of objects which from experience we know not to be transparent. Many people, indeed, are convinced that there must be some trick or mistake in the actual drawing. Their eyes simply refuse to accept what seems to be strange or absurd.

The explanation for these riddles of perception may be easier for us to understand if we first take a look at some more pictures that illustrate the same problem.

In front or behind?

Paradoxical situations similar to those described in the last paragraph also occur in other types of illustration. The picture at top left of this page shows a fisherman with his typical pipe

and cap patiently waiting on the quayside for a bite; and some distance away we see three sailing boats. Oddly, however, the fishing rod seems to pass behind one of the sails. Experience, expectation and the laws of perspective will combine to tell you that this cannot be; yet the more closely you stare at this detail of the picture, the more obvious it will be that the fishing rod seems to be behind and not in front of the sail.

Now look at the picture beside it: the aeroplane appears to be flying in front of the radio aerial, yet the proportions indicate that this is impossible. Here, too, we are confronted with a situation which patently contradicts everyday experience, and our sense of reality and probability.

Finally, in the picture at the bottom of the preceding page, where does the umbrella seem to be in relation to the girl's head? Undoubtedly we get the same impression as in the other drawings: the umbrella handle appears to go right through her hair, unlikely as this may seem.

The explanation for these phenomena, in terms of the psychology of perception, is in itself quite simple: if there are two figures of different shapes and sizes, but lacking outline, the fact that we may see one figure in front of the other, behind it, or merged with it depends on its relative size and structure, even if this defies logic. As an example, take the two figures below. We can see that at the points where they overlap their outlines cannot be separated, but which of them is placed in front of the other? To most people there will be no doubt that the figure formed by a vertical stripe crossed by three horizontal stripes passes behind the disc, in the same way as the ring and length of thread appear to lie behind the rectangle.

We can now better appreciate what seems odd about certain details of the preceding pictures. The fishing rod passes behind the sail because it is thinner; the radio aerial seems to be behind the aeroplane for the same reason; and the umbrella handle is, in a manner of speaking, "forced" behind the girl's head because it is thinner than her mass of hair.

All these examples appear ridiculous and illogical, yet this does not in any way alter our perception of the figures as related to each other. They go to show that in deciding what we perceive, the manner in which the visual information is organized is more important than past experience.

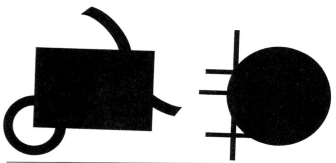

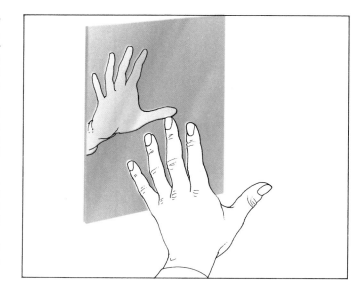

"Mirror, mirror on the wall . . ."

There is no end to what can be done with mirrors; and perhaps this is why in fairy tales such as "Snow White and the Seven Dwarfs" they are endowed with magical properties. Every enchanted castle is provided with mirrors that can reflect all manner of images which, according to circumstances, will evoke love, jealousy, greed, terror, horror or laughter. Indeed, the belief that mirrors faithfully reproduce images is itself an illusion. Even the simplest types, the plane mirrors which we use in everyday life, perform at least one kind of transformation, reversing left and right (see above illustration).

Looking at mirror images is so much a part of everyday life that we tend to take it for granted and assume we understand it. Yet there are problems here which are not easily resolved. For example, why do flat mirrors only reverse left and right and not top and bottom?

If you want to see yourself as others see you, have a look in one of those big, movable flat mirrors which tailors or dressmakers use to reflect the whole person. Arrange two of these mirrors at right angles to each other, as in top right figure on opposite page and place yourself in front of the angle; you will see that your image is no longer reversed. The same thing happens with a concave mirror (top left figure on opposite page), in which, if you rotate it through 90 degrees, you will see the image inverted.

There is no trickery involved here: these are phenomena of the physical world which occur in accordance with laws that are complex but not impossible to describe. Broadly speaking, by introducing various curvatures to a given reflecting surface, it is possible to create mirrors which in various ways modify the shape, dimensions and orientation of the objects reflected.

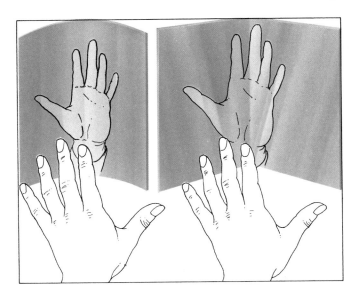

Mirror images

These introductory remarks about mirrors will have convinced you that the problems in this field are not as simple as they may seem. It is, therefore, worth looking at them in rather more detail.

For a start, what exactly is a mirror? Broadly speaking, it is a flat or curved, smooth surface which reflects images. And just as curved surfaces can be infinite in number, so too can mirrors. However, for practical purposes we cannot deal with an infinity of mirrors: we must pick a few simple forms for purposes of generalization and comparison.

There are six commonly recognized *fundamental surfaces*, each described in terms of a pair of perpendicular axes (see illustrations below) passing through the center of curvature. The directions of these axes are determined by the directions of minimum and maximum curvature of that surface. The shape of either axis may be convex, concave or straight. These six types of reflecting surfaces are: the *plane* mirror, which is the most common, in which both axes are straight; the *convex* mirror, in which both curvatures are convex; the *concave* mirror, in which both curvatures are concave; the *convex cylinder*, in which one curvature is convex and the other axis straight; the *concave cylinder*, in which one curvature is concave and the other axis straight; and finally the *saddle-backed* mirror, in which one curvature is concave and the other convex.

The figures below show the ways in which the capital letter E is distorted when reflected in mirrors such as these. The following remarks, we should emphasize, apply mainly to images reflected in a plane mirror.

Let us therefore try to understand what happens in this type of mirror. If an object is placed in front of it, we see what is commonly called a *virtual image*, a direct and symmetrical image of that object. The term "virtual," signifying something that is not true or real, but potential, simply indicates that the image seen by the eye appears to be behind the surface of the glass. Thus the light rays reaching the eye seem to come from a real object located behind the mirror. So there is clearly an element of illusion and deception here. The reflected object appears to be the same distance behind the mirror as the real object is in front of it. For example, if we set an object a couple of feet from a plane mirror, it appears with the same dimensions, shape and orientation (though with the right in place of the left) as an object set a couple of feet behind the mirror. This is simply an immediate consequence of the general law

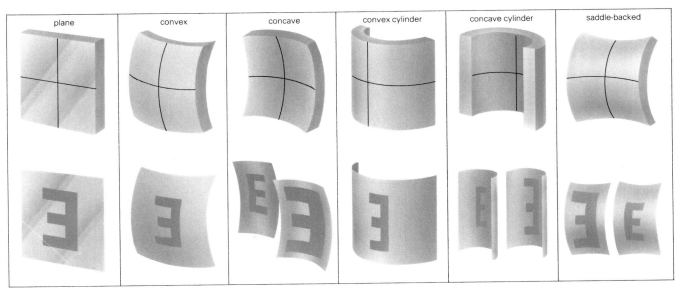

of reflection, which states that the angle of reflection of a light ray is equal to the angle of incidence.

Why is it, however, that such a mirror exchanges left for right and vice versa, but not top for bottom? Take a book and place it upside down against a plane mirror: the individual letters appear upside-down and the sequence of words runs from right to left instead of left to right; yet the order of the lines from top to bottom remains unchanged. What can be the reason for this apparent contradiction?

The explanation is to be found in the confusion between left and right in an image and its orientation. For an observer placed in front of a plane mirror, directions from left to right are not altered any more than those from top to bottom. But the fact that light is propagated along straight lines, as, too, are images, causes what is above and what is below to remain as such in a plane mirror, whereas what is on the right side of the observer is transferred to the left, and vice versa.

Mirror games

Here are some puzzles with clocks to test your ability to read reflections in a mirror. The first ones are easy, but they become more difficult as you go on. The answers can be found on page 117.

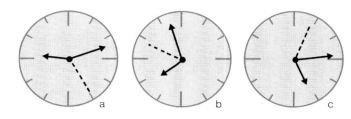

3. This is even more complicated: given the same conditions of reflection in a plane mirror, you must now work out not only the hours and minutes but also the seconds (as indicated by the dotted lines).

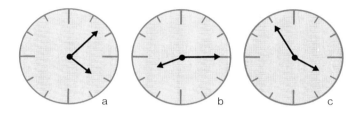

4. Say, at a glance, on which of these reflected clock faces the time is closest to 16.00.

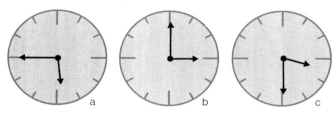

1. The three clocks are reflected images in a plane mirror. Can you tell the real times (supposing it is afternoon or evening) from the positions of the hands?

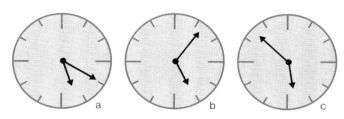

5. And again: which of the three is closest to 18.20?

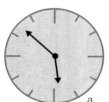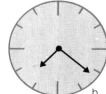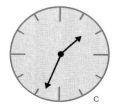

2. The faces of the clocks are similarly reflected, but the exact position of the hands is rather more difficult to determine. Can you tell the times (again p.m.) to the precise minute?

6. Finally, on which of the clocks is the time closest to 22 hours, 50 minutes, 28 seconds?
(The position of the second hand is still indicated by the dotted lines).

It is an illusion to believe that mirrors faithfully reflect images: even the commonest type, the plane mirror, reverses left and right. A deforming concave or convex mirror makes it evident that every different type of mirror surface reflects a different image.

"Mirror games" – Answers

1. Clock *a* shows 18.15; *b* 21.00; *c* 20.30.

2. Clock *a* shows 18.08; *b* 16.39; *c* 22.26.

3. Clock *a* shows 14h, 48' 35"; *b* 16h, 3' 11"; *c* 18h, 46' 56".

4. Clock *b*, which shows 15.45; *a* shows 19.52 and *c* 20.05.

5. Clock *c*; *a* shows 18.40, *b* 18.54 and *c* 18.08.

6. Clock *c*, which shows 22h, 45' 5"; *a* shows 13h, 14' 49", and *b* 13h, 45' 50".

It needs a bit of imagination to read the times on clocks in front of a flat mirror without being able to see the numbers indicating hours, minutes and seconds. There is, however, a little trick to help you solve these puzzles easily; try raising the page to the light so as to read the time transparently from the other side.

The faulty mirror

The drawings on the following two pages illustrate a typical family scene. It is night, as indicated by the moon and stars outside the window, and all members of the family are absorbed by a television programme. Even the dog lying on the floor seems to be taking a keen interest although he looks more relaxed than the others.

Only the grandmother, standing at the back, appears a bit bored, politely stifling a yawn with her hand. Behind the viewers, undetected even by the dog, is a bespectacled burglar in a balaclava, holding a necklace. Such is the power of television that even he seems momentarily drawn to the screen and forgetful of the work in hand.

On the wall facing the television set is an old mirror which every now and then, as if tired of the unvarying routine, amuses itself by altering certain details of the reflected images of objects and people in the room. Only those who are aware of this know not to believe everything they see reflected.

So in this situation, with everyone huddled around the screen, the mirror reflects the scene but makes a few changes, thirteen in all. Can you spot all of them? Check your answers with those on page 120.

A strange art form: anamorphosis

In a plane mirror, as we have seen, the image directly reflected shows a reversal of left and right, and vice versa, but leaves everything else, shape and dimension, unaltered. In other types of mirrors (see page 115) the images undergo distortion both of shape and dimension; they are made bigger or smaller, longer or shorter, wider or thinner, turned upside-down or arranged in some other manner which fails to reflect reality. Yet there are certain mirrors which do the exact opposite; they show images in their correct sizes and positions but, seen from the front, they appear distorted. We know that the surfaces of objects, when viewed from an angle, undergo deformations which can be corrected by compensatory mechanisms of perception: a door, for example, seen from an angle, takes on the shape of a trapezoid, yet we continue to see it as a rectangle.

The kind of distortion that we propose discussing, however, is rather less familiar. It is, in fact, a specialized art form, known as *anamorphosis*, which emerged in the early Renaissance period and spread through Europe especially in the seventeenth and eighteenth century. The term ''anamorphic'' is derived from the Greek *anà*, meaning ''upon, again,'' and *morphé*, which means ''shape''; and anamorphic art deliberately distorts the perspective of images (people and land-scapes) so as to make it more difficult for the observer standing in front of the picture to recognize the subjects represented. The distorted image can be restored to reality only by being viewed from a particular angle or with special glasses. As a simple example, place the book on a table, hold this page in an almost perpendicular position between both your eyes and then look at the above picture, foreshortened, with one eye.

You will clearly see the face of a child, an image which from the front you can only vaguely make out. This is, in fact, a drawing from the *Codice atlantico* by Leonardo da Vinci, who was one of the first students of geometrical perspective. It is not by mere chance that the beginnings of anamorphic art coincided with the period when Renaissance painters were beginning to master the laws of perspective in such a way as to give an impression of depth. The effect of anamorphosis is

''The faulty mirror'' – Solution

therefore the very opposite of perspective. Whereas the latter entails modifying the shape and dimensions of objects represented in a drawing or painting, with a view to transmitting an impression of depth to someone standing in front of it, anamorphosis is an intentional distortion of perspective designed to appear correct and true only when viewed from a particular angle, which is never directly from the front. A famous example of anamorphic art is that of Hans Holbein's *The Ambassadors*, painted in 1533, with a deliberate distorting effect (bottom right of opposite page). To recognize the object thus distorted, you must hold the page at a steep angle, close one eye and look at the picture with the other eye from a distance of about 15 centimeters (6 inches). Go on trying until you have identified the object concerned. If you cannot, we will provide the answer later, after some more discussion about the nature of anamorphic art.

True art or a mere game?

Anamorphosis is a curious but fascinating pictorial technique, which combines the fun of a game with the expressive niceties of art. It originated in the sixteenth century (although the ancient Greeks already understood how it worked) and it allowed Renaissance painters to distort the figures in their frescoes so that these appeared in their true guise only when viewed from below or from one side. The corridor walls of great palaces were adorned with pictures containing deformed figures which were meant to be observed only from either end of the corridor. Anamorphic art became even more fashionable in the succeeding two centuries, when such pictures, containing special images or messages, found a ready sale. The fact that these could not be directly recognized and could only be deciphered by resorting to special devices, helped to give this technique of painting a magic, mysterious significance.

So far we have discussed distorted images which can only be seen in ordinary terms when approached from certain angles. But there are instruments, easy to construct, which will transform anamorphic images into normal ones. Take a small can (such as that commonly used for preserved fruit or other foods), remove the label and wash the outside thoroughly so that it reflects objects. Alternatively, take any kind of transparent cylindrical container and stick a sheet of black paper round the inside. What you have made is an *anamorphoscope*, a kind of cylindrical mirror designed to provide a correct view of certain anamorphic images. It is surprising how a distorted figure is transformed into a normal one (see the illustration on this page). Try placing your cylindrical mirror in the center of the figure on page 122, and you will see the curved motif transformed into a pattern of repeated blocks.

Because anamorphic images cannot immediately be recognized and need to be corrected with instruments, they have been used over the centuries as a means of conveying

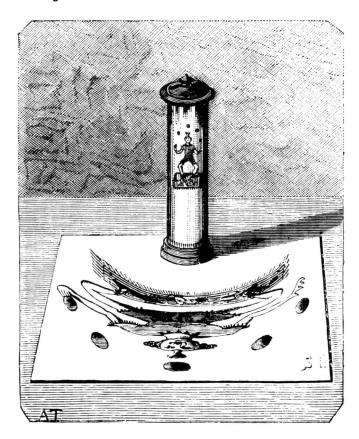

esoteric messages, not to all and sundry, but to a chosen few. Certain monstrously deformed images have been transformed by the anamorphoscope into elegant erotic scenes. Chinese art, in particular, has specialized in erotic anamorphic pictures. There are, too, certain distorted scenes and figures which have to be corrected by conical rather than cylindrical mirrors.

Anamorphosis in other fields

Anamorphic distortion is not the exclusive province of a specialized art but is also to be found in other areas of human activity. Cartographers engaged in preparing maps use transformations and principles of anamorphic art when projecting the surfaces of the Earth on to a cylindrical or conical surface. The technique of cinemascope, which projects images on to a screen much wider than normal, is likewise based on a sophisticated system of anamorphic lenses. An ordinary caricature is really an anamorphic exaggeration of certain physical traits, designed to make us laugh, affectionately or scornfully, at particular aspects of personal behaviour.

The concept of anamorphosis extends beyond art and graphics to the realms of science. Certain animal forms can be explained as the result of an evolutionary process which has gone through a succession of anamorphic distortions of an original form. There are, for instance, some types of fish which, if observed from an angle, or in a cylindrical mirror, take on the appearance of other fish species. Even the evolution of the human brain can be seen to illustrate a series of anamorphic deformations stemming from an original form.

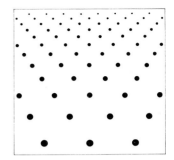

If you look carefully at these two figures you can easily identify the features which give the impression of depth in space. In the one on the right it is the different arrangement and sizes of the dots, which become increasingly small and crowded with distance. In the lower figure it is the converging lines which have the same function.

The secret of "The Ambassadors"

Did you manage to identify the anamorphic detail of Hans Holbein's painting, reproduced on page 120? It represents a human skull with its typical cavities, as can be seen in the

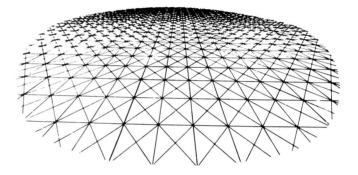

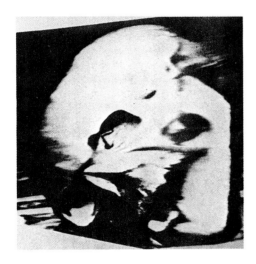

figure below which is an optical rectification of that object.

Perception of a deformed image is a strange yet fascinating experience; and those who wield the instruments which create such distortions seem to possess some secret, mysterious power. This may be the reason why certain artists have not been satisfied merely to represent outward reality but have amused themselves by deforming it, and in so doing have exercised full mastery over the image.

Perspective

Anamorphism, as we have said, is a deliberate bending of the rules of perspective. We shall now take a look at these rules, again without going into technical detail (there are plenty of books on the subject). Here we intend to consider perspective

as language, a code devised for communicating messages. Knowledge of its rules will help us to understand better the phenomenon of anamorphosis. So let us examine the practical use of perspective in relation to everyday experience.

The more we distance ourselves from things, the smaller they appear. It is not by chance that objects vary in shape and size depending on our own movements; it happens in accordance with certain precise geometrical rules which collectively make up *perspective*. By applying these rules it is possible to represent objects, on a plane surface, so that they conform to reality, namely in such a way as to ensure that they retain their dimensions in relation to the space around them. In practical terms, perspective dictates that a given object has to be drawn larger or smaller in relation to another which is nearer or farther away.

Now it is easier to understand anamorphic art. The basic law of perspective states, in fact, that in order for images to be perceived most effectively in three dimensions, they must be projected on to a plane perpendicular to themselves. But what happens if we look at them from one side? When you visit the cinema, try sitting in the end seat, right or left, of the front row: the images on the screen will be uncomfortably distorted and you will soon switch your seat. But as we have already pointed out, anamorphic images are intentionally created to be seen from the side.

Cinemascope is an example of the application of anamorphic principles: in it the images are, so to speak, squeezed sideways on the film, which is then run through a projector

equipped with an anamorphic lens, that is a cylindrical lens which widens them again, so restoring them to normal proportions on the screen.

You will probably have noticed that signs written on the surface of roads, such as motorway exit directions, are often anamorphic. They are, in fact, designed as if they were on an inclined plane and not perpendicular to the eyes of the observer.

Playing with faces

Distortion of images in perspective adheres to certain laws and natural proportions, so that the figures thus produced are perceived as real, pertaining to what is true. The sense of

A photograph of a film shot in cinemascope (left): the image comes out horizontally compressed. It is projected through an anamorphic lens which, having a reverse effect to the one used in taking the shot, restores the image to its normal proportions (right).

perspective is an integral part of our capacity to see. Perhaps this is why we regard as odd or unusual any deviation of images from the normal principles of perspective. As a practical example of what we have been discussing, here is a game.

In the sequence shown below the illustration at top left shows a drawing on a regularly squared grid. The following four figures show how the head is distorted in various ways according to changes made in the pattern of the grid. Take a pencil and try tracing the heads as they might appear on the three remaining empty grids.

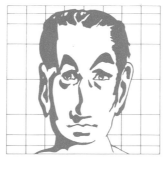

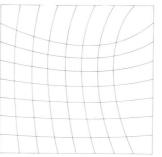
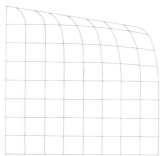
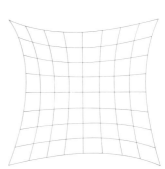

The distorted room

The following curious experiments were first thought up by the American psychologist Albert Ames. He altered certain parts of a normal room, "distorting" the walls, the windows and the doors so that the room was shaped like a trapezoid instead of a rectangle. Yet when this strange room was observed through a hole, it appeared perfectly rectangular, with the walls parallel and the floor horizontal (see figure on the right). The image thus formed on the retina was that of a normal, rectangular room. Just as a wide variety of objects gives a single retinal image according to their orientation in space, so it is possible to construct any number of "distorted rooms" which, when observed from the right position, give retinal images equivalent to those of normal rooms.

There is nothing very strange or surprising about this: the "distorted rooms" are simply the consequence of applying certain principles of perspective. More bewildering, however, is the fact that if we put objects in this room, those placed in the farthest corner appear much smaller than might be ex-

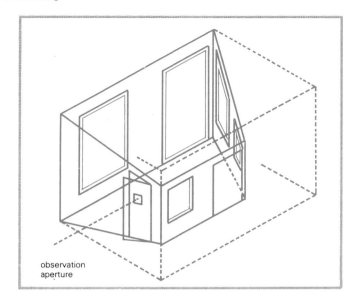

observation
aperture

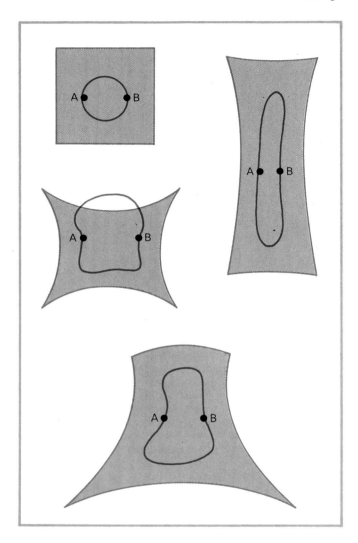

One final strange aspect of Ames's room is that if the observer looking through the hole is able to put in his hand and touch the walls with a stick, the distorting effect, whereby objects and people are made to appear unduly large or small will gradually be reduced. After a thorough exploration he will realize clearly that it is the room which is distorted and not the objects.

Fun with topology

When is a square the same as a circle? Can a right glove be transformed into a left glove? And how can a coffee cup bear a closer resemblance to a vase of flowers than to the saucer on which it stands?

These are not just idle, whimsical questions. There is a serious reason for asking them. Images reflected in concave, convex and cylindrical mirrors, and anamorphic art in particular, ought to convince us that the deformation of images is part of common experience, even if we are not usually aware of it.

What does deforming an image really mean? As a rule we might say that it implies varying its form, in the sense of departing from what is familiar and normal. There is a branch of geometry, called *topology*, which is concerned with those properties of a figure that are not influenced by changes of shape and size: it is involved instead with the properties of "position," as is suggested by the name of the discipline, which means "study of places."

To get away from the abstract, let us imagine a geometrical figure made of deformable matter, which can be stretched in any direction but to which nothing can be added or subtracted. However much we lengthen or shorten it, certain geometrical properties of the figure, the so-called *topological properties*, remain unchanged. This merely provides a general idea of the nature of such properties, and to go into the matter more deeply would be inappropriate here. So let us look at a concrete example of topological properties. In the illustration on this page, the figure at top left shows a square containing a circle with two points (A and B) marked on its circumference. Let us imagine that the figure is a thin rubber band which we can make as long as we wish. The figures on the right and at the bottom show deformations (more properly described as *transformations*) of the original figure, whereas this does not apply to the figure at center left, because the original circle does not cut through the sides of the square at any point. In a topological transformation, the marked points remain unchanged.

Now, using only your intuition, try to solve the topological puzzles on the following two pages: they are designed to test your ability to spot the unvarying properties of certain figures in spite of the changes of form they have undergone.

In each of these examples the first figure *a* has been transformed; in which of the other figures *b, c, d* or *e*, can you recognize it? The answers are on page 128.

pected, considering the actual distance, while those placed in the nearest corner appear gigantic. The room thus seems to be made for giants and dwarfs, because objects of the same size, although very close together in terms of distance, appear much bigger or much smaller than they really are; the same is true of people, as can be seen from the photograph on the preceding page.

In terms of perception, this is interesting on several counts. When we introduce objects into a "distorted room" they take on contradictory dimensions. Our visual system is thereby faced with two conflicting possibilities: either the objects in the room are distorted, or the shape and dimensions of the room itself are deformed. But we are so accustomed to seeing rectangular rooms that we prefer to see people themselves transformed into dwarfs and giants rather than think that the room is distorted.

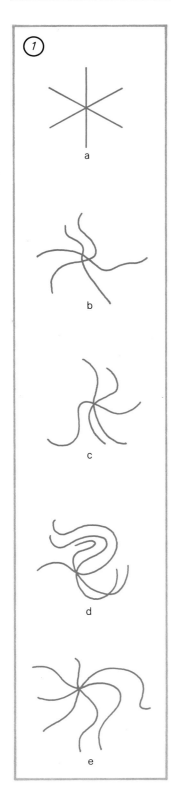

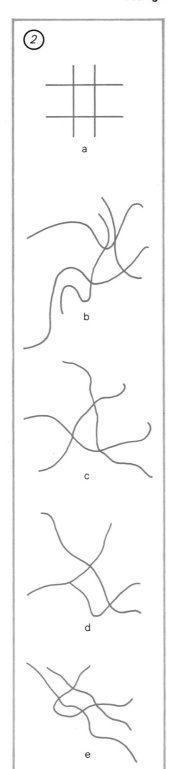

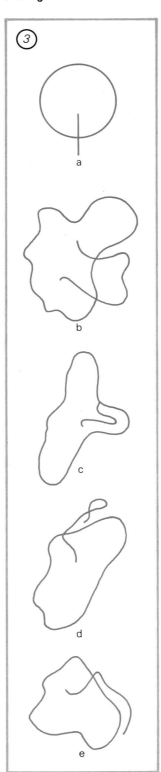

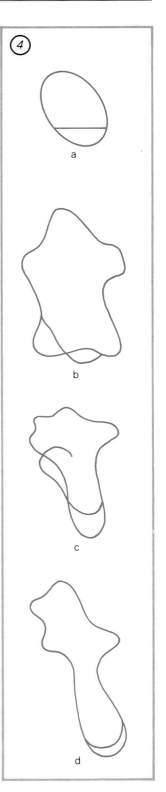

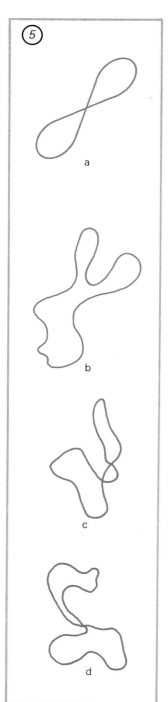

⑤

a

b

c

d

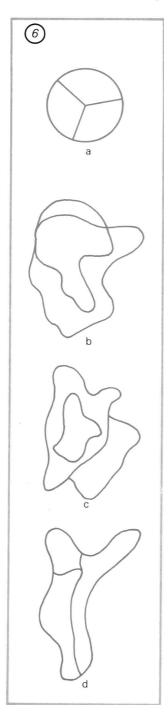

⑥

a

b

c

d

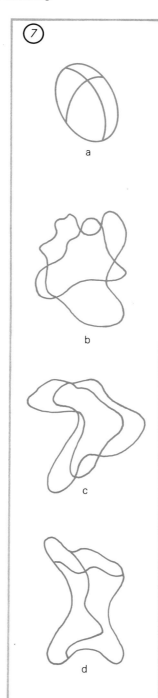

⑦

a

b

c

d

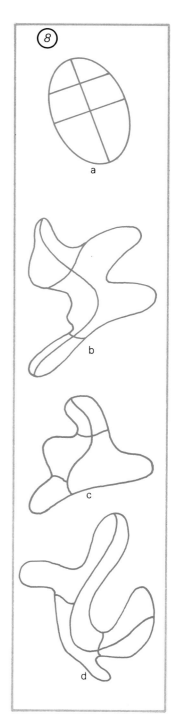

⑧

a

b

c

d

Solutions

1. *c.*   2. *b.*   3. *e.*   4. *d.*   5. *d.*   6. *d.*   7. *d.*   8. *b.*

Things are not what they seem

As the trees swayed in the wind,
it seemed as by a visual illusion
that this swaying
communicated itself to all things.
(Gabriele D'Annunzio, Prose di romanzi)

The striped dress

That evening Sue was in a bad mood. She didn't know why but the prospect of the coming party made her feel uneasy. Last time, at the birthday of her closest friend, she had refused to join in, watching the others dancing and eventually getting thoroughly bored. She shuddered at the thought of going through such a miserable experience again. On that occasion something had gone wrong. A lot of her friends had been there, the atmosphere had been happy, yet. . . . Was the fault with herself, Sue wondered? She gazed at her image in the mirror and for the first time had the feeling that she was getting rather fat. From time to time she had worried, as all girls do, about putting on weight, but never before had she felt so self-conscious.

Fortunately Sue had a willing and understanding listener in her mother, who hastened to reassure her daughter and took her along the following day to her dressmaker. There Sue tried on a long dress, simple yet elegant, with a vertically striped floral pattern. Accepting the present gracefully, Sue resolved to wear it for the party.

To her relief and delight, the evening proved a great success. Although she was unaware of being different, she soon sensed, from the attitude of the boys, the smiles, the invitations and the easy chatter, that she was being accepted in a manner she had almost forgotten. She was the center of attraction and spent a happy, carefree evening. The new dress took much of the credit. Sue was the same person, a good-looking girl, not fat but with an attractive figure, and the

dress made her look even slimmer. Sue's mother, in fact, had solved a potentially distressing psychological problem in a rather unusual way. Its basis was a perceptive effect familiar in the field of optical illusion, and put to practical use in the world of fashion.

Look at the illustration on the preceding page: the female silhouette on the left appears to be more slender than that on the right, but actually they have precisely the same measurements. The illusion is derived from the different arrangement of the lines.

Deceiving the senses

Things we see, but which are not what they seem at first sight, are called *optical illusions*, and they are among the most fascinating aspects of the psychology of perception. Some people experience the sensation powerfully under the influence of drugs, or if mentally sick, conjuring up what appears to be a real world entirely from the realm of their own imagination. Hallucination of this kind is completely different from what happens to individuals affected by drinking too much alcohol, when they say they are ''seeing double'' and complain that nothing around them will stand still. What we are concerned with here are those experiences related to perception whereby certain objects, figures and images appear to undergo distortions which are not actual deformations but merely illusions.

The arrow illusion

One of the best-known of optical illusions, the *arrow illusion* or the *Müller-Lyer effect* (after the name of the psychologist who specialized in these studies), is shown in the illustration on the right (Fig. 1). Two segments (*AB* and *A'B'*) of equal length are bounded in different ways by arrows, so that one appears shorter than the other.

This optical-geometric illusion has led to closely related variants. Fig. 2, for example, seems to consist of an arrow, the tip (*A*) at one end, the notch for the bowstring (*C*) at the other. *B* is the exact midpoint of the line *AC*, but we perceive the half *AB* as shorter than *BC*, so that the entire segment *AC* does not seem to be divided exactly halfway. It is clear that this distortion of our perception is due to the addition of the auxiliary lines. The arrow *AC* can, in fact, be analysed more precisely: it is possible to measure the illusion by calculating by how much *AB* should be increased, or *BC* diminished, for the two sections to appear equal to each other. And thus an indicator can be established: the percentage of deformation to which a geometrical figure has to be subjected so that it is perceived according to objective geometrical standards.

In general one can say that, given a geometrical figure with determined characteristics, the addition of other lines will

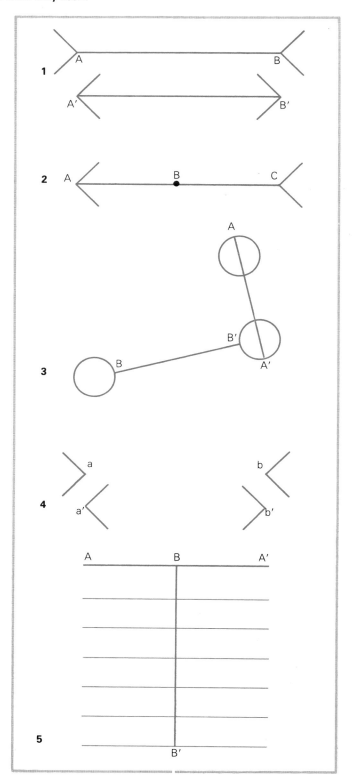

modify its apparent properties, particularly in terms of size, shape, direction etc.

Fig. 3 illustrates the diverse arrangement of circles for perceiving the two lines AA' and BB' as different in length, whereas they are really equal, as can easily be checked. In the case of AA', the two circles give the impression of closing off the ends and thus of shortening the whole line, whereas in BB' the circles, shifted so that the line does not intersect them but merely touches their circumference, appear to have a lengthening effect. Perception of AA' and BB' as equal is therefore disturbed and distorted by the varied positioning of the circles at the ends of the two lines. In Figs 1 and 2, on the other hand, it is the oblique lines which perform the same function in perception as do the circles.

To help understand the role played by these lines and circles, try taking away from Fig. 1 the right angles AB and A'B', thus creating the new Fig. 4. What do we seem to perceive? In the first place, we notice that the illusion remains: although these are only right angles with symmetrical tips and sides, we see that the distance between a' and b' is markedly shorter than that between a and b. We have to consider that our previous experience in analysing Figs 1 and 2 may be a determining factor in perpetuating the illusion. We can see that the angles a'b' seem to close off and limit an area, whereas a and b together appear to open up a potentially limitless space.

The phenomenon of optical illusion is of great theoretical importance. We have to bear in mind that illusory effects are not restricted to visual sensations: it is possible to experience illusions of hearing and of touch. But it tends to assume greater significance in the visual sphere because here, more than in areas related to the other senses, we can show that the illusion, i.e. what is apparent to the eye, is quite independent of the physical reality.

Another geometrical illusion, in which the deforming function of the visual stimuli is performed by parallel horizontal lines, is illustrated in Fig. 5. Here the lines AA' and BB' are actually equal in length, but because of the structure of the figure they appear different, with the line BB' seemingly longer than AA'.

Convergent or parallel?

Take a look at the first of the two strange figures at the top of this page; what is the illusion it contains?

The oblique lines, enclosed in a square, lie parallel to one another, but this is a property that we are unable to grasp visually because they are interrupted by lines which intersect their entire length. Even with a great deal of concentrated effort, it is hard to isolate the diagonal lines and to see them as parallel. The loss of parallelism is even more striking in the second figure, which reproduces _Hering's illusion_: the two parallel lines appear to be curved under the effect of the rays which run across them.

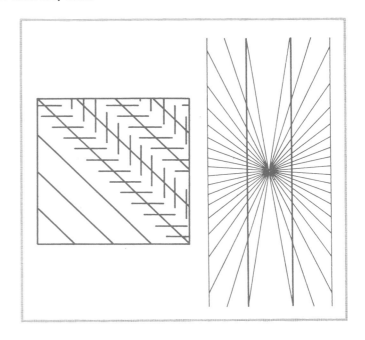

A break in direction

Here is a further example of visual illusion. In the figure below, the two oblique lines on either side of the rectangle do not seem to be extensions of the same line. This is because our perception of a continuous line is interrupted by the rectangle over it. In other words, the two oblique lines apparently lose alignment, one of them seeming to have shifted away from the other. This figure is known as _Poggendorff's illusion_, from the name of the German physicist who first identified and described it.

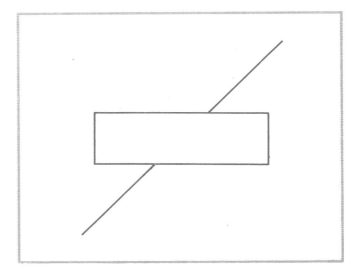

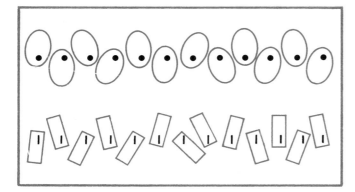 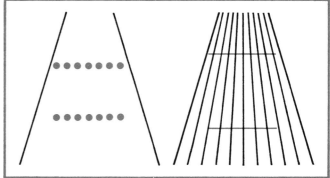

Broken lines

Optical illusions are images capable of giving our visual system a false idea of the form, distance or direction of one or more objects. They are directly caused by certain geometrical features of the figures themselves which disturb correct vision and suggest misleading relationships between the various parts. In Poggendorff's illusion, for instance, the oblique line is disturbed by the rectangle which interrupts it halfway, preventing the continuity of the line being perceived. To express this in proper visual terms, we would say that there is some "noise" (see page 22) in optical illusions which precludes correct representation.

In the two figures at top left there is also some "noise" which prevents us recognizing that the dots and vertical bars are indeed geometrically arranged in a straight line: nor is it difficult to understand why we get this impression. In the first figure the positioning of the small ellipses produces the effect of breaking the straight line of dots; in the second, it is the irregular arrangement of the rectangles which appears to alter the alignment of the vertical bars.

These simple figures, which seem to be no more than diverting, are really elementary illustrations of more complex visual situations, helping us to examine and understand normal phenomena of perception. Have another look therefore at the preceding optical illusions and try to identify the "noise" in each of them. This is a useful exercise in becoming aware of things that may at first glance have gone unobserved; and, if nothing else, it will serve as a reminder that we should always be on our guard against illusions in the boundless world of visual experience.

The railway lines illusion

The illustration at top right is an example of a very strange effect on visual perception, known as the *railway lines illusion*. The two rows of horizontal, parallel dots in the first figure are of the same length, yet this is not apparent to the eye: the row of dots closer to the point where the two straight lines start to diverge appears longer than the other one. This effect remains no matter which way the figure is pointed. It is obvious that the element deforming correct perception of the image is the inclination of the two straight lines. From a geometrical viewpoint we can affirm that the figure is made up of two horizontal dotted lines, which are equal and parallel, and two equal, convergent straight lines. It is the particular arrangement of the two latter lines which distorts our vision of the others. The figure on the right is another representation of the same optical illusion.

The illustration at the bottom of the page shows the same kind of distorting effect, but in an even more striking manner, for the familiar geometrical figures here seem to be deformed in two ways. Firstly, the two rectangles appear to differ from each other, the one on the right, nearer to the meeting point of the converging lines, seeming larger. Secondly, their shapes also appear distorted, so that at first glance they are seen not as rectangles but as trapezoids. In this case too the deformation is caused by the particular arrangement of the convergent lines in relation to the rectangles. This example is known as *Ponzo's illusion*.

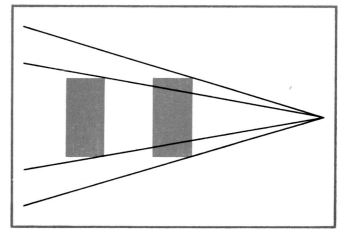

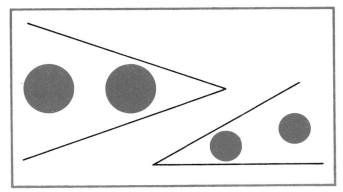

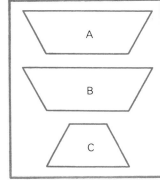

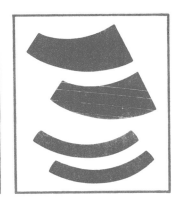

Why is the sun bigger on the horizon?

Most of you will have noticed, after a fine day, that as the sun sets on the horizon, its red disc appears to be much bigger than it was around midday when at it was at its zenith. In simple terms, the *zenith* is the point of the celestial sphere which is vertically above any point on the Earth's surface and thus vertically above the observer. So the sun is at its zenith when directly overhead. If you compare it at this moment with the way it looks, hours later, as it sinks below the line of the horizon, you will notice that its circumference, as it sets, appears much larger.

The explanation of this phenomenon is interesting because it too has something to do with Ponzo's illusion, mentioned above. Look at the first figure in the illustration above: the two circles are the same size, but the one on the right gives the impression of being bigger. Now take a close look at the second figure: although the lower side consists of a horizontal line, the illusion is still there. In fact, the circle situated closer to the sides of the angle appears larger than the other. This, in simplified form, is exactly what happens when we look at the sun on the horizon. It is further proof that the study of optical illusions, far from being a mere pastime, can be valuable in understanding everyday visual phenomena.

Equal or different shapes?

Let us now consider the two illustrations at top right. In the first, which depicts three trapezoids set above one another, there is a double effect of illusion. If we look at figures *A* and *B*, they appear not to be equal, although actually they are. This is because of the different way in which they are placed, one above the other. This factor of different positioning is easier to comprehend in the pairs of figures in the other illustration, where the second figure of each pair, having been placed below and slightly to the right of the other, seems to be smaller, whereas it is really equal to the one immediately above.

If we look once more at the illustration of the trapezoids, we see that the base line of figure *C*, which differs from those of *A* and *B* in being longer than the top line, appears shorter than the bases of *A* and *B*, even though measurement will indicate that all three are of equal length. What makes the bases of *A* and *B* look longer is that, together with the other sides, they enclose a bigger area than *C*. Perception of the larger dimensions of *B* gives the illusion of its base also being longer, whereas this is not so. Broadly speaking, the illusion, therefore, arises not so much from a factor of dimension as from the fact that the sides of trapezoid *B* enclose a larger space than that of *C*, and thus none of its parts appear to be equal to those of *C*.

The fan illusion

Having identified the factors which create the "noise" in the simpler optical illusions, we can now take a look at others of a rather more curious and complex nature. One of these is undoubtedly the *fan illusion*, otherwise called *Oribson's figure* (illustrated at bottom left).

Here we can recognize elements of both the Hering and the Ponzo figures. The illusory effect consists in the fact that the black square and circle appear to be deformed; and the "noise" is caused by the radial arrangement of the lines which

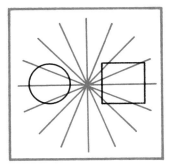

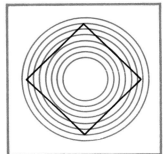

run through the two geometrical figures and which resemble the shape of a fan.

They may, nevertheless, be regarded as examples of *broken form* (see the right-hand figure at the bottom of the same page).

Impossible figures

"There was something uplifting about the scene, but football is going through a lean period." Whoever made this statement would seem to be jumping quite haphazardly from one topic to another. What is the sense of such reasoning, and what connection can there be between the uplifting scene and football? None whatsoever.

The sentence consists of two disconnected phrases and it is possible for us to translate this apparent illogicality into visual terms, using special types of images. Look carefully at the figure at bottom left and try to "read" it: the lower part, with those three circles, resemble three tubes, but as we transfer our gaze upward, the figure looks more like a container or some sort of magnet. The parts in the middle, as they merge into one another, appear simultaneously to be full and empty, curved and flat. If we try to give the figure a single, overall meaning, we soon see that we cannot decide which of the two likenesses to choose. So we feel confused and uncertain, perhaps rather uneasy. And this happens because we are unable to provide an unambiguous definition to the figure, which is therefore unacceptable, just like the sentence quoted at the beginning, consisting as it does of two statements each of which makes sense on its own but not if taken together. What is the meaning, above all, of the adversative conjunction "but" between the two phrases?

Let us come back to the figure we were discussing above. The vertical segments seem to belong both to tubes and to a magnet; and this very fact, namely that the figure consists of

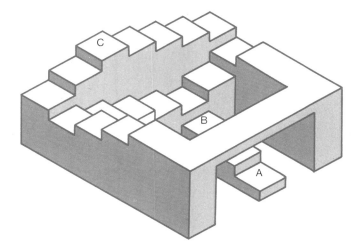

two fundamental sections which have different meanings, explains why it is impossible to give an overall interpretation. We have to realize, however, that the impossibility is not one of perception: the figure, in fact, is before our eyes in its entirety, with all its characteristics. What we are unable to do is to make any sense of it, to think it out. Again, if we look at the second figure at the bottom, we perceive something but cannot say what. We can certainly distinguish a triangle but its shape is strange, the sides solid but with no clear indication as to which are in front and which behind.

Both these examples are known as *Penrose figures* (named after L. S. Penrose, the British geneticist, and his son Roger, a mathematician, who specialized in these forms of optical illusion). From such a triangle are derived other "impossible" figures, like the one illustrated above. It is no use trying to walk up or down this kind of staircase for the steps lead nowhere. You could, if you wanted, travel from *A* to *C*, assuming there were three steps between *A* and *B*; you could also try walking around the bridge, counting the steps that go up and those that go down. But no matter how often you try, you will probably find that the reckonings always give a different answer.

Fraser's spiral

Here is a figure which, without exaggeration, can not only baffle your eyes but drive you crazy! What, in fact, can you see on the opposite page? A spiral flowing into a central vortex? Very well, try to trace it with your finger, it will simply go round the same point without following the course of the spiral. Take your finger away and look more closely; you still get the strong impression of a spiral. Try once more with your finger: this is certainly no real spiral. In fact Fraser's spiral is one of the most surprising of optical illusions: the deception is brought about by a series of concentric circles.

The world: an enormous illusion!

"Everything is illusion, including what you are reading!" This notice appeared outside the laboratory of Richard Gregory, professor of Bristol University, one of the great scholars of perception and inventor of new types of microscope and telescope. It was a deliberately provocative statement, designed to stimulate and condition the mind of anyone venturing inside. But how often have we rummaged around for an object we have lost and which was really there, under our nose and in front of our eyes, all the time? Have we not watched the moon racing over the clouds, or been in a train which we thought was moving, only to realize that it was really the train on the next platform pulling out? And we have surely noticed (as was described and illustrated at the beginning of this chapter) that a girl will tend to look slimmer in a dress with vertical stripes or in one that is coloured black. As a final example, look at a photograph of a city street, and notice how some of the people and buildings appear closer and others farther away, even though the photograph is flat and all the visual details strike our eye from the same distance.

In our innocence, we all believe – as has already been pointed out – that what we see faithfully mirrors the outside world. This is a superficial attitude. Things are indeed very different; and if we look at even the most familiar objects with a more critical eye, we shall soon recognize that these are not as simple as initially they may have seemed. Optical illusions clearly demonstrate that what we see is in no way a faithful mirror of reality: there are innumerable instances where the perceptive results do not correspond to the objective facts. It is true that optical illusions are extreme cases, but we have seen that even the perception of reality under normal conditions is conditioned by the observer's own personal experiences and preconceptions: it is the conclusive result of a series of operations involving the reception, transmission, elaboration and organization of the visual messages that reach us. So can we still claim that what we see is the faithful reflection of reality?

Taking all this into account, Gregory's pronouncement seems rather less paradoxical than when first encountered. This does not imply that we see nothing, rather that we see things wrongly, as in a conjuring trick where we are deceived into experiencing unreal situations. Our senses convey to us information about our surroundings which enables us to take the correct actions and to adapt as necessary to the circumstances. Things themselves do not actually deceive us; we merely have to rid ourselves of the illusion – for such it is – that what we see is indeed the world as it exists.

Optical illusions have been a topic of major interest in the psychology of perception ever since studies in this field commenced around the middle of the nineteenth century. Early research suggested that such illusions were exceptional but that they were useful for the better understanding even of normal phenomena.

Later it became evident to the scientists that optical illusions, far from being marginal experiences, occurred much more frequently in the realm of perceptive phenomena than had ever been imagined. They aroused a great deal of interest and curiosity, naturally, because of their entertainment value. Yet these diverting puzzles proved to have a more serious purpose, representing, in simplified form, problems of far deeper complexity and significance.

The moving train

The train we are on is standing in the station. For a brief moment we raise our eyes from the book we are reading and glance across at the stationary train on the next platform. Then our attention is again distracted by an odd-looking person who happens to be walking past the train window. Suddenly, switching our gaze once more away from this curious individual, we get the strong impression that we are moving past the carriages and compartments of the other train and conclude in a flash that our train is pulling out. In fact, as we soon realize, it is the train on the adjoining platform which is passing us. We have fallen victim to an illusion of movement.

The wandering moon

It is evening and the moon will shortly come out. The sky is clear but a chilly breeze warns of an impending weather change. Gradually the first thin clouds appear and float overhead. When they reach that part of the sky where the moon hangs motionless, a strange thing happens: the clouds, which were unquestionably on the move, have suddenly come to a halt, while the moon, which previously seemed immobile in the sky, appears quite clearly to be racing along above them.

This is, of course, yet another illusion of movement, common enough to have inspired song writers and poets, including Milton who, in *L'Allegro*, wrote of ''. . . the wandering moon, Riding near her highest noon . . .''

Illusion and movement

Movement is probably the area of everyday experience in which perceptive illusion is most powerfully apparent, demonstrating, better than by any other means, how our senses deceive us. And considering that movement is the essential element in the rhythm of daily life, it is easy to understand what we mean by saying that illusions of perception, contrary to what was once believed, are far from rare. But it is important to specify exactly what kind of movement we are talking about because movements are, so to speak, infinite. Let us therefore narrow the argument by discussing only those forms of movement, such as journeys by car or by train,

Look, for example, at the above illustration: the image of the woman on the right is two and a half times bigger than that of the woman in the background. Yet the only difference that we can say exists between them is that the first seems nearer to us and the second farther away. But actually this is an illusion; both the female figures represent perceptive data which reflect identical conditions. Both, in fact, are situated in two-dimensional space, as is normal with photographic images, and are at the same distance from our eyes. The type of information we receive in these instances is called "relative size": particular objects, set in their normal spatial context, are perceived in their real dimensions, despite the fact that the sensory messages imply a difference. This is a very common everyday experience. Yet there are circumstances in which "relative size" does not give us correct information about distances and dimensions.

We have already referred to movement as one of the most important factors in correctly perceiving distance and depth of objects. But even movement itself may be a source of illusion, as is shown by the following small experiment.

which all of us have experienced time and time again and which are a part of our daily life. However, in order to comprehend these optical illusions, we need to bring a more reasoned approach to our observation of everyday objects. We shall soon understand why, but at this stage we will merely say that in some part of our brain the received information is corrected and that we are convinced of having true sensations.

The wayward cigarette

Light a cigarette, puff on it a few times so that the tip is glowing, and place it in an ashtray. Switch off the light and close the curtains or blinds so that there is complete darkness; then, standing a little distance away, look hard at the red spot represented by the cigarette tip. Very soon you will get the impression that this spot is moving in the room. No need to worry, however; this is no ghost which has picked up your cigarette and started to smoke it. The movement is merely an illusion, and a very familiar one, for which there have been various explanations. The most likely one is that the phenomenon is caused by a change in the functioning of the visual system, that occurs when it is made to work in abnormal conditions.

The spinning spiral

Another strange sensation of movement had been known since the time of Aristotle. It is well demonstrated by placing a standard disc on the turntable of a record player. Start it up and as the record revolves stare for half a minute or so at the central pivot. Stop the record suddenly and keep looking at the pivot: you will notice that the record still seems to be revolving, but in the opposite direction.

The same effect is more clearly evident in another experiment. Take a drawing of a spiral, like the one illustrated on the left, and rotate it: it appears to get smaller or larger according to the direction of rotation. When you stop, the spiral seems to continue moving, but, as in the former case, in the contrary direction.

Tricks of movement

The phenomenon of the spinning spiral which, when stopped, appears for a while to be still rotating in an opposite direction is known in psychology as the *consecutive negative effect*. Such illusions also occur with colours, and we shall discuss these more thoroughly in the next chapter. For the time being we can state that this illusion consists in the perception of movement even when the stimulus (the moving object) is no longer in operation: the term "negative" indicates that the illusory movement occurs in the opposite direction to the actual one.

Various illusions of movement can be produced in the laboratory and even at home. Try this next experiment yourself. Below left is an illustration of a circle in the form of a sunburst, with rays emanating from a central point. Make a copy of this and rotate it on the turntable of a record player at a speed of 33⅓ rpm. Look hard at the center for about five minutes, perhaps less. Then switch your gaze to the center of the immobile figure on the right. You will get the brief impression that this is revolving in the opposite direction.

The next illusion is another curious example of consecutive negative effect, which is not directly related to movement but certainly associated with it. In the top illustration look patiently for a few minutes at the slanting lines on the left and then quickly transfer your gaze to the vertical lines on the right. How do you see them?

These effects have been given a neural explanation (to do with the nervous structures of the visual system) in which a fundamental role is played by the reciprocal processes of

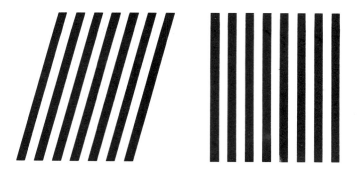

excitation and inhibition in the cell layers of the retina and of the cerebral cortex. There may also be a component which is due to adaptation, the phenomenon whereby if a certain stimulus strikes our receptors for some length of time, the latter respond powerfully at first and then ever more weakly until a normal level is reached.

So far we have described consecutive negative effects in the perception of movement as reproduced in an artificial situation, such as the laboratory. Although rare, similar illusions can also be found in everyday experience. Should you ever have the opportunity to admire a beautiful waterfall, look for a few seconds at the water cascading down and then quickly transfer your glance to nearby objects such as rocks or plants. These will seem literally to be moving upward. This, too, is pure illusion which, like other examples, proves how imperfectly our eyes mediate between ourselves and the outside world.

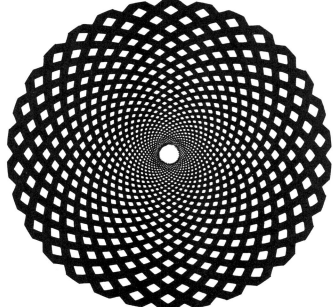

A car journey

As most of us will have discovered, a car ride provides excellent opportunities for observing various kinds of illusions. Let us look at some common examples, first from the viewpoint of the driver, then of a passenger gazing out of the window.

Imagine, then, that you are driving along at a fairly reasonable speed, but not too fast. Ahead in the distance are two lampposts (see Fig. *a* below). Look at the one closer to you, and what do you see? As the car gets nearer, the lamppost seems to advance toward you and to grow steadily bigger; yet you know that it is stationary and unvarying in dimensions. The second lamppost then undergoes the same kind of transformation. The movements and changes in size are obviously illusions. But, in fact, every object we perceive, as we drive along, is in some way subjected to the same illusory effect: trees, houses, hills and mountains, traffic signals, the shape of the road, and so forth. This is important in order to understand the phenomena we have been describing. Fasten your gaze on anything straight ahead on the horizon and as you get closer the surroundings will not only appear to be growing in size but also to be coming at you more and more rapidly (see Fig. *b* below).

Now, still looking directly ahead, see what happens to the two sides of the road: these seem to be racing toward you, rearing up and flashing past in continuous motion. But of course everything is really immobile and absolutely unvarying in size.

In the passenger's seat you will see things differently but still get illusions of movement, for trees, houses and other details of the landscape will appear to be moving in the opposite direction to that in which you are travelling. The interesting difference is that things seem to be passing more and more slowly as the speed of the car decreases, and also the farther away they are from you. When they are virtually at an infinite distance (like the stars in the sky) they may appear quite motionless.

If you have travelled by air, you will have noticed the extremely powerful sensation of speed at takeoff; but when the aeroplane has gained height and is cruising, at a speed far greater than it was at takeoff, there is, paradoxically, no sensation of movement. If you look down at the landscape below, it gives the impression of moving past very slowly. When coming in to land, it is difficult adjusting to the movement, so much so that things seem to be rushing toward you, rather than the contrary. Illusions are frequent in these circumstances; and nobody knows this better than the pilots of aircraft who rely on instruments more than on individual perceptions.

The fact that objects seen from the window of a car appear to move at a speed inversely proportional to their distance from us helps us to judge their distances correctly, and it provides further proof that movement is a fundamental factor in our perception of the third dimension.

Constancy of perception

How can we explain the fact that, in spite of all these illusory effects, we generally perceive the objective world as it actually is?

In the figure at the top of page 137, we do not see two women of different sizes but two women of approximately the same size but positioned at different distances from us. The reason why an object is seen in its true dimensions, despite all the changes it undergoes in the formation of the image on the retina, is the effect called *constancy of size*. So when our eyes move, the images of various objects alter position on the retina and undergo changes in shape and size (getting bigger or smaller), yet we still see these objects as unchanged in form and dimension, and furthermore motionless in space. Therefore in addition to constancy of size there is so-called *constancy of position*.

Perception of movement

Many of the image games included in this book have been set up in somewhat artificial conditions; the figures of which they are composed are static and we, looking at them, are more or less sitting still. But in real situations movement is normal and immobility exceptional. This applies, in fact, to most forms of life. If we look carefully, we see that there are no absolutely

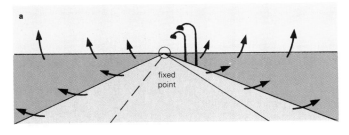

a

fixed
point

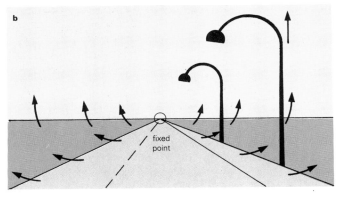

b

fixed
point

focus in order to produce two-dimensional images on the retina. But a deeper examination of the structure and workings of the eye shows it to be a far more complex and versatile instrument than a camera. It is more like a computer programmed to act in accordance with mathematical and geometrical rules (a relativistic type of geometry, similar to a projective type) and capable of continual adjustments. And it is these rules which make it possible for an acceptable correspondence to exist between the physical world and the world as we perceive it.

A system which reasons

The analysis of optical illusions demonstrates clearly that vision is not an automatic operation which works without our being aware of it, but an active process of inference, in which the visual system does not merely transmit signals passively but organizes and interprets these signals. We know that images are formed on the retina upside-down and on a two-dimensional plane; yet we see them the right way up and in three-dimensional space. It is obvious here that the visual system, consisting of the eye and the brain, intervenes and acts on what is to be seen in the surrounding world, and gives it a meaning. And it is easy to recognize this active mental contribution in the case of certain images, such as optical illusions, which in themselves are highly ambiguous. It would, however, be true to say that all images are in a sense basically ambiguous.

Thus the perceptive process starts with a mass of data and narrows it down to pieces of information which have a meaning for us. Just as in mental reasoning we progress from a set of premisses to a conclusion, so from a collection of visual data we progress to what is properly called perception. And, to continue the analogy, just as when we reason we abide by certain rules, so when we look at things, making the transition from mere sensory data to perception (i.e. interpreting them), we do it by observing certain rules, or laws, which already exist in the outside world.

Finding out how the system uses these rules may help us to understand not only the phenomenon of optical illusions but also the way in which, in spite of the fundamental ambiguity of retinal images, it establishes a correct and certain relationship with the outside world.

immobile animals in completely still surroundings. Movement therefore takes on a special significance in the animal world. And the eye itself is the result of a long process of evolution which has culminated in a system specialized, above all, in the perception of movement. There are some animals which react only to moving objects. Place a dead fly in front of a frog or a chameleon and they will not notice it, even if they have gone without food for some time. This is not because they prefer to eat fresh food; it is simply that if the prey is not moving, they are unable to see it.

The frog's eye and, in a more perfected form, the human eye are provided with a retina which, rather than reflecting static images, serves to analyse the changes in the flux of light that are caused by moving objects. And indeed even motionless images may convey the illusion of movement. Look at the figure above, don't you get the impression that something is moving, rotating, sometimes clockwise, sometimes anticlockwise? The perception of movement here is due to the combination of contrasting light in a fairly broad field of vision.

In our own visual system it is very important that the information concerning the structure of what we perceive should be separated from the information concerning its movement. Human beings, in the course of evolution, must often have found it more important to recognize the direction in which a particular object is moving, even if that object is not clearly defined, and to react accordingly, than to stop and study its details. And it is in analysing movement that the average camera is shown to be totally inadequate. It may be useful to make a superficial comparison between the eye and the camera, especially to explain how light rays come to a

Deceptive curves and cubes

Take a look at the figure at the top of the opposite page and describe what you see. You will most probably perceive a series of concentric curves in relief, their edges marked by coloured circular lines which lie in the trenches formed between the curves. But now take the book, turn the page upside-down and have another look: the lines which

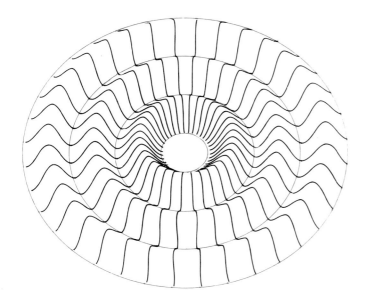

two surfaces of different form penetrate each other, their meeting point invariably creates a concave discontinuity of their tangent planes. In the case of the sinusoidal surface, transverseness provides a basic unity which explains its division into sections of both continuous and discontinuous surfaces.

The so-called *rule of partition* which operates in the cases of Schröder's staircase and the illusion of the cubes (page 75) is based on transverseness. With regard to Schröder's staircase (first figure at bottom left), the parts of which it consists are obviously the steps, and each step is divided by two lines of concave discontinuity. If the staircase is inversely perceived i.e. looked at as if from below, the boundaries between the steps necessarily change as well. This can be checked by looking at the coloured zone which, in the first case, seems to form part of a single step, but which, when the figure is inverted, appears to belong to two adjoining, successive steps.

In the illusion of the cubes (second figure at bottom left) the same phenomenon occurs: the three rhomboidal faces in colour at first seem to be part of a single cube, but when inverted are seen as three sides of separate cubes.

previously lay in the trenches have now bounced up to the crests formed by the curves.

A number of varied processes of revision and reorganization are involved in deriving perceptive meaning from the visual data in this figure, which in technical terms is formed by rotating the line of a sinusoidal wave around a vertical axis in accordance with a given rule. This results in a sinusoidal surface which, drawn on a piece of paper, is two-dimensional. But although we know it to be on a two-dimensional plane, we see it in relief. It is evident that in this example the perception of three dimensions is caused by a process of inference on the part of our visual system.

The law which appears to govern the perception of sinusoidal surfaces is that of *transverseness*, a type of rule which is frequently encountered in everyday life. Thus when we dip a straw into a drink, we form a circular concave discontinuity where the straw breaks the surface, and the same thing happens when we pierce a steak with a fork or place a candied cherry in a mousse. The rule may be expressed in this way: if

Ghostly shapes

An unlikely event perhaps but have you ever spent a night in a castle? Unable to sleep, have you risen some time after midnight and roamed the ramparts? In the small hours of morning, have you perhaps heard sudden rustling movements or, peering in the gloom along the line of fortifications, caught a glimpse of a fleeting shape, covered in a white shroud? Well, such experiences are given to few, and whether ghosts actually exist is not what concerns us here. Yet some of you may have been aware, in certain conditions of heavy shadow or dazzling light, of having seen objects or figures which are not really there.

Have a look, for example, at the illustration below. The chances are that you will see two figures, the one on the left of a comet and the one on the right of a pear. You may say that

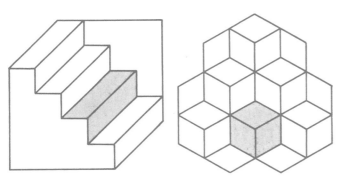

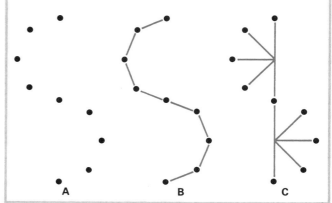

not only can you definitely see a comet and a pear but that the images stand out more clearly than their backgrounds. What is surprising, however, is that although you are aware that neither the comet nor the pear exists, you would not admit to seeing, say, arrangements of small tarts from which irregular slices have been removed. Despite the fact that we acknowledge there is no comet and no pear, we still continue to see them.

This resistance of the perceptive system is interesting in that it helps us to understand what we mean when we say that our mind builds images. Perception is the final product of a whole series of activities involving the reception, interpretation and transformation of incoming sensory messages.

Outlines

What is an image? Some will say that the answer is obvious. An image is there, you can see it; so why bother to define it? But an analytical approach to questions that seem elementary often reveals aspects and problems which are quite new and very interesting. So, to return to our original question, let us say that a figure is defined by its *outline*, which as a rule is taken to mean a line or series of lines which form a boundary around the figure we recognize as being significant. However, we have already seen examples of figures which lack outline, and yet we have still recognized them as real figures. To understand this fact, let us go back and try to work out, from the physiological point of view, what happens when we see the outline of a figure.

Look at the figure at top left: our perception of its outline

stems from a sudden change of stimulus in two contiguous zones of the retina. The result of this transition may be a difference in clarity, as in A, or an unexpected change of colour, as happens in the perception of the grey circle within the dark green square (B).

In a sense the very words you are reading in this book can be regarded as outlines, since they consist of a mass of fairly regular, dark-coloured lines which, standing out from the white background of the paper, give rise to continuous retinal stimulations. Seeing outlines is necessary for perception, which organizes visual stimuli into figures.

Let us now consider the illustration below: in A we see dots, which can be logically linked, as in B. Nobody would ever think of joining the dots as in C, where it is almost impossible to recognize the constellation of the Great Bear or the Plough. Obviously one can join the dots representing the stars of the Plough in innumerable ways; but one feels almost compelled to keep to the familiar arrangement, whereas the infinite number ways in which the lines could be linked are simply abstract possibilities.

Now take a look at the series of dots in the illustration above: in A the vast majority of people would admit to seeing a wavy line roughly in the shape of a capital "S," as outlined in B. But again, there are countless other ways in which it would be possible to join the dots, as, for example, can be seen in C. So why do we go for the wavy line rather than for the myriad of other arrangements?

The psychological term for this phenomenon is *virtual* or

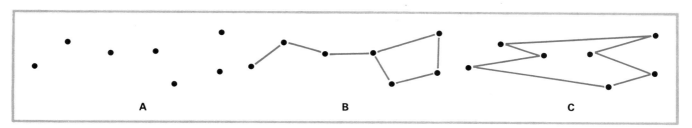

amodal lines, because, although they are not perceived to be present in the visual sensory pattern, they do determine the organization of the visual field in a much more forceful manner than the other lines which can be worked out only as a result of a conscious mental process.

Stars and constellations

When we look at the starry sky on a calm, moonless night, the sight of those numberless twinkling dots in space fills us with a sense of the infinite, of awe but seldom of fear. A determining influence on our feelings in these circumstances is that of culture, the knowledge that has been built up over the centuries. But try to imagine what our distant ancestors must have felt as they gazed at the thousand upon thousand specks of light in the sky. Might it not have been one of sheer confusion, even anxiety? They saw a mass of lights arranged chaotically, without any apparent order or meaning; and it would hardly be surprising if this strange perception of a myriad of undefined objects did not arouse in their minds a feeling of unease or even terror.

Seeing is in a sense bringing order to what strikes the eye. Primitive man, confronted by an apparently confused and chaotic jumble of images, surely felt the necessity of giving some form to the infinity of luminous dots in the heavens, of arranging them in accordance with familiar and easily recognizable patterns and contexts. We are probably not far from the truth in imagining that the *constellations* came about in this way. The need to overcome that impression of confusion and mystery conveyed by the heavenly sphere induced prehistoric man to fill the sky with everyday objects, bestowing the shapes of familiar animals and beings, real and imagined people on the thousands of stars. From these the constellations eventually received their names.

The division of the sky into constellations also had a practical purpose: grouping together stars, even if the links between them were imaginary, comparing them to objects of everyday experience, made it easier for them to be recognized. Furthermore, given that they were apparently immobile, they could be used as constant points of reference by travellers and navigators at sea. It is interesting to realize that such needs were felt in the same way by people and races from every part of the earth: the Chinese, the Chaldeans of Mesopotamia, the American Indians, the Incas and the Mayas all grouped the stars of the sky into their own constellations, even though these would often be arranged in different ways, with different names and meanings.

From the simple viewpoint of perception, the constellations are no more than patterns of virtual lines, which over the centuries have been given real and concrete meanings. Virtual lines are, in fact, binding links which our visual experience tells us are real, unlike the infinite number of lines which are geometrically possible but which we can only imagine and not perceive as actually existing.

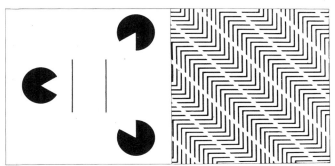

Whiter than white, blacker than black

In the two figures at the top, one is the negative of the other. The one on the left clearly shows a white triangle in the foreground, its three corners resting on three black discs. We notice too that we seem to see this triangle as whiter than the other white zones, although the conditions of stimulation are identical. The white of the background and the white of the triangle are exactly the same; yet because of its apparent whiteness, the triangle is perceived as being "above" or "in front," as if there were an opaque surface between us and the other figures. Perhaps even more surprising is that the triangle seems to have proper outlines although, as can be verified, this is an illusion, since there is no qualitative change of stimulation for most of the length of the triangle's sides.

What about the figure alongside on the right? Look carefully and you will see clearly a black triangle in the foreground, blacker than the black of the background. Here too the same remarks apply as for the adjoining white triangle. These properties might appear to be simple optical illusions, but some authors, particularly Gaetano Kanizsa (an Italian psychologist who has specialized in the problems of perception raised by such figures) prefer to describe them as "anomalies." The reason is quite simple: when we look at these drawings, we get the impression of the anomalous or abnormal appearance of figures with their own perfectly visible outlines, even though there are no conditions of stimulation that determine our recognition of outlines and edges. In terms of phenomena there is no difference, in fact, between these outlines and those corresponding to actual discontinuities in stimulation: the anomalous feature is the mechanism whereby the outlines are formed.

To what extent are these anomalous figures present under different conditions of stimulation? We can get a good idea of this by examining the two lower figures on the preceding page. You can probably recognize the first as an example of Ponzo's railway lines illusion (page 132); the line on the left appears longer than that on the right, although both are the same length. Take away the oblique lines and the effect of illusion remains (see illustrations on page 132). The second illustrates Hering's illusion (see page 131), in which the transverse segments obstinately refuse to look parallel although they really are. This distortion is produced by anomalous stripes, without any borders, just as occurs in the case of lines that are physically real.

The fact that these effects of perception persist even in more complex situations such as optical-geometric illusions is proof of the "resistance" or functional capacity of such patterns. Considering that Ponzo's illusion gives the same effect, this implies that we really do see the outlines of the figure. Is there a reason for this?

A puzzle of perception

Some of the figures we have just been examining are truly puzzling; it is difficult to convince ourselves that the various outlines are not physically present, for the harder we look, the more real they appear. And the figures as a whole look lighter than their light backgrounds or darker than their dark backgrounds. The perception of such anomalies has been attributed by some to a contrast of brightness, meaning that a white surface contiguous to one or more dark surfaces appears even whiter than it really is. This implies that the phenomenon of anomalous lines is a direct result of such a contrast. But let us take a look at the left-hand figure in the illustration below. Unlike the figure shown at top left of page 143, there are no black discs here to contrast with the white

square, so that there is a marked reduction of the dark areas. Even so, the perceptive effect of anomalous surfaces remains. If the increased brightness of the anomalous surfaces were to depend on the contrast between white and green, the circles on the right in the second figure ought to appear brighter, given that they are surrounded by dark outlines. Instead, as you can see quite clearly, it is the circles on the left which look brighter. This example shows that contrast in brightness is not a necessary condition for the formation of anomalous outlines and phantom figures.

It is not easy to explain these effects of perception, but it is worth mentioning a few theories which have the merit of being reasonably simple to understand. Phantom shapes, without real outlines, are apparently due to the tendency of our brain to "complete" the shape in the simplest possible manner. In other words, if we perceive certain figures as incomplete, we tend to fill in the missing parts. But although this tendency may be the principal factor in our perception of phantom outlines and figures, it is only the first step towards understanding the phenomenon.

Science works in the following way: once an explanation has been found, and a hypothesis formulated, it needs to be confirmed by the definition of new concepts connected with it. So, having attributed the perception of phantom lines and figures to the completing tendency of the brain, we have to clarify when and in what circumstances an object which we observe is perceived as "complete;" and this question leads to the more general consideration as to what we mean by this very term. When is a figure defective or incomplete? What is a lacuna or gap? Answers to these questions are needed in order to arrive at a scientific solution of this interesting problem of perception, but within our present terms of reference we cannot pursue the matter further.

Hidden messages

Examine the figure below, which at first glance appears to be an indistinct jumble of geometrical shapes. Actually it conceals the title of an extremely well-known play, and the aim of the puzzle is to try and decipher it.

The problem is complicated by the fact that the letters of the words that together make up the title of the play have been very simply but cleverly disguised so as not to be immediately legible.

VIOLONCELLO

The puzzle, which represents an example of perceptive camouflage, can be solved only by identifying the factor which prevents us seeing the phrase or phrases in their entirety. If you have not yet discovered the title of the play, cover the upper half horizontally with a non-transparent sheet of paper. You can now see clearly that the play is "Romeo and Juliet" by William Shakespeare.

The camouflaging element consists in the fact that the line of capital letters at the bottom has been repeated in a symmetrical and specular (mirror-like) fashion on top. The odd thing about the puzzle is that if we remove the piece of paper used for covering the top part, the letters once more disappear. In other words, having identified the individual letters composing the proverb, we are no longer aware of them when the factors originally disguising them are restored. What we perceive are circles, lozenges and various other kinds of geometrical shapes, all of which in some way prevent us recognizing the words. Some of the constituent letters are admittedly easy to make out even when symmetrically repeated, but other examples can be cited in which the camouflage factor operates to greater effect.

Can you read what is written in the figure at the top? By way of a clue we can tell you that it is the name of a musical instrument. Only after eliminating the camouflage factor is it possible to read "violoncello."

The perceptive phenomena represented by these elementary puzzles have been much studied and analysed. They prove that past experience exerts a powerful influence on the way in which we perceive objects, but only up to a certain point. When confronted by strong disturbing factors, as in the specularly symmetrical repetition of the letters in our examples, familiar objects are no longer recognizable and lose the meaning given to them by past experience.

Mimicry: one of nature's tricks

The disguised play title is an illustration of artificial camouflage. But nature provides innumerable instances of camouflage which we, with so many other things on our mind, simply do not notice. We all know that in spring woodland birds build nests in which to lay their eggs and raise their young, but these nests are not easily detected, for the birds conceal them most effectively in the trees, usually in the fork of several branches. From the ground it is almost impossible to see them, for not only are they the same colour as the branches but also hidden by the leaves. Only in late autumn, when most of the leaves have fallen, is it possible to see the places which the birds chose for building their now-deserted nests. Some species, such as magpies, and certain mammals, like squirrels, which are unable to hide their nests sufficiently well, build them instead at the top of high trees, as far as possible from likely predators.

The most widespread and interesting form of natural camouflage is *mimicry*, a form of adaptation whereby certain animals (and also plants), in order to protect themselves from predators, take on the colours and shapes of their surroundings. It is difficult, though not impossible, to detect a green praying mantis as it hops to and fro in a meadow; if we are looking carefully, we may catch a glimpse of it only at the very instant it moves, for when at rest it blends perfectly, in shape and colour, with the surrounding grass. Even more remarkable are the stick insects and leaf insects, so named because they imitate so perfectly the twigs and leaves on which they respectively settle. Those of our readers who go in for scuba diving will know from experience how difficult it is to spot an octopus clinging to a rock, or a flatfish, such as a sole, lying on the sandy bottom, and will perhaps have been deceived by fishes which look exactly like certain forms of seaweed. And there are of course countless other wonderful examples of natural camouflage.

Examples of animal mimicry. Left to right: a squid, whose body displays patches very similar to the vegetation on the sea bed; insects closely resembling thorns on twigs; a grasshopper from Borneo, capable of blending perfectly with the dead leaf on which it is resting.

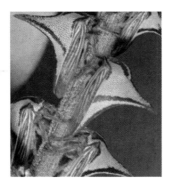
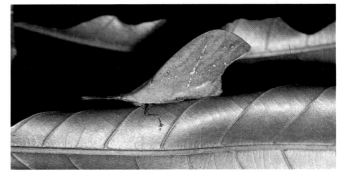

Military camouflage

The use of military camouflage to deceive the enemy is a practice that has been employed for many centuries and by many different armies. In modern times, however, it has become very sophisticated. Whether for personal use by infantrymen and commandos, or employed to disguise the whereabouts of important industrial or military installations, transport vehicles, aircraft, hangars and the like, it consists as a rule of irregular patches, mainly green and brown, so as to blend with the natural tones of the landscape. Camouflage of this type is widely employed in wartime to afford some protection against enemy air attacks, since it makes reconnaissance and accurate targeting difficult. For the same reason naval warships are generally painted a uniform light grey, which helps to conceal their outlines against sea and sky. The camouflage principles deliberately adopted for military purposes are the same as those which have evolved naturally among certain animals and plants.

It is possible, however, to create other situations, analagous to those already illustrated, in which invisibility depends not so much on colour as on general pattern. But these, too, are genuine examples of camouflage.

In the upper illustration, below, the hexagon on the left is contained in the figure on the right, yet is not perceived as such. Its presence can be verified by tracing its outline with a pencil, but it remains "invisible." The hexagon, in fact, is camouflaged inside the overall pattern in such a way that it cannot be singled out as an independent geometrical form. It is evident that the hexagon is completely contained within the

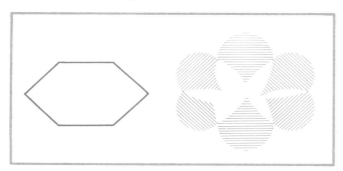

right-hand figure and that no part of its perimeter has been removed or altered. To put it in other words, the "noise" (see page 22) which prevents us seeing the hexagon is the new pattern of which it forms a part. This pattern is made up of lines which, taken together, give even the hexagon itself a new significance; and our eyes are compelled to accept it in this new context.

The first of the two figures at lower left may appear to be a large square with oblique lines arranged in smaller squares superimposed on the corners; but what you are seeing is actually a simple octagon, namely a regular polygon with eight sides and eight equal angles. Perception is here disturbed by the sets of parallel lines which, so to speak, remove the four faces of the octagon and incorporate them in another structure, causing them to change their function and their figurative significance.

We have already seen another example of camouflage in our "hidden play title" (page 144), where the "noise" is provided by the specular repetition of the letters. It is interesting to note, however, that a different and unusual arrangement of the same letters does not camouflage the phrase and make it hard to read (top figure).

Our conclusion is therefore that certain familiar shapes and figures lose their meaning and take on a new one when they are incorporated, wholly or partially, in new structures.

Past experience

The manner in which we perceive objects is largely conditioned by past experience, namely all those occasions on which we have repeated the same perceptive experience. Somewhere in our brain there is, figuratively speaking, a

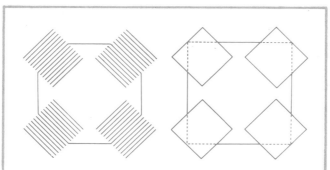

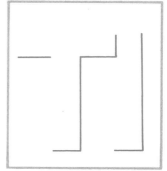

ABCDEF

II I2 I3 I4 I5

bundle of accumulated experience which imposes itself strongly whenever the same stimuli strike the field of vision. In other words, past experience in some way directs our capacity of perception, enabling us to recognize certain objects, or certain details, and not others, furnishing them with a particular meaning.

When we see an apple, we perceive a meaningful object, and not an indistinct mass of visual stimuli. Perhaps an example from the realm of language will more clearly illustrate our argument. When we say "pen," the word strikes a chord in our intellect, in the sense that we all think of a precise object of characteristic shape and, possibly, colour. But if we read the same word the wrong way round, from right to left, i.e. "nep," it has no meaning for us; it is merely a jumbled arrangement of verbal stimuli. The same goes for, say, a house, a person or a work of art, which are not vague, indistinct elements of shapes and colours in the field of vision, but precisely a "house," "person" and "work of art."

As an example, look at the two figures at the base of the second column of the opposite page. The one on the left seems to be a confused jumble of random lines, without any meaning, whereas the one on the right is an ordered arrangement of the same lines which can be recognized as the capital letters "TI."

An object therefore has its own significance because our perception identifies it as such, but this depends to a large extent on our heritage of acquired experience and our individual needs and desires.

Although past experience is undoubtedly important, it is intermingled with other factors, among which a prime role is played by context. Look at the illustration above. Scanning the top line, you will read the second figure from the left as the capital letter "B"; but when you glance along the bottom line of numbers, you will identify the third figure, not as a "B" but as the numeral "13." Obviously, the difference between the two symbols, which are exactly alike, is their context. The same situations also apply to language, in which homophones (words with the same pronunciation, though not necessarily the same spelling, such as "fair" and "fare," "bow" and "bough," "right" and "write") take on different meanings according to the phrase or sentence (i.e. the context) of which

they are part. So the conclusion is that the same signs in different contexts have different meanings.

How good an observer are you?

Camouflage often assumes forms other than those already examined. Some figures look so complicated that one may easily overlook certain data. The capacity to see may also be defined as the ability to identify details of an image which are inconspicuous, insignificant or virtually camouflaged in the overall context.

Here is a little test to determine your capacity for spotting details. If you want to find out whether or not you are a good observer, examine the illustration below for about five minutes, then turn the page and have a look at the picture at bottom left. Take as much time as you need with this one: it is the same drawing, yet not exactly the same. Certain details have been changed in more or less obvious ways. Without turning back to the previous page, jot down those you have been able to discover. If there are nine changes on your list, you can count yourself a good observer (there are, in fact, twelve in all); if you have found more than nine, your capacity for observation is excellent. Should you only have spotted five or six, don't worry; it is all of matter of visual memory, and memory, as even the ancients knew, is a faculty which can be improved with exercise. Check your answers on page 150.

The poser of problems

To end this chapter, here are a couple of absorbing and surprising "camouflage" puzzles devised by Samuel Loyd (1841–1911), an American puzzlemaker who was keenly interested in problems and games that tested the mind. Born into a well-to-do family from Philadelphia, he was educated at public school up to the age of seventeen, but he never went to college; in fact, he was so obsessed with playing chess that for the next ten years he had little time for cultivating other interests. Loyd's chess problems and solutions made him famous wherever the game was played. In addition he devised thousands of puzzles and brainteasers, most of them mathematical, which are still remembered to this day. His

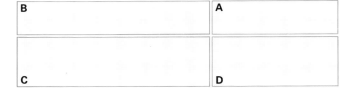

son, also named Sam, took up his father's work after the latter's death, but he was not such an original thinker and his books were little more than revisions of his father's works.

The vanished girl

Sam Loyd Sr is credited by enthusiasts with the following little-known puzzle, though it is not absolutely certain that he devised it.

The figure at the top of this page shows fifteen girls in various poses. If we rearrange the group, cutting the drawing into four rectangles as shown by the dotted lines and positioning them according to the pattern below the illustration itself, we can verify that there are, in fact, no longer fifteen young women, but only fourteen (see top of opposite page).

What can have happened to the girl who has vanished? If you try to solve this apparent paradox simply by checking the girls and the parts of them which have been fitted together, you will soon find that this is a blind alley. Actually, the question as to which girl has disappeared is itself misleading. The solution may appear more convincing if we first take a look at another similar puzzle.

Teddy and the lions

Probably the most famous puzzle to have been devised by Sam Loyd dates from 1896, and is called *Vanished from the Earth*. It

consists of a square sheet of cardboard with a circle in the middle, cut out so that it revolves smoothly: thirteen warriors are drawn in such a way that a part of each appears on the fixed square and part on the circle. When the circle is rotated, the parts can be rearranged so as to make one of the warriors disappear.

There are several versions of this puzzle; the one illustrated below is known as *Teddy and the lions*. If you count the number of lions and hunters in the left-hand drawing, you will find there are seven of each. But if you rotate the central disc so that it conforms to the illustration on the right, you will be able to count eight lions and six hunters. How is this possible? Where has the seventh hunter gone, and where has the eighth lion come from?

All is revealed

As we said before, such questions are no help at all in solving these puzzles. The very fact that the disappearance of one hunter is compensated by the addition of one lion should demonstrate that in fact nothing and nobody has vanished. At the instant of rotating the central circle, all the lions and all the hunters disappear together. When the disc comes to rest in the proper position, the various parts combine to form a new pattern because there is a different arrangement. The second drawing actually consists of a group of eight lions which are smaller than the original seven, while the hunters are slightly bigger. In other words, there are more lions, but smaller in size, and fewer hunters, but with bigger dimensions.

The reasoning is the same in the case of the vanished girl, for her apparent disappearance is likewise caused by the rearrangement of parts in the transition from the first to the second figure. When section A is put in the place of B, and vice versa, the entire figure is muddled up. There is no vanishing act here either; in fact, in the second one part of the girls is increased in size. If you compare the first girl in the first figure with the first girl in the second figure, you will see that the latter towers above the head of the former. In the second figure too the sizes of the fourth and the seventh girls (from the left) are also markedly larger in comparison with the corresponding girls in the first figure. So in this puzzle as well the disappearance of one girl is compensated by the increase in size of the others. Still unconvinced? Compare the dimensions by tracing the corresponding figures and placing one on top of the other.

The disappearing line

The foregoing explanation may perhaps have left some of our readers unsatisfied. Admittedly, the figures used as examples contain so many details that it is not easy to understand the solutions and see clearly just how the individual parts are combined and compensated. We have therefore devised

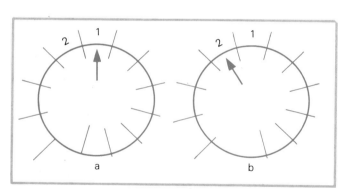

another version for you in which it is easier to see exactly what is happening and come to the correct solution. By posing this problem we are again following the basic method of scientific inquiry. When the factors involved in verifying a phenomenon become so numerous as to make its analysis difficult, if not impossible, the scientist recreates a simpler version of the same thing in the laboratory; simpler in the sense that it isolates the factors or reduces their number in order to make the inquiry easier.

Look carefully at the two circles in the figure above: their circumference is divided into segments by various perpendicular lines, the arrows indicating no. 1 in the first circle and no. 2 in the second circle. If you cut circle a along the circumference so that it can be rotated until it reaches position

b, you will find that one of the segments dividing the circumference has disappeared. When, in fact, the circle is in position a, with the arrow pointing to no. 1, you can count twelve lines; but when it is rotated so that the arrow points to no. 2, there are only eleven lines.

Where has the line gone? Actually it has not vanished at all. We can show this by resorting to one of the most elementary principles of geometry which states that *the whole is always equal to the sum of its parts, no matter how the parts are rearranged.*

Let us now go back to our puzzle: the transition of circle a to circle b does not result in the loss of any part but only in a new arrangement. In other words, when the circle moves from the first to the second position, the twelve segments are arranged so as to give only eleven, each of them a little longer than the original twelve. This one line which appears to have disappeared has really gone to join the others. To check this and to understand it even more clearly, measure each of the segments dividing the first circumference and calculate their overall length; then do the same thing with the segments of the second circumference, and you will see that the total length of the segments is exactly the same as in the first case. This is only one example of a problem or a puzzle in which the solution may not be found because we fail to apply some fundamental principle.

"Are you a good observer?" – Solution

The interplay of light and colour

*Experience. The shadow thrown
by the light of the candle and illuminated by the natural light
of morning turns blue; the shadow thrown by daylight
(a shadow which is weaker and becomes deeper the farther
you distance yourself from the light)
and brightened by candlelight turns red.
The shadow thrown by candlelight,
very close to the light source, has glints of green.*
(Friedrich Hegel, Jena Aphorisms)

Light and shadow

The following experiment is easy to carry out but you need to have a keen eye. If you stand with the sun behind you and look at the shadow thrown on the ground by your body, you will notice, if you look carefully, a zone of half light between the area of deep shadow and the area of full light. Now observe how the light is distributed in these three zones: in the area of deep shadow it is uniformly weak, in the half light it is gradated, and in the zone of full light it is uniformly strong. What is particularly interesting, however, is that in the darker part of the zone of half light you will see that a narrow band, similarly dark, has formed, and that in the lighter part a thin bright band has appeared. If this experiment proves difficult to follow there are other ways in which the same effect can be more clearly demonstrated.

The blue strips

In everyday life we normally perceive things in their entirety: only for practical purposes of work or research are we likely to analyse them in terms of shape, size, colour and other constituent elements. Thus genuine optical illusions can also be produced by colour, as is well known by painters who use such effects skilfully for expressive ends. Look carefully at the figure on the right: the series of strips ranges from light blue to dark blue through varying shades (left to right). The interesting thing to notice is what happens to the left-hand edge of each band; the colour appears brighter on the left and darker on the right part of the strip, although the shade does not actually vary at all from one side to the other. To confirm this, take two sheets of paper and place them on either side of any band; contrary to what you saw before, the variations of shading vanish and the colour is uniformly distributed. Now remove the pieces of paper and look at the overall figure once more; the borders of each strip again appear to be shaded.

This is a very important phenomenon in the study of perception. Consider that when we begin a drawing, we almost always sketch an outline. Many prehistoric drawings and certain pictographs demonstrate that the technique of sketching things in outline represents one of the earliest developments in the history of art. For more than a thousand years painters have been aware of the importance of outlining adjacent areas to heighten the contrasts of colour and luminosity (brightness). It is only in fairly recent times, however, that this problem has become a subject for scientific discussion.

The Mach bands

Ernst Mach (1838–1916), as many readers will know, was an Austrian scientist, primarily a physicist, but keenly interested as well in philosophy and psychology. We have already drawn attention to his dihedron, one of the most typical reversible figures, on page 76. But his name is also associated with the analysis and description of the phenomenon known in the nineteenth century as the *Mach bands*. It is worth describing these briefly here, if only because it is one of the most convincing examples of the subjective contribution to perception. As with all phenomena which are outside everyday experience, this one can only be appreciated by personal testing. So we suggest treating this experiment as yet another interesting game. It will convince you of the existence of certain perceptive realities.

Take an opaque card and place it under a normal fluorescent tube, as illustrated in the figure below; the effect will be even

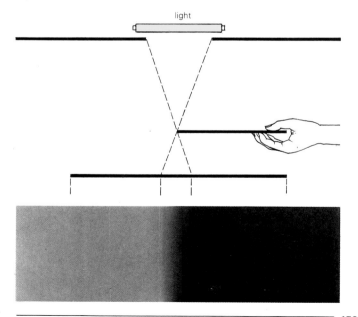

more striking if there are no other lights in the room and if you cover the two ends of the tube. The light is projected on to a sheet of white or grey paper from a height of about 30 centimeters (12 inches). Part of this sheet is illuminated by the light coming from the entire length of the fluorescent tube. Now hold the opaque card about 2 centimeters (1 inch) above the paper: between the illuminated area and the dark part there is a zone of half light. Logically, the light ought to have a uniformly bright distribution in the illuminated part, a uniformly weak distribution in the dark area, and uniform shading in the transitional zone. But concentrate your attention on that zone of half light: at the outer edge, where it tones into the illuminated area, you will see a thin but conspicuous bright band, while on the other side, where it blends with the dark area, there is a thin dark band. These are the Mach bands, which are the result of purely subjective intensification and thus not real, caused by the manner in which we perceive light with our eyes and by the structure of the lighting used.

The effect is so striking that some people cannot believe it to be merely a subjective fact. The bands appear vertically in the center of the figures at the top of this page. They are explained by the mechanisms of excitation and inhibition to which the cells of the retina and the brain are subjected, cells which are responsible for the reception and organization of the visual stimuli emanating from the contrasting zones. To venture more deeply into these questions would entail discussion of neurophysical theories which lie outside the province of this book and which could be tedious. Suffice it to say that in everyday life we experience comparable effects of contrast without being aware of them.

Artistic effects

The phenomenon we have just illustrated in the form of a game has long been utilized by artists, but only recently has it been scientifically analysed. We do not know exactly when the effect of outlines on the perception of contrast was first discovered, but it is very likely to have been associated with the development of some new technique in the visual arts, and not only in this field. Once verified, such a technique would then have been consolidated and transmitted from generation to generation. And one may suppose that, being known, it would have been applied to other areas of activity as well. Thus there is evidence of its use in China near the end of the tenth century; and it is still employed generally in oriental art. The outline-contrast effect has been widely exploited too

Below: if we look at a photograph in which the subject is illuminated from the side, it is clear that the light has the effect of bringing out shapes, giving them volume and weight by alternation of light and shade.

Right: a photograph in which the plastic effect of the forms is obtained by soft lighting carefully set up in the studio. As a rule, we can say that light determines the way in which we perceive objects.

in certain ceramic processes since antiquity: and many pieces of pottery owe their particular appeal to such procedures.

The French neo-impressionist painter Paul Signac (1863–1935) was a keen observer of the effects of contrast in shade and half light. Indeed, the principal key to understanding his works resides in the luminous contrasts of adjacent areas and the outlines derived from them.

A few words on light

In describing these special perceptive experiences, we have frequently mentioned light, which gives prominence and consistency to the objects that surround us and enables us to see their shapes and judge their dimensions.

Let us ask ourselves, however, in what way light gives "body" to things. If we look at the pictures on this page and, even more particularly, things around us, we can easily understand that they acquire volume from the contrast of brightness and darkness. Simple observation of objects shows that parts are illuminated and parts are in shadow. The contrast of light and dark, in turn, varies according to the intensity of the light source and the shape of the objects concerned: the greater the light intensity, the greater the contrast.

No doubt you will have noticed that if an object is angular in shape, the contrast is sharp, whereas if it is round, the contrast from light to dark is gradual. Chiaroscuro (the distribution of light and shade) also determines the volume of things; and volume, as we know, can be measured in height, breadth and depth i.e. in three dimensions.

All these aspects, which combine to make up visual experience, depend on light. And if we remember, as we shall soon see, that light is broken up into colours and therefore can be defined essentially as colour, we can appreciate in what sense it is the constituent element of vision.

An amusing experiment

Have you ever looked closely at a glass of water from above? Do it now and you will notice that the bottom of the glass seems to be much closer to the eye than the surface it is standing on, although this is not really so. Take a felt pen and, from the same position, mark on the outside of the glass the point where the bottom seems to be situated; you will find that it is some way from the actual bottom. If you have difficulty in locating the exact point, find it with the help of a drinking straw. You can also measure the deviation by comparing the levels of water below and above the pen mark. More precise measurements are needed of course for other parameters such as the velocity of light in water, but this is obviously a far more complicated matter.

The explanation of this phenomenon has to do with the light waves emanating from the bottom of the glass, which are deflected when they pass through water. As a result, anyone observing the glass from above gets the impression that the light waves stem from a point situated higher than the actual base of the glass. You may have experienced the same kind of illusory effect when diving into water; although it may look quite shallow as you look down, it often turns out to be considerably deeper. In a swimming pool the depths are of course marked; but if you want to avoid a rude shock, think twice before jumping into an invitingly clear pond or lake.

The paradox of colour

Readers will surely be convinced by now that perception of objects, despite superficial appearances, is not a simple phenomenon. And perhaps no aspect of the perceptive process is as paradoxical as the sensation of colour. Light, which our eye sees as colourless, is in fact a synthesis of all colours. There is no actual colour, say, in a bar of soap, even if it appears to be pale pink or lavender; the colour exists only as a sensation.

Although we move about in a world of many varied colours, this does not imply that things are, in reality, coloured; it means simply that objects reflect part of the light which strikes them and that these radiations produce our perception of colours.

The light of the sun, which we see as white and which, although white is a colour, we take to be colourless, is actually the source of all colours. Yet this is only one small aspect of a highly complex and fascinating subject. Some objects have a "chameleon" effect, appearing at some given moment to be one colour and then, an instant later, another colour. And what of two colours which, when mixed together, produce a third colour?

Light cannot truly be a combination of all colours because of the variations of the actual sources of light and the diversity of reflecting surfaces. Most of you will have seen what happens when drops of petrol are spilt into sea water or just into a

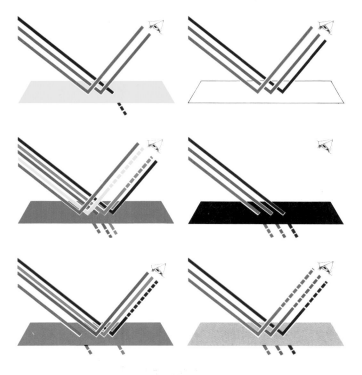

The three diagrams on the left show that when light strikes an object (which does not reflect it perfectly as in the case of a mirror) some luminous frequencies are absorbed and others reflected, so that the object appears to be coloured according to the frequencies it reflects and according to the proportions in which they are reflected.

Here, we see how three surfaces, which appear respectively to be coloured yellow, magenta and cyan, absorb and reflect radiations of different wavelengths.

The three right-hand diagrams, from top to bottom, show how an object appears white if it reflects uniformly and in a very high percentage the incident rays, black if it absorbs almost all the rays, and mid-grey if it absorbs fifty per cent of them.

Opposite page: the breaking up of white light by means of a prism.

puddle of rain. The effect is very similar to that of a miniature rainbow in which you can see all the colours of the spectrum.

Merely a sensation

The truth, hard as it is for us to grasp, is that colour does not itself exist. It is we who see things as coloured, although they are not. Ask anyone what colour leaves are at night, when there is no light, and the answer will be green, even though nothing can be seen. And the reply will be unhesitating and positive, as if green were an intrinsic quality of leaves, an essential component of their being. Yet colour is no more than a collection of electromagnetic waves which, when they strike our retinal receptors, produce coloured sensations. Leaves transmit to us only certain types of radiations, that convey to us the sensation of green, but if the radiations were different, the leaves too would appear a different colour. We call leaves "green" only by convention, meaning that this is the name we always apply to a certain type of sensation.

Our normal attitude to colour, and to perception in general, as we go about our daily affairs, is thus based on misconception. Simply because leaves provide us with the sensation that we are in the habit of calling "green," we assume that this "green," rather than being a subjective experience, is a vital component of leaves, along with the water, carbon and other elements of which they consist.

A grey world

According to some religious doctrines, the soul, after the death of the body, continues to live, entering into other living creatures. Whoever has been good and virtuous is transformed into another human being and will live happily, but whoever has done evil and is unworthy of his fellow creatures, will not deserve human form and will become an animal, such as a dog, a cat, a horse or something else.

There is always some vestige of truth in myths and strange beliefs. Man's insuppressible instinct for justice has fed his imagination and led him, through religious faith, to devise all manner of special punishments for those who have transgressed. Whoever returned after death to live as a dog, a horse or another mammal was subjected to a particularly heavy form of punishment: he was destined to see the world as grey. Justice for those who had not done good in their earthly existence thus entailed the loss of chromatic vision. Science suggests, in fact, that mammals below the rank of primates do not see the world in colours but everything in grey. This is curious because other animals undoubtedly possess chromatic vision.

Let us try to imagine what it would be like to see the world without the colours which have so much influence on our moods and emotions. We can see the advantage of perceiving things in colour by comparing a film or television programme in colour with one in black and white. A world that was prevalently grey would be poor and dull indeed compared to the rich and colourful variety of the world we actually inhabit, for it is colour that gives it life and beauty.

We rightly attribute enormous importance to our perception of colour, which is a fundamental aspect of vision and which affects our sensations to such an extent that it is virtually impossible to imagine a grey world.

A word on theory

We can better understand the behaviour of light and some of its strange and paradoxical effects if we pause for a moment to consider some elementary theoretical notions.

Light is simply a form of energy consisting of electromag-

netic waves, which travel in a straight line and with an undulating motion in all directions at the extraordinary speed of 300,000 km (186,281 miles) per second. When you look at the red disc of the setting sun, you are seeing something that is no longer there; the sun has already disappeared, but the light it sends out takes about eight minutes to reach the earth. The wavelengths of the electromagnetic rays range from a maximum to a minimum and, like all measurements of length, are measured on the metric scale in km, m, cm, mm and μ: the last letter indicates a *micron* i.e. one-thousandth of a millimeter. It is difficult to imagine a millimeter divided into a thousand parts, but you must in fact go further and think of it as divided into a million parts, because the human eye perceives wavelengths ranging from 380 millimicrons (the colour violet) to 780 millimicrons (the colour red); and the millimicron (mμ) is the measure of length indicating one-millionth of a millimeter.

A miniature rainbow

If you look at a waterfall crashing down into a chasm and rebounding in clouds of tiny droplets of water, you may see, if you are standing in the right position, a miniature rainbow in all its colours. It is a very fascinating and beautiful sight.

It is possible to recreate the colours of the rainbow in their order by using a simple device known as an *optical prism*. The light travels in a straight line, but if a ray strikes a piece of glass at an acute angle, its trajectory is deviated or, in scientific terms, is subjected to *refraction*. If a piece of glass has the form of a triangular prism (illustration above), the ray travelling through it is slowed up: encountering a new surface and passing into a new medium, it is thus refracted and then resumes the direction of its incident path. In so doing, the light is broken up into a multicoloured band, just as we see in a rainbow. The tiny drops of water suspended in the air resemble miniature prisms which together break up the light of the sun and then form the phenomenon known as the rainbow.

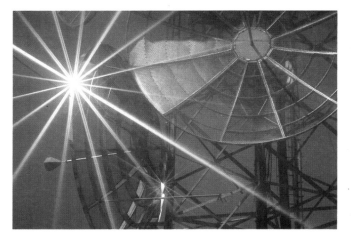

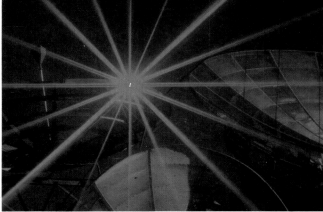

The band which recreates, in sequence, the colours of the rainbow when a ray of light passes through a prism is known as the *solar spectrum*.

Actually we do not see all rays, only those that stimulate our retinal receptors.

The colours of the spectrum correspond to various wavelengths: the longest produce the red extremity of the rainbow, the shortest the violet extremity.

The effect of light on colour

You may often have seen a woman who, before buying a dress or length of material, takes it outside the shop to examine it by daylight. She does this for a very sound reason, namely to see the "true" colours in natural light, knowing full well that certain shades, such as red, are falsified under the fluorescent lights of the shop, whereas sunlight brings out the colours even more.

The electromagnetic waves of the artificial lighting are, in fact, concentrated in certain regions of the spectrum, whereas solar light distributes luminous energy uniformly throughout the spectrum thus giving things the right quantity of light for reflection. Colour therefore is better observed in daylight, although obviously it will undergo considerable variations according to season, weather, cloudiness, atmospheric conditions and, above all, time of day: as the hours of the day vary, so too does the angle of inclination at which the light rays strike the ground. It is not advisable, for example, to examine coloured objects when the sky is calm and clear, and the rays travelling perpendicularly i.e. with maximum intensity; light which is too intense diminishes the capacity to distinguish all colours properly, for they seem to become rather whiter. Ideal conditions are provided by sunlight in a sky with only a few clouds, coming from the north and in a vertical direction: the optimal colour of an object will therefore be evident in such conditions of optimal light.

In the tunnel

Modern life, especially in cities, moves at an ever faster pace, and increasing pressures sometimes disturb our peace of mind. However, something that is not sufficiently realized is, that of all the human senses it is our vision which every day comes under the heaviest pressure and which is most easily impaired. Artificial lighting, computers and activities such as driving, reading, writing and typing all place a strain on our eyesight and test our visual capacity to the limit.

To take a concrete example, let us reconstruct the work that the eyes of a car driver are expected to perform in the

Above, in bad weather, at night and in tunnels, the eyesight of a car driver is subjected to continuous strain as a result of having to correct stimuli which are often deceptive.
Top left: a non-neutral light falsifies perception of colours; in the right-hand photograph the light exposing the film is modified by means of a red filter placed over the lens, thus resulting in a major change of colour: the light blue sky has been transformed into a black night sky and the solar reflections (involving a cross-screen) seem to be rays emitted from a red beacon.

course of travelling through a tunnel lit by sodium lamps.

The lights are positioned at regular intervals in one or two lines. As the car moves along, the lights seem to come toward the driver. The closer he gets, the greater appears to be the distance between them; and those that are farthest away appear to be moving slowly, increasing speed as the car passes beneath them. Once past, they appear to slow down and as they recede they get smaller. In addition, the rows of lights and the gleaming mosaic of tiles on the roof and walls of the tunnel are reflected in the shining bonnet of the car, forming an inverted image which also appears to be moving. The driver is also usually aware of the red tail lights of the car ahead, and calculates his distance from their size and brightness. To his left or right (depending on the rules of the road) are the headlights of approaching cars. These lights, when very close, vanish and are replaced by the red tail lights in the rear mirror, which also reflects the headlights of the cars behind.

There are other visual illusions that could be mentioned, but here we are concerned only with those relating to colour. To the driver the colours of the other cars travelling through the tunnel look strange; it is evident that his eyes cannot be trusted and that the true colour of these cars cannot be judged until he is out of the tunnel. The same applies to night driving wherever sodium vapour lamps are used to illuminate roads and highways. These lamps emit a very strong monochromatic yellow light which is visible for a considerable distance even in adverse weather conditions such as snow and fog. Their light causes a marked modification of colours: thus a yellow car will gleam an even brighter yellow, but red and blue cars appear to be grey. In fact, sodium vapour lamps emit almost all their energy in two wavelengths located in the yellow part of the spectrum, which is why little of the colour of red and blue cars is left for reflection.

Travelling through a brightly lit tunnel can therefore give rise to a number of illusory effects which simultaneously involve shape, movement and, as we have seen, colour. So a series of visual mechanisms must come into play very rapidly in order to correct the stimuli deriving from the special conditions of such surroundings.

The play of colours

If you take a fairly large magnifying glass and put it up against your colour television screen, you will observe numbers of small dots made up of the three fundamental colours, red, green and blue, which are successively repeated. All the variously coloured pictures that we see on the screen are the result of the mixture of these three colours alone. Television is merely the technological application of a principle of the *trichromatic theory*, which in simple terms says that only three colours, red, green and blue, are needed to obtain all the others. The theory of colour vision, first formulated by the English physicist Thomas Young (1773–1829), was further

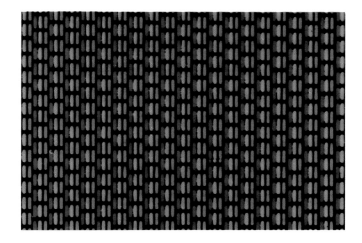

Above: an enlarged image of the phosphors of a colour kinescope. Below: additive synthesis obtained by projecting lights in the primary colours of red, green and blue-violet. The superimposition of the three coloured circles in the center of the screen gives an area of white.

developed by the German physicist and physiologist Hermann von Helmholtz (1821–94). His hypothesis was confirmed by studies of the nervous structures responsible for the functioning of vision, and to some extent it is still valid today. Von Helmholtz stated that there are three *primary colours*, blue, green and red, and that these are associated with three types of cones (see page 60), namely three types of retinal receptors "programmed" to receive these three colours;

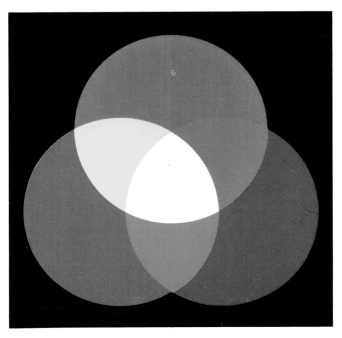

perception of colour therefore is the result of the most varied stimulations of these three receptors. Thus red and green together give the sensation of yellow, while yellow and blue produce grey. When the colours are produced by two or more coloured light rays, we call it *additive synthesis*. If the three primary radiations are projected on to a screen (lower figure on preceding page), we get a white light, equivalent to that which is obtained from all the rays of the spectrum.

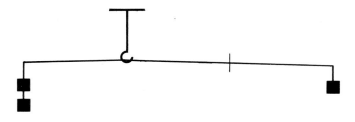

Colour composition and measurement

The trichromatic theory can be expressed visually in the following way. The figure at top right shows a rod. If two equal weights are placed at either end, the barycenter or center of gravity is in the middle, but if the weights are different, the center of gravity will shift to the side of the greater weight. Now we progress from the rod to an equilateral triangle, made up of narrow meshes, with weights hung from its corners. If the three weights are equal (lower left figure), the triangle's center of gravity will be at the geometrical center of the figure. But if three different weights are hung from the corners (lower right figure), the center of gravity will no longer be as before but will be shifted. The whole triangle will thus appear to be made up of an almost infinite number of points or centers of gravity.

Now let us revert to the trichromatic theory. The fact that every colour can be obtained by the additive synthesis of the three primary colours is the basis of the model known as the *barycentric triangle* (shown below). The vertices here represent red, blue and green; the mixture of different quantities of these colours gives another colour; the center of the triangle represents white, where the quantities of these three constituent colours are equal; the points forming the sides represent those colours formed by the mixture of only two colours, the so-called *secondary colours*: the central point of side *RV*, for example, is yellow, of side *BV* peacock blue, and of *RB* violet. It is interesting to note that the *complementary* of a colour, in this example represented by point *H* on side *RB*, is point *K*, where the extension of straight line *HO* intersects side *BV* of the triangle. Thus every segment which passes through the center *O* and touches the opposite side links two complementary segments. Each colour has its complementary: blue-yellow, green-violet and so on.

Symphony of colours

Walt Disney's famous cartoon film *Fantasia* underlined the links that certainly exist between music and colour. Our

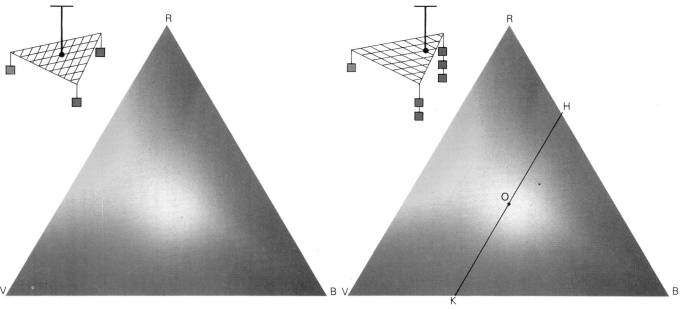

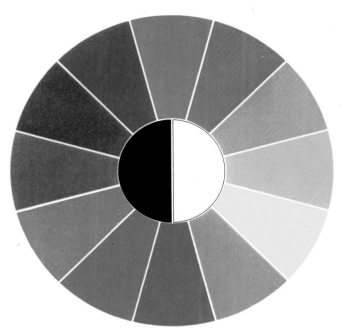

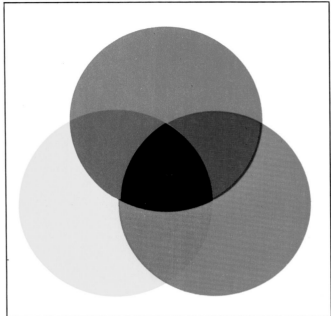

Above: chromatic circle divided into twelve sections; each colour is situated opposite its complementary colour.

Right: subtractive synthesis of primary colours (cyan, yellow, magenta). The area in the center is black.

senses of vision and hearing have something in common, as this analogy will show. If we strike all the keys of a piano together, we do not hear music, but an indistinct and indeed rather unpleasant noise; and if we combine lights of every colour, we see the colour white, which we perceive to be colourless. Just as music is created by playing a few notes at a time in succession, so we see colours by assembling (or, as will be shown, subtracting) only a few colours. The play of colours is, in fact, infinite; as infinite as the combination of notes that make up music.

The majority of colours which we see in nature are nevertheless formed by subtraction or, in other words, by the filtration of certain radiations and the reflection of others. All things, in fact, apart from transparent media, possess molecules known as *pigments*, which have the power to absorb specific waves of the spectrum and to reflect others. And we see things that are naturally coloured not because of the radiations which they "subtract" from solar light but because of those which they send back. Thus we see the leaves of trees as green because they absorb all the other radiations and send back only those corresponding to "green." This is the principle of *subtractive synthesis*, the basis of the mixing of colours and varnishes on the palette. In contrast to additive synthesis, it is easier in subtractive synthesis to predict the colour that will result. Blue and yellow, for example, commonly give green, while red and yellow produce orange, and so forth.

Tonality, luminosity and saturation

There are certain basic characteristics of colour which we need to be aware of in order to get a better understanding of chromatic perception. When we perceive a colour, the experience is conditioned by three fundamental qualities: tonality, luminosity (brightness) and saturation.

The term *tonality* describes the colour tone or shade, the quality which makes a yellow differ from another colour such as an orange or a green etc. *Luminosity*, as its name suggests, is the quality which makes one colour more luminous (brighter) or darker than another; it may depend on the intensity of the light, but also on the condition of the eye. A third parameter used to define colour is *saturation*, which is the true and actual measurement of the colour of a given subject. When we say that one red is deeper than another red, we refer in the main to its saturation. Colours with little saturation are greyish, near to grey, while saturated colours appear to contain no grey. It should be emphasised, however, that saturation is a matter of perception and has nothing to do with the composition of colours.

These three qualities may vary individually but it is obvious that they are jointly determined by the conditions of light and by the eye.

"Colourless" colours

"Colourless" is a simplified translation of the term "achromatic," from the Greek *a-chroma*, meaning "lacking colour."

So how can colours be described as colourless? It seems to be a contradiction in terms.

The colours commonly described as achromatic are those which are considered only in terms of the criterion of luminosity, from very dark, or *black*, through the range of *grey*, to very bright, or *white*. So are black, grey and white therefore colours or are they not? The answer is that it all depends on the point of view. We feel the sensations of grey, white and black, so psychologically they exist. But they do not exist physically, because white light is made up of all the radiations of the visible spectrum, whereas black, in fact, respresents the absence of light.

In terms of pigments, however, black, grey and white are regarded as colours and hence they do exist: white is a primary colour because it is not obtainable with other colours, whereas black is a secondary colour because it is a mixture of other colours.

Why is the sun red when it sets?

We can now understand why certain natural phenomena occur. At dusk, when the sun sinks slowly over the horizon and its rays strike the surface at an increasingly oblique angle, the blue and violet radiations, with their short wavelengths, rapidly disappear because the atmosphere through which they have to travel is thicker and does not permit them to penetrate; so they undergo filtration in favour of those radiations with longer wavelengths (from red to yellow), which, possessing more penetrative force, spread in all directions. This is why, as it sets, the sun first appears yellow on the horizon, and then red, until it vanishes, while the clouds turn red and pink until darkness falls.

. . . and why is the sky blue?

The sky appears blue particularly after a storm but also on some windy days when the air is clearer and seems to be rid of all impurities.

Broadly speaking, the blue colour of the sky is the result of a combination of related phenomena. The sunlight which reaches our eyes goes through a series of transformations: changes of speed, diffusion and direction, depending on the nature and composition of the medium through which it passes. This medium is usually constituted by the atmosphere, which teems with an infinite number of the minutest solid or liquid particles: gas molecules, dust, seeds, pollen, water droplets and so on. The last, present in vast amounts, may assume small dimensions, as in clouds and mist, or larger ones, as in rain. They refract light in different ways, according to their size. The irregularity and variety of the particles suspended in the air cause irregularities in the diffusion, dispersion and reflection of the light; all of these phenomena

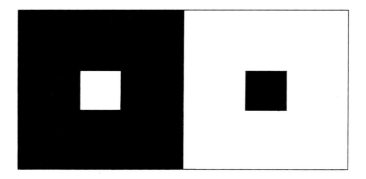

together create the characteristic blue colour of the sky. So when we see it as blue, it is because the innumerable tiny particles in the air, struck by light containing a preponderance of blue and violet rays, give out this colour. For similar reasons the sky sometimes seems to change to a very pale blue sometimes appearing almost white.

Half full or half empty?

Take a liter bottle containing exactly half a liter of wine and ask someone whether it is half full or half empty. The initial reaction is likely to be, "Surely it's the same thing?" Yet the question is not as silly as it sounds. If, in fact, we set the bottle among a series of bottles full of wine, the answer will probably be that it is half empty; but if it is put in the middle of a lot of empty bottles, the likely reply will be that it is half full. These are shades of emphasis which nevertheless have a very different psychological significance. What makes the two situations different, that of the half-full bottle surrounded by empty bottles and the half-empty bottle surrounded by full bottles, is the different context in which the key object is placed: when the background changes, the object too is perceived to be different, although actually it remains the same.

This phenomenon also explains what happens when we perceive colours.

A matching game

Here is an experiment which you can treat as a game and which will show you just how subjective colour perception really is.

Take two sheets of paper, one white and the other black: they will serve as backgrounds for squares of various colours. To begin, take a white square and place it on the black sheet, then take a black square of the same size and place it on the white sheet. The first square, the white on the black, will appear bigger than the other (see the figure above). What is it that conditions such perception? Obviously the apparent difference in size is due to the difference in background: the black ground makes the white square appear larger, even though this is not, in fact, the case.

Now cut out a grey square and place it alternately on the white and black sheets of paper: here, too, the grey square on the black sheet is perceived to be markedly bigger than when it is placed on the white sheet. And the black background also makes the same square look brighter. The same thing happens when you take squares of other colours, such as yellow, red, green or blue: the colours will look appreciably brighter on the black sheet than on the white. And the reason is the same. This matching game becomes more complicated when the background sheets are themselves coloured. If you take a blue square and place it successively on a green sheet and then on a yellow sheet, the square will first appear brighter and then darker. Similarly, a yellow square placed on a blue sheet will appear more luminous than when it is set on an orange sheet.

Even colour changes

The manner in which we perceive colours is influenced by a number of subjective factors. Look at the two squares shown

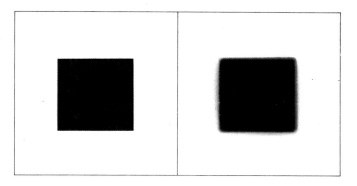

in the illustration at the top of this page: the colour of the left-hand square is clear, like its outlines, which makes it stand out sharply. But the outlines of the square on the right are rather blurred, and as a result there is a change in the way we see the entire surface. It even looks as if the two squares are painted in different colours. The right-hand square appears almost opaque and fuzzy, as if it were sprinkled with dust, whereas the one on the left is clear, compact and solid. Yet the two squares, apart from the difference in outlines, are absolutely identical in colour and the apparent difference is merely a consequence of the subjective manner in which we see them. If you don't believe it, cover the blurred parts of the right-hand square with two pieces of paper, and you will see that its colour is exactly the same as that of the other square. This shows that although only the edges of the square differ,

Below: a grey, a yellow, a red and a light green, when seen on a white ground, appear darker and less luminous than the same colours on a black ground.

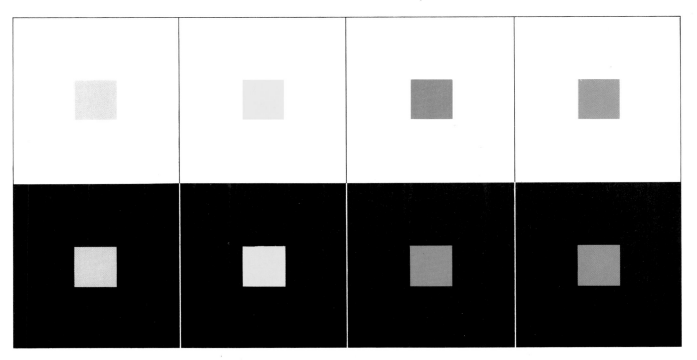

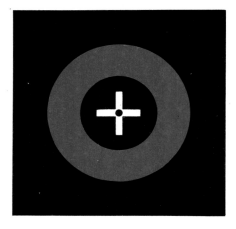

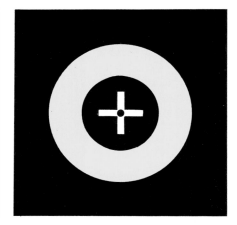

this factor extends its influence to the overall perception of the figure's colour. The same effect is to be seen with any other colour.

Consecutive images

If we stare for a long time at the setting sun and then quickly shift our gaze to another spot, we will notice that the image of the sun lingers, its outlines toned down, for about two minutes. At first it retains its initial colour, but gradually it changes to a darkish blue, which is the complementary colour

of the original stimulus. This type of experience has long been recognized and was described by observers such as Aristotle, Leonardo and Newton. In the vocabulary of the psychology of perception there is a distinction between a *positive post-humous image*, which forms as soon as the stimulus ceases and which appears with the same colour features, and a *negative posthumous image*, which appears afterwards in the complementary colour of the positive image.

A test of this can be made by observing the illustration above. Look hard for about twenty seconds at the black dot in the center of the cross inside the blue circle, then shift your gaze to the dot in the center of the grey square. You will get the sensation of seeing a yellow circle around it. Pause a while

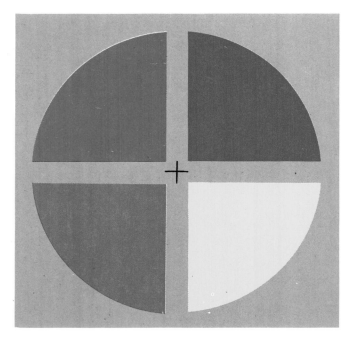

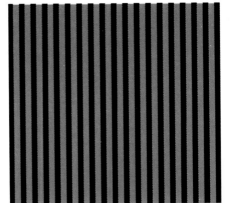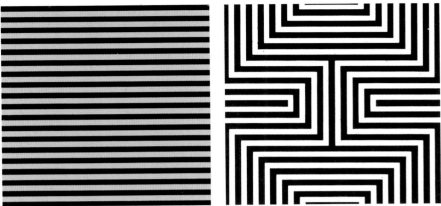

and then look for twenty seconds or so at the dot inside the yellow circle, move your eyes as before to the dot in the middle of the grey square, and you will see a blue circle. This is a simple example of consecutive negative images, which means that the image appears immediately in the complementary colour of the colour under observation.

If you now look at the two figures at the bottom of the opposite page, following the same procedure, you will see the same thing happening simultaneously in the complementary colours of red, green, blue and yellow.

The phenomenon of consecutive negative images relates not only to colour but also to other aspects of the visual stimuli, such as form and movement.

Linked consecutive images

In the sequence of figures shown above, look at the first grid for ten seconds and then at the second one for the same time. Do this consecutively for about ten minutes and then look at the black and white pattern: the horizontal lines will appear reddish and the vertical lines greenish. If you rotate the page through 90 degrees, you will readily see that the colour relationship is reversed.

The mysterious city

Our next diversion is a kind of holiday in colour. Some time ago a travel agency offered an interesting package to its more adventurous clients: a visit to a mysterious city which in addition proved to be an adventure in self-discovery. Having arrived at their destination, each person had the choice of entering the city by any one of three entrance gates. What happened next was up to each individual. When their trip was over and they had returned home, all the clients met to exchange views on their experience. At the same time they

reconstructed the details of the unknown city, locating the places where various events had occurred. The outcome was the map reproduced on the following double page. You now have the opportunity to examine the map and to ponder on the conclusions to be derived from it.

Note. To interpret the legends on the map, we suggest that you look at it under a red light or under a small sheet of transparent plastic of the same red colour as has been used for the red writing. The red light or plastic sheet will serve as a filter and will remove the disturbance caused by the superposition of writing in two colours.

Our imperfect eye

The camera captures things as they are at a given moment; the eye, however, has not evolved as a system for gathering static, uniform stimuli but rather for collating them in space and time. And we have already noted that subjective elements play an important role in the process, causing us to delude ourselves that we see the world as it really is.

The eye is a wonderful intermediary between ourselves and the world, but it is far from perfect. It often deceives us into seeing things that are not there or not allowing us to see things that are there, and it also tires easily. When, for instance, we gaze for some time at an object which is constantly moving, the speed seems to decrease. And when we look attentively at a coloured surface, the colour appears to become less and less saturated. If you don't believe it, take a piece of grey paper and cover partially one of the coloured squares shown on page 161. Look closely at the colour for about thirty seconds and then whip away the paper. The part just uncovered will appear to be brighter than the rest. The fact is that when we look at a colour we immediately perceive it as being brighter, but when the stimulus is removed it gradually loses this quality.

This can be explained by the process of adaptation which our eyes undergo when exposed for some time to a given

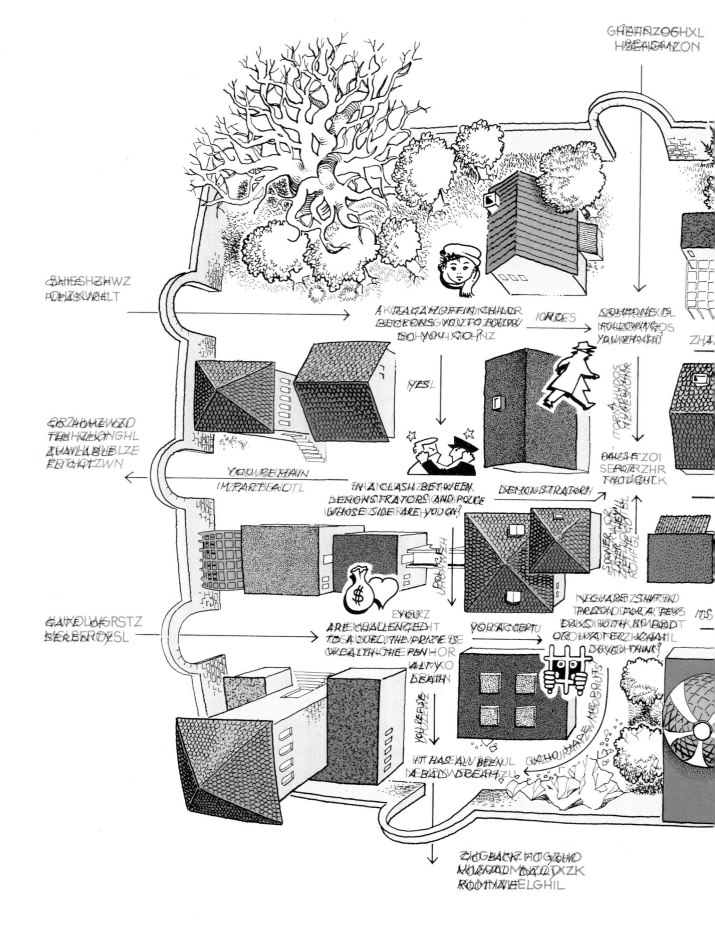

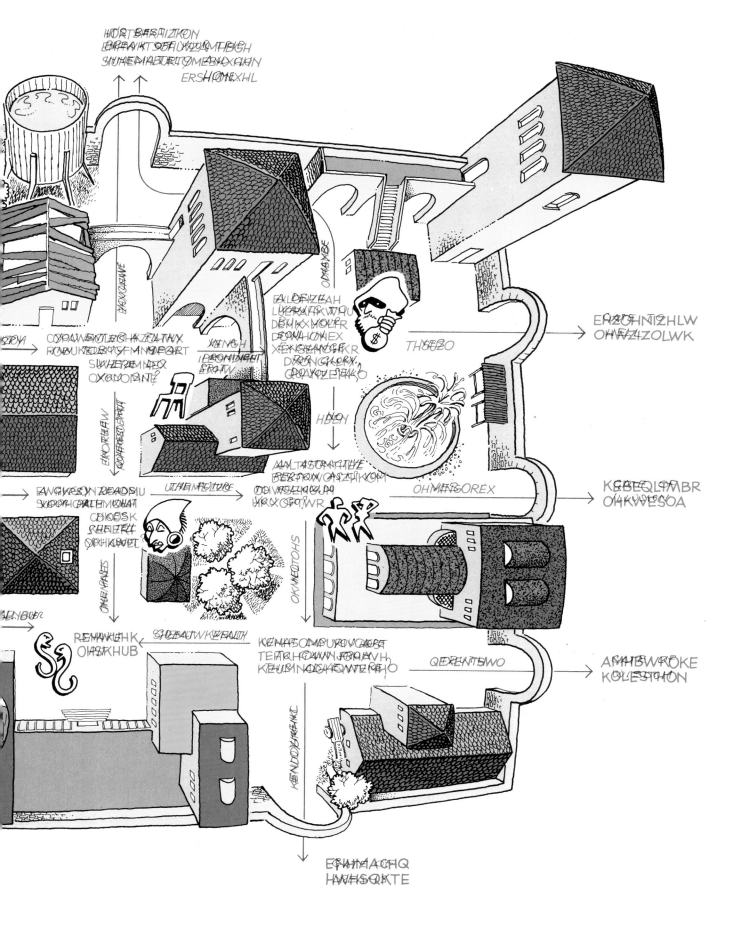

the world in which he lives. The arts of painting and sculpture offer convincing proof of this. But the notion of fixing images mechanically, by using some kind of instrument, did not come about until the eighteenth century, when scientists began experimenting with the "camera obscura," a small chamber furnished with a hole through which light penetrated, throwing images of the outside world on the opposite wall (see page 56). The first photographs date only from the middle of the nineteenth century, after various attempts to fix images on metal plates covered with light-sensitive materials. When such a plate was placed in a black box (a miniature "camera obscura") and put in front of a scene, a landscape or an object, the forms were gradually reproduced on the plate. The first *daguerrotypes* (named after their inventor, the French painter L. J. M. Daguerre) consisted of images produced on copper plates covered with iodized silver; and from then on photography progressed rapidly to become the vital instrument of expression and communication with which we are all familiar today. It is now used in every field of human activity, whether it be newspapers and magazines, mass entertainment, science or industry. Photography, in one form or another, is an integral part of our daily lives; and from the earliest experiments it has developed into an infinitely versatile and creative technique available to us all.

The reason we have referred back to the beginnings is to remind ourselves of the fact that photography is, first and foremost, a technical achievement. There are countless manuals on the subject and we do not need to go into details. We are more concerned here with the creative possibilities of photography and the manner in which it has enriched the language of imagery.

Communication by photography

The essential condition of course for taking a photograph is light, either natural or artificial. In a sense, the art of photography is a form of composition with light, taking account of its quality, intensity and direction. The word itself is derived from the Greek *phòs*, which means "light," and *gráphein*, which means " to write;" so to "photograph" is to "write with light."

It is possible through photography to express one's feelings, to create an atmosphere or to highlight certain details rather than others. For example, there is often an extra dimension of interest or aesthetic appeal in a picture taken *against* the light.

These introductory remarks will show that photography is not just a simple copy of reality. It is an illusion encouraging the belief that it represents the subject being photographed as if we were actually seeing it ourselves. The photographic image is by and large a means of communication and expression, and consequently can be used as imaginatively as any other medium. And the message it sends out can be manipulated and packaged, so to speak, as the fancy dictates.

stimulus. This is what we meant by saying that the subjective factor plays an important part, too, in chromatic perception: the sensation of colour depends not only on the physical characteristics of the stimulant light but also on the fact that it is in the eye that the stimulating action of this light begins and ends.

Photographic images

From the very earliest times man has used the language of imagery in order to communicate and represent the objects of

When we take a photograph we do not merely freeze a moment of reality but by deciding how to frame it we also make a selection, choosing to represent only a certain part of that reality. To this end, the photographer can select the most suitable lens aperture which, combined with the focal length and thus the angle of the visual field, will determine how much or how little of the scene appears in the finished picture. So, at opposite extremes, we have the extremely detailed, wide-angled *fish-eye* shot, and the very narrow shot through the more powerful telephoto lens, which brings out details by getting as close as possible to the object and showing it much larger than

when seen by the naked eye. The photographs on this page are all taken from the same spot, without changing the perspective. But by varying the distance of the shot, it is possible to make use of the various focal lengths to alter considerably both the relative perspective and dimensions, while ensuring, if so desired, that the size of the principal subject in the picture will be unchanged.
Opposite page: a photograph taken against the light, with the sun already low, thus accentuating the glowing tones of the sunset.

Innumerable examples could be given of this capacity, but only a few can be mentioned here. Consider, for instance, how a camera represents reality. The lens does not show things in their entirety, but sets it in a frame, selecting some parts and excluding others, exhibiting it at a distance or in close-up, enlarging or reducing, even deforming objects we can all see. It only represents a part of reality, taking it out of context, never reproducing it faithfully but giving it new, varied and different meanings.

Without venturing unduly into abstract and problematical areas, we shall review in the following pages some of the more familiar ways in which one can amuse oneself with photography.

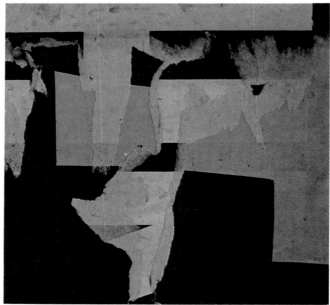

Collage

Look at the above illustration and try to describe it; it could be a pictorial translation of the written metaphor: "This girl is a flower." You will note, however, that the arrangement of petals around the face of a beautiful girl conveys its meaning far more strongly than do the simple words. The message it communicates is immediately understood and emotionally effective.

This image has been built up according to the technique of collage, by which pictures are composed, more or less at random, by sticking together disparate materials. Among those commonly used are pages taken from newspapers or magazines, various types of cardboard (thick, thin, corrugated etc.), wrapping paper and tissue paper. It is a technique which allows full play to the imagination. As a rule, once the shapes have been cut out, they are not immediately glued together but arranged in several different ways, tried out again and again, and finally assembled in what seems to be the most satisfying or striking way. Photographs can also be used in conjunction with a wide range of materials, including plastic, cloth, pieces of wood, parts of flowers and so forth. The only limitation, obviously, has to be bad taste. Once stuck

Above: the collage on the left identifies the girl with a flower; on the right are posters ripped from a wall to form a random decollage reminiscent of informal paintings, a technique used by the famous photographer Ernst Haas. Right: an imaginative collage created by Bruna Bagli.

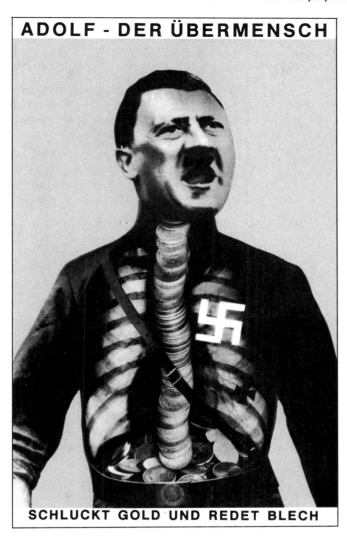

ADOLF - DER ÜBERMENSCH

SCHLUCKT GOLD UND REDET BLECH

head of a noted politician on the body of a donkey). This is the technique known as *photomontage*. You can use posters or any type of publicity matter for basic material, and exercise the imagination freely to obtain striking and often amusing results. Photomontage is widely employed in advertising and

Left: a celebrated anti-Nazi photomontage from the 1930s by John Hartfield.

Below: an eyecatching photomontage used for an advertisement by a cosmetics firm.

together, the materials can be painted or varnished to make them last longer.

Interesting results can also be achieved by experimenting with the reverse procedure, whereby a collage is taken apart. The technique (known as decollage) is to strip away glued and superimposed parts so as to obtain unusual and striking combinations of images, like the one illustrated at top right of the opposite page.

Photomontage

Another way to have fun with photographs is to cut out various kinds of advertisements from magazines and stick together different parts so as to form original images (like the in some contemporary art. Indeed, we see examples all around us in daily life.

Photomontage enjoyed a considerable vogue prior to World War II. It is worth mentioning the work of the photographer John Hartfield in Germany during the 1930s. Hartfield used this technique with great skill to express his hostility to the Nazi regime, notably producing posters and covers for the radical magazine *AIZ*.

One of these covers, reproduced on the preceding page, showing a rather controversial image of dictator Adolf Hitler, carried a caption which translated: "Adolf the superman swallows gold and spews out lead." By cleverly combining a number of visual elements (the chest opened as in an X-ray image, with coins piled up in the oesophagus and stomach), Hartfield communicated a visual message of strong political content, implying that Germany's resources were being converted into lead, in other words, death-dealing arms. In other photomontage images Hartfield portrayed the Nazi leaders as bloodstained butchers, open to corruption and capable only of squandering public money.

The language of photography

People all over the world communicate in countless languages, and these languages of course consist of spoken and written words. Used in an infinite variety of combinations, these words enable us freely to express our thoughts, feelings and ideas. Yet words have their limitations, for they cannot readily communicate meaning unless they are understood; and few of us can command, at best, more than a few languages in addition to our mother tongue. The language of images is a far more universal means of expression. In its varied forms – drawing, painting, sculpture, architecture, mime, dance, photograph, advertisement, strip cartoon, cinema, television etc. – it breaks through the barrier of verbal communications.

Photography is thus an all-purpose language, and the camera an instrument of considerable versatility. The technique has been perfected to such an extent that the camera can nowadays be used to create *special effects*, thus extending the potential expressive range of the medium itself. It is

Left: there are innumerable ways of "playing with pictures" by taking photographs through creative filters. In this shot a filter finely engraved on the surface has broken up the sunlight, creating an unreal multi-coloured halo. Above: a photograph taken with an infra-red colour film, giving a false colour effect. The resulting pictures are unusual, interesting and to some extent unpredictable, but this type of film is not easy to use; correct exposure is critical and there are many factors which can influence the results.

true that the camera, when compared with the wondrous complexity of the human eye, reveals its inadequacy. But like all instruments invented by man, it is capable of performing astonishing tasks and in its most sophisticated and advanced forms can discern objects which are almost and, in some cases, totally invisible to the naked eye.

We have seen that if we break up sunlight by means of a

prism (see page 155), we get the colours of the spectrum, with violet and red at either end. Beyond these two limits the human eye is incapable of perceiving any other radiations, even though the electromagnetic rays do not terminate with the violet and red wavelengths.

Special films exist which are sensitive to infra-red radiations i.e. those beyond red. It is possible with these to obtain special photographic effects, for they reveal things that we cannot normally see, so that the data has to be read and deciphered. In a sense this constitutes an entirely new branch of the general language of photography. Infra-red films come in black and white and in colour. The latter can produce many unusual and fascinating effects: it is made up of three layers, which are not intended to be exposed to blue, green and red light, as in normal films, but to green, red and infra-red. All three layers, however, are in varying measures exposable as well to blue light, in which case this light has to be blocked with a dark yellow filter. If the film is to be used for "creative" purposes, it can also be exposed without filters, or with filters in different tones of yellow, which make it possible to obtain

arterial blood as greenish. So the photographic language here is quite novel, in that colours different from the actual ones enable the images to be correctly read and interpreted.

Picture puzzles

The illustration below shows a detail of a famous painting in the form of a jigsaw puzzle in which two of the pieces are missing. See if you can guess the identity of the painting. The other illustrations on this and the following pages are photographs cut respectively into rectangles, circles and strips. They have then been rearranged so as to alter them and make them difficult to recognize.

What you have to do is to sort them out and describe the subjects they depict, which needs a little ingenuity and imagination. Obviously you cannot juggle round the individual pieces as in a regular jigsaw; so you have to work them out in your mind. The solutions are on page 174.

many varied and unusual colour effects. If such film is used to photograph green grass, rich with chlorophyll, the grass looks red. And if you take a snap of a person, the flesh will appear a cold greenish or bluish colour.

Infra-red photography is also used in the scientific field and for military purposes. In pictures of blood circulation, for example, it shows up the venous blood as brick-red and the

"Picture puzzles" – Solution

On the right is the detail of the painting in the puzzle, Leonardo da Vinci's *Mona Lisa*. The other solutions are self-explanatory.

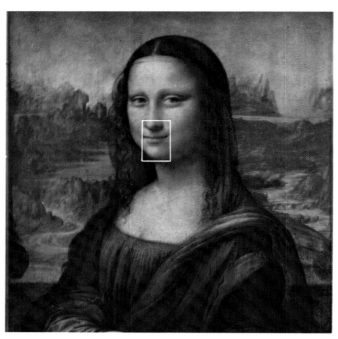

The moving picture

Cinema, television and, most recently, the video-cassette are means of communication which could not have come about without photography. Yet even before the invention of the photograph, attempts were made to communicate visually by conveying an impression of *movement*. The reason is easy to fathom and we will only mention it briefly here.

Photography provides a static picture of reality whereas our experience consists mainly of things that are moving. Around us everything moves: people, nature, the universe. Perception of static objects in immobile surroundings is an artificial experience, which can only partially be recreated in scientific laboratories. So at various times attempts have been made to depict motion by somehow animating figures and forms. But such pictures provided only a vague and illusory idea of movement. Not until the present century did it become technically possible to reproduce perfectly the perception of movement using two-dimensional images.

There is thus no contradiction in the fact that cinematographic pictures, which by definition move, are seen and experienced as the most faithful and convincing representations of reality. Indeed, their capacity to fascinate and their power to attract, undoubtedly superior to that of simple photography, depends on this very attribute: such pictures seem to convey actions and events with unrivalled accuracy and can be reproduced wherever and whenever required.

Let us take a closer look now at the way in which movement is perceived. Already we can define it as the result of a sequence of dynamic structures, even if their arrangement is fixed. To be more precise, if we break down the moving picture representation of a given action (say, a child running), we see that it is made up of a number of static photographs, each of them separate and each following the other. It is their rhythmic sequence that creates the movement.

To understand how this is achieved, let us examine some of the structures of the eye. When on a sunny day we look at objects out of the window, and then suddenly close our eyes, we still get the impression for a brief moment of seeing those images, although not clearly and with somewhat blurred outlines. The phenomenon is even more striking if we gaze at the sun when it is rising or setting, namely when its rays strike at an oblique angle or are filtered by the thickness of the atmosphere: as soon as we shut our eyes, we still seem to see its bright light, which almost appears to be moving. These fairly commonplace experiences show that perception of images does not cease at the exact moment when we no longer look at them, but still continues for a very short while. The phenomenon whereby images remain fixed on the retina is the very basis of cinematography, enabling single pictures to be linked together and projected so as to convey the sense of movement.

So much has been written about the cinema that we do not propose to discuss it here; instead we shall suggest a few entertaining ways in which you can create movement yourself with pictures drawn in two dimensions.

The thaumatrope

The thaumatrope, derived from a Greek word meaning "marvellous movement," is an instrument which can create the impression of movement. It consists of a disc of cardboard or of some other stiff material (as shown in the illustration below), to which are attached two pieces of string. Different pictures are drawn or stuck on either side of the card. If you rotate the card by tightening and pulling the pieces of string, you will see the two pictures merge into one. So you can draw a picture on one side with some details missing and then draw these features alone on the opposite side.

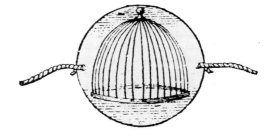

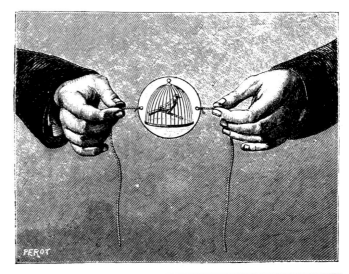

The flying bird

The thaumatrope is an amusing gadget which produces the sensation of movement, if only in elementary form. This is because there are only two images superimposed upon the retina and therefore the elements that make them up and differentiate them are strictly limited. But if the number of successive images is increased, there is a much more persuasive sense of movement. Let us try to construct a more sophisticated type of thaumatrope. Cut out two pieces of cardboard or stiff paper and fix them together as shown in the illustration below. Then stick the four pictures which represent the actions of a bird in flight on to the four sides in the order indicated. By using a piece of string or long elastic band, you can now rotate the pieces of cardboard and get the impression of the bird actually flying.

You can create other examples of four-action movement without making the individual pictures too complicated.

The phantascope

The phantascope, popular in the nineteenth century, was one of the first devices based on the persistence of the image on the retina to give the perception of movement.

To make your own phantascope, take an average-sized piece of cardboard and stick on it ten pictures representing the successive phases of a complete movement, as illustrated on the opposite page. Cut out and very carefully stick the disc with its circle of pictures on a sheet of black cardboard; then, using scissors or a sharp knife, make holes in the original disc so that there are ten black rectangles showing through between each picture. Put a pencil or similar object through the center of the two discs, stand in front of a mirror, and rotate the top disc. If you look at the images through the openings round the edge, the figures will seem to be moving.

The first phantascope was invented by the Frenchman J. Plateau in 1833. Similar to it was the tachyscope, consisting of

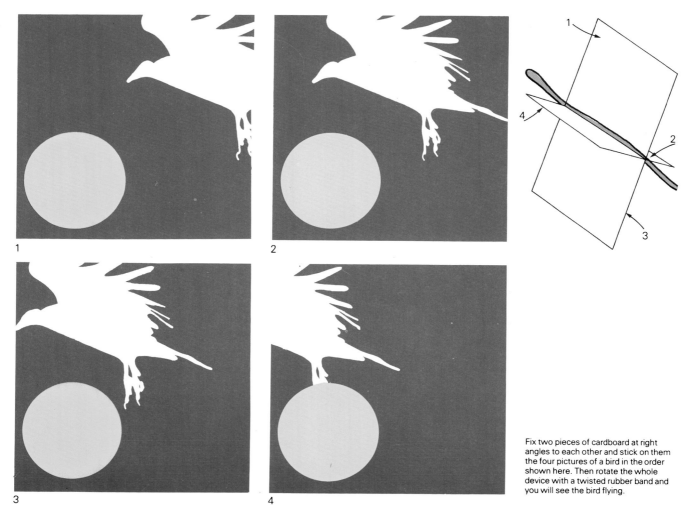

Fix two pieces of cardboard at right angles to each other and stick on them the four pictures of a bird in the order shown here. Then rotate the whole device with a twisted rubber band and you will see the bird flying.

1

2

3

4

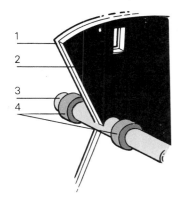

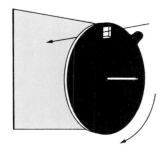

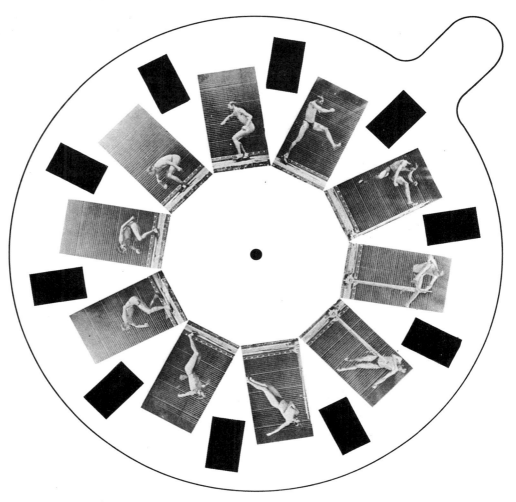

Right: the phantascope, one of the instruments which preceded the invention of the cinematograph, consisted of a disc of cardboard on which were stuck a series of pictures, illustrating successive phases of a complete action.
Above: the upper diagram shows the parts making up the phantascope: 1. printed disc; 2. black cardboard; 3. wooden rod; 4. rubber stoppers. The lower drawing shows one of the openings through which the pictures are observed in the mirror.

a large rotating disc, manually operated, with a series of scenes on it; the succession of fixed images was illuminated by lights coordinated by the action of the wheel, with a brief interval of darkness between one picture and another. All these curious games were derived from optical studies which led, in 1895, to the invention of the cinematograph by the brothers Louis and Auguste Lumière.

The tricks of the cinema

The cinema, together with the cartoon strip, is a fairly important example of multiple language, whereby pictures linked to movement are combined with gestures, the spoken word, sound and music. No other modern medium can rival it for eloquence, for it is an independent and original synthesis of different forms of artistic expression – painting (composition of images, colour values etc.), literature (dialogue and dramatic interpretation) and music (sound is an indispensable accompaniment to film narrative). In terms of the cinema, however, all these arts are dependent upon imagery and movement. Without discussing the merits of film language, it is worth emphasizing that of all the languages which rely on the visual element for expression, probably none more than that of the cinema incorporates the mechanisms and laws of perception for the purposes of communication.

The cinema creates its special effects by various means, but among the most important principles are the constant size and relative distance of objects. When in films we see huge palaces burning to the ground or battleships being sunk by hidden submarines, although we are excited and moved, we know deep down that it is all illusion, all make-believe. We know that the palaces and the warships are no more than miniature models photographed from a position and distance which makes them seem life-size and real.

Select Bibliography

General books
De Grandis, L. *Theory and Use of Colour*, Poole and New York, 1986
Gregory, Richard L. *Eye and Brain. The Psychology of Seeing*, London 1971
Köhler, Wolfgang *Gestalt Psychology*, 1929

Articles taken from the *Scientific American*
Gregory, Richard L. *Visual illusions*, November 1968, page 66
Young, Richard W. *Visual cells*, October 1970, page 80
Attneave, Fred *Multistability in perception*, December 1971, page 62
Ratliff, Floyd *Contour and contrast*, June 1972, page 90
Pettigrew, John D. *The neurophysiology of binocular vision*, August 1972, page 84
Gombrich, E. H. *The visual image*, September 1972, page 82
Rock, Irvin *The perception of disoriented figures*, January 1974, page 78
Metelli, F. *The perception of transparency*, April 1974, page 90
Teuber, Marianne L. *Sources of ambiguity in the prints of Maurits C. Escher*, July 1974, page 90
Campbell, Fergus, & Maffei, Lamberto *Contrast and spatial frequency*, November 1974, page 106
Julesz, Bela *Experiments in the visual perception of texture*, April 1975, page 34

Gardner, M. *The curious magic of anamorphic art*, January 1975, page 110
Johannson, Gunnar *Visual motion perception*, June 1975, page 76
Beck, Jacob *The perception of surface colour*, August 1975, page 62
Hess, Eckhard, H. *The role of pupil size in communication*, November 1975, page 110
Kanizsa, Gaetano *Subjective contours*, April 1976, page 48
Favreau, Olga Eizner, & Corballis, Michael C. *Negative aftereffects in visual perception*, December 1976, page 42
Sekuler, Robert, & Levinson, Eugene *The perception of moving targets*, January 1977, page 60
Nussenzveig, H. Moysés *The theory of the rainbow*, April 1977, page 116
Siegel, Ronald K. *Hallucinations*, October 1977, page 132
Land, Edwin H. *The retinex theory of colour vision*, December 1977, page 108
Thomas, David Emil *Mirror images*, December 1980, page 158
Rock, Irvin *Anorthoscopic perception*, March 1981, page 103
Wolfe, Jeremy M. *Hidden visual processes*, February 1983, page 72
Hoffmann, Donald D. *The interpretation of visual illusions*, December 1983, page 137
Cooper, Lynn A., & Shepard, Roger N. *Turning something over in the mind*, December 1984, page 114
Wallach, Hans *Perceiving a stable environment*, May 1985, page 92

Photographic sources

a = above; b = below; c = center; l = left; r = right. Stelvio Andreis, Verona: 153b, 166. Ardea Photographics, London: 27cr, 174c (J. P. Ferrero). E. Arnone, Milan: 117. Beeldrecht, Amsterdam: 80, 81a. A. Bertolasi: 57, 60b. Canon, Verona: 167. G. Cavallero, Savona: 137a. B. Coleman Ltd., Middlesex/M. P. L. Fogden: 145br. C. Delle Cese, Verona: 10, 24ar/b, 27al, 156a, 170. Jerome Ducrot: 60a. Lionello Fabbri, Rome: 67r. Ken Haak: 59b. Andrew Lawson/John Brennan: 68. Enzo Magni, Milan: 32. Magnum Photos, Milan: 155. 168ar (E. Haas). Mansell Collection: 52br. Marka Graphic, Milan/Z. Leszozyski: 145bl. G. Mazza, Montecarlo: 103. Norman Parkinson: 174b. Photo Researchers Inc./R.C. Hermes: 145bc. Martin Robbe: 59a. F. Roiter, Venice: 156b. Studio Inside, Milan: 153a. The Exploration: 125b. The Image Bank, Milan, H. Fujii: 27bl. Time Life, New York: 62–3b. Twentieth Century Fox, U.S.A.: 124a. M. Vautier, De Nanxe, Decool, Paris, 27br. All other photographs are from the Mondadori Archives.